THE OLD POOR LAW IN SCOTLAND

THE EXPERIENCE OF POVERTY, 1574–1845

Rosalind Mitchison

Edinburgh University Press

© Rosalind Mitchison, 2000

Edinburgh University Press Ltd
22 George Square, Edinburgh

Typeset in Ehrhardt
by Hewer Text Ltd, Edinburgh, and
printed and bound in Great Britain by
The Cromwell Press, Trowbridge, Wilts

A CIP record for this book is
available from the British Library

ISBN 0 7486 1344 7 (paperback)

CONTENTS

To past and present members of the Economic and Social
History Department of Edinburgh University, who have given
me support and companionship over many years.

ACKNOWLEDGEMENTS

I owe thanks for help, information, references or hospitality to many people: in particular to Michael Anderson, John Ballantyne, G. M. Birnie, Gordon Desbrisay, Helen Dingwall, John Dwyer, Edward Hodgkin, June Irving, W. W. Knox, Leah Leneman, Lt. Col. T. K. Macfarlan, Ailsa Maxwell, Lord Moncrieff of Tulliebole and the late Lady Moncrieff, Charles M. Morison, Athol Murray, Willie Orr, Janet Pearce, Nicholas Phillipson, Christopher Smout and David Stevenson. But in a study which has occupied me for more than twenty years I am sure that other, forgotten names should figure in this list. To them I give apologies as well as thanks. I am also grateful for anonymous help from the staffs of the Scottish Record Office, the National Library of Scotland, Edinburgh University Library, Strathclyde and Central Scotland Regional Archives, Aberdeen and St Andrews University Archives and Edinburgh City Chambers Archive.

ABBREVIATIONS

APS	*Acts of the Parliaments of Scotland*
ECA	Edinburgh City Archive
EUL	Edinburgh University Library
KSR	Kirk Session Register
NLS	National Library of Scotland
NSA	*New Statistical Account*
OSA	*Statistical Account of Scotland*
PP	*Parliamentary Paper*
RPCS	*Register of the Privy Council of Scotland*
SHS	Scottish History Society
SRO	Scottish Record Office
SRS	Scottish Record Society

AUTHOR'S NOTE

The £ sign in this book has been used exclusively for sums in sterling, and so has the / sign for the separation between sterling shillings and pence. Scottish currency from 1600 was worth one-twelfth of sterling. It remained the normal currency in speech and writing till the mid-eighteenth century, and so in Chapters 1–6 the words pound, shilling and pence are used for Scots money without qualification. So is merk – two-thirds of a pound. By the nineteenth century it was no longer common parlance, so in Chapters 7–10, except for reference to the striking of the county fiars, all money references are in sterling.

References to *The Statistical Account of Scotland* unless otherwise stated are to the modern edition of this work edited by Donald J. Withrington and Ian R. Grant (Wakefield, 1974–83).

The older names of Mearns and Angus have been used for the counties of Kincardineshire and Forfarshire.

Most of the material used in this book is from the Kirk Session Registers of the parishes of the established Church. All these can be found through the Scottish Record Office, renamed in 1999 as the National Archives of Scotland, which carries either the registers themselves or photocopies. I have not, therefore, burdened the note structure with specific references to these.

INTRODUCTION

This is the first modern study of the whole life of the Old Poor Law of Scotland which stretched from 1574 to 1845. It is a subject worthy of study: how a society deals with its less fortunate members tells us a good deal about the values of that society and the links or barriers between the classes. The story of poor relief in Scotland also has features of special interest. Originally set up as a copy of the developing English Poor Law, it grew in a very different way. In England the Poor Law became the most important element of local government and, enlarged by further statutes and an enormous body of case law, a system by which the better-off members of a parish tried to limit their financial obligations and the labouring population endeavoured not to be restricted in its choice of where to live and work. In Scotland the administration of the law was taken over by the Church because no other body had an effective system of local government, but it was also of concern to landowners and their lawyers. Landowners were often, but decreasingly, able to evade the explicit demand in the initiating statute that they pay a rate. For much of the life of the Scottish Poor Law the financial base of poor relief was charitable giving. It was therefore particularly under the influence of changes in social and religious thought. Intermixed were charitable impulses, the Protestant desire for a well-ordered society, the fear among landowners of a regular tax on land combined with a wish to appear generous and open-handed, and the emphasis of the evangelical movement on personal independence and responsibility. Educated and uneducated opinion both had their influence.

Yet when the need came for revision of both Poor Laws it was the English one that succumbed to doctrinaire views. The difference in dates between the two reforms, the English Act of 1834 and the

1

Scottish of 1845, explains this. In 1834 a Royal Commission could be set up simply to produce one kind of evidence: by 1845 the statistical movement had become stronger and more sophisticated, requiring more than partisan information.

Historians have an interest in relief systems and not simply to measure their capacity to keep people alive. Such systems have a part to play in many historical questions: for instance, did poor relief have a bearing on economic or demographic growth? was Protestant Europe a more effective base for social support than Catholic? what was the effect of state-ordered relief on the relations between classes? Historians have debated whether the English Poor Law hastened or delayed the Industrial Revolution. How much was the eventual freedom of Europe from crises in mortality due to the improvements in the organisation of relief? There are many other questions, for all of which we need the evidence of as many countries as possible. This in itself is justification for producing the evidence of this particular country, Scotland.

It has been usual when historians look at the Old Scottish Poor Law for them to take their evidence from statements or monographs by either lawyers or ministers of the established Church. But by the late eighteenth century both these professional groups had a vested interest in providing misinformation. The Scottish legal principle of 'desuetude', the ruling that if a statute could be shown not to have been used it lost force for the future, meant that it was worth the while of an advocate to assert, on no basis of fact, that parts of the various statutes about the Poor Law had been ineffective. Ministers holding strongly by the individualist ethic of the evangelical movement and enthusiastic for voluntary aid could discount evidence about the past raising of poor rates in their parishes. Both groups were aided by a limited grasp of historical fact and have been a rich source of mis-statements. One or two good monographs have been successfully steered through the misleading literature by going to primary material. This study has also been based on primary material at parish level. There were approximately 900 parishes in early modern Scotland and of these I have studied parts of the registers of activity of near 300. I have supplemented this by the scraps of Justice of the Peace records, the register of the Privy Council, legal processes, contemporary pamphlets, books and newspapers. There is still a large amount of untapped source material for others to work on and I hope that some will do so.

CHAPTER 1

GETTING STARTED

In the sixteenth century the concern of thinkers for the poor in many European countries is a redeeming feature in a civilisation of aggressive egoism and ruthless expansion. From Poland to Spain men in varied countries produced serious arguments about the best way to ameliorate the miseries and squalor of the poor. Two centuries earlier poverty had been seen as an admirable and saintly characteristic, particularly manifest in Jesus Christ. In the sixteenth century it was seen with greater validity as a block to education and training, and so to economic usefulness and religious commitment. The new emphasis was not simply theoretical. It produced various schemes, sometimes for cities, sometimes for states, for support and education of the poor.[1] The most effective of these, the Old Poor Law of England, lasted for two and a half centuries and became a dominant feature of local government.

There were major changes in the sixteenth century which were likely to have affected the scale and nature of poverty. There was a European-wide rapid population growth after a long period of demographic stagnation. This led to changes in the various economies enhancing the value of productivity. Partly caused by the increase in population but also drawing from elements we do not fully understand came the rapid inflation of the period, which has become known as the price revolution, a drastic change in the relationship between silver and the necessities of life, a change enhanced by some unscrupulous governments indulging in deliberate adulteration of their coinages. It was a century of frequent wars, and the warfare was on a raised scale. More men were drawn into armies and more injured or discharged soldiers were left to find some sort of living when the campaigns ceased. To those used to looting and to short periods of intensive activity, the work patterns of civil life, long hours and limited reward, whether in craft or farm work, did not appeal. The march of armies living on local food supplies may have forced on many families the choice between vagrancy or starvation.

Besides economic change there was the great split in belief and religious practice within Christianity, the shattering of the unity of western Christendom into the opposing camps of Protestantism and reformed Roman Catholicism. Both of these placed a new emphasis on the need for active and committed belief. This new divide was a further cause of war. There is a current debate on whether the religious divide enlarged or decreased provision for the poor. In Protestant Europe monastic charity, an irregular supply depending on specific endowments and the scale of food leftovers, disappeared with the Reformation, and Protestantism dismissed the idea of earning merit by charitable gifts. It is claimed that for England charity did not regain its pre-Reformation level until the later seventeenth century. But there was more organised poor relief, based on a strong discipline in the Protestant churches concerned to see that communities supported their poor.[2]

The word 'poor' had two distinctive meanings and indicated two different types of need, on very different scales of urgency. The obvious group of 'poor' was those with no immediate prospect of supporting themselves: cripples and people with other obvious handicaps such as the blind, the very old, young orphan children, lunatics. The size of this group was relatively static; its needs could be foreseen and materials or money collected. But there was a much larger population living very near the edge of poverty, which could be tipped into destitution by some external disaster destroying the means by which a living was put together. Events such as harvest failure, war, plague, urban fires could not be foreseen, and the people who might be at risk from such disasters might be as much as one-third or two-fifths of any community. A recent analysis of the returns from Edinburgh to taxes of the 1690s shows that more than a third of the city's households were classified as too poor to contribute.[3] It was this dark shadow of potential destitution which made the setting up of poor relief systems so difficult. The elements that might cause surges in destitution varied in their predominance across Europe. In the Low Countries and parts of south-east England the local economy had developed far enough for there to be areas, large towns or industrialised villages, with many families working in industry, usually textiles but sometimes in metals or mining. Such areas were susceptible to distant disturbances, famines, wars, plagues, which could cause interruptions in demand and thereby throw many hundreds of people into unemployment.

It was also an age in which the claims and functions of states became enhanced. Almost all of these were monarchies, and their fortunes were consequently at risk with their dynasties. Marriages could be arranged but other features of the life cycle could not, and were a source of insecurity. Civil war could result from a ruler's choice of religion.

These features of early modern Europe may do something to explain contemporary concern about the poor. The articulate and lettered men who expressed it had many opportunities for seeing the scale of need and of experiencing the risk of aggression by beggars. People who faced the choice between starving or begging might well prefer the latter option, and had little reason to hang on to subservience. Families forced off the land by changes in ownership or use could join together in bands seeking support, and not always peaceably. Injured soldiers in some countries were supported by pensions, but these might lose value. Most of those who had been mercenaries were left to their own devices to stay alive. Vagrant groups, where they have been examined, appear to have consisted mainly of young, single men, but there were also some deserted wives, married couples or prostitutes, and sometimes there were children. In England the groups were small in the sixteenth century except for gypsies, but they enlarged in the seventeenth century.[4]

All the great religions of the world stress the desirability of kindness and charity to the poor. (The Jewish tradition of this is expressed in the Apocryphal book Ecclesiasticus: 4.) What was new in the sixteenth century in many countries was the decision that this could not be left entirely to personal philanthropy. Among the enhanced activity of nation states or of cities was to be provision for the destitute. Traditionally it had been held that some part of the tithe or teind of a parish should be used by the priest for this purpose. But in many places much of the teinds had been withdrawn from the parish priest to sustain other developments, monasteries, universities or collegiate churches. Other sources of help, such as confraternities and guilds, had taken over care of some of the poor in towns and even in some country areas. The bigger cities had themselves given aid; private charity had founded hospitals and leper houses. Monasteries had received legacies for charity. There were many ways in which help was provided, but it still did not meet the needs of the sixteenth century.

Scotland had a share in many of the features enhancing poverty, though for the most part in only a limited way. The later fifteenth and the sixteenth centuries saw drastic changes in the tenurial rights of the peasantry, as feuing was introduced and the strength of the old 'kindly' tenures, based on kinship, weakened. Her rulers and regents, who had no understanding of the economy, were irresponsible in their debasement of the coinage, so that during the later sixteenth century inflation was particularly severe. The nominal cost of basic food went up by six times, for some foods by as much as eight times. There was little established industry that could absorb surplus labour: the country's primitive exports were the products of farming, hunting or mining only. As a northerly country her harvests were always at risk of bad weather. The function of the town was to meet the needs of its locality for tools and clothing. What we know of the activity of town guilds suggests some care for their own members and their dependants in sickness or old age but on a very limited scale. The structure of society meant that those governing it knew little of the life of those who worked with their hands. Parish life particularly suffered from neglect – 87 per cent of Scottish parishes had had the teind deflected to the support of monasteries, universities or collegiate churches. These distinguished buildings had been achieved by robbing the parishes, and the effect of the Reformation was to move much of these resources into the hands of the aristocracy.

A relief system or poor law has to have two aspects. One is to arrange for the support of those in need on some local or central base. The other is to control who are to be the recipients, to decide on the qualification which will define the poor. In the past the resources had to be local, and so, therefore, was the qualification. Hence the denial of relief to those from other places, who were called by various offensive names; vagabonds, sorners, beggars. Only in a person's 'own' parish, that in which he had been born, should relief be available. Both the English and the Scottish Poor Laws made this initial rule. People who roamed, who had no stake in any community, no employer, master, lord, who might or might not be fit to work, were seen as outsiders and a menace.

The first statute in Scotland which fulfils these requirements was made by Parliament in 1574. It was a temporary Act, and largely a copy of the important English Act of 1572 which really set up the English Poor Law.[5] The essence of the Acts was the same. The poor, aged and impotent of parishes or towns were to be supported by a local tax or stent in proportion to the payer's resources. Vagrants or sturdy beggars were to be arrested, imprisoned, branded and sent away unless some local citizen would take them into service. The differences between the Acts were trifling: the size of the iron with which vagabonds aged between 14 and 70 were to be branded was not specified in the Scottish Act, and the students, wandering and begging were labelled with the Scottish Universities, not Oxford and Cambridge. The Scottish Act even took its title from the English. It was an 'Act anent the punysment of strong and ydle beggars, and provision for sustenance of the poor and impotent'. The priority of both Acts was to control beggars. There was, however, one significant difference which had a long-term effect. English parishes were ordered to provide work and work materials for those needing employment. Scottish parishes were not.

The other difference between the Acts lay in the likelihood of application. Unlike its Scottish replica, the English Act was founded on experience and activity. The English Act built on previous sixteenth-century statutes which forbade begging by the 'sturdy', ordered cities to provide charity and collect alms on a regular basis and arrange the compulsory apprenticing of vagrant children. There is evidence of attempts to obey these requirements, and in some well-populated rural areas confraternities had worked as in cities.[6] It is easy to understand why the Act of 1572 became the foundation statute of a system of relief which endured for over two centuries, accumulating an enormous body of law by accretion, statutory additions and modifications and case law.[7] It became the basis of local government in the English countryside. The Scottish Act, merged in the permanent Act of 1579,[8] has left no such trail of amendment, amplification and use, yet its development, despite its weakness, shows that it had a part to play in the country's story.

Though it would be a great oversimplification to claim that English statutes were obeyed and Scottish ones were not, there was a vast difference between the powers, resources and expectations of the central authorities of the two countries. The government of England had means of extracting obedience which that in Scotland did not.

There were monarch's courts available for the whole country, Justices of the Peace with administrative as well as judicial functions, and the Star Chamber to push for the enforcement of statutes that met resistance. In Scotland approximately half the country was not under royal jurisdiction, but held in large franchises by the nobility. In the Highlands and western islands clan chiefs and clan nobility were the effective rulers; elsewhere the great families, or surnames, controlled society, the Hamiltons, Stewarts, Douglases, Campbells and Gordons. The priorities of the leaders of these and lesser surnames did not include obedience to the orders of Privy Council or Parliament.[9] In 1609, when James VI set up an imitation of the English Justice of the Peace for Scotland, the office carried very little authority. Its powers did not include supervision of the Poor Law, and in all spheres were restricted by the franchises. James, when he had reached the relative personal security of the English throne, was to claim that he could govern Scotland by his pen: a wiser statement would have used 'influence' rather than 'govern'. The important element in the differential development of the two Poor Laws was that, though Scotland had little in the way of effective secular government, she had a much more powerful Church.

At the time of the initiating Act Scotland was recovering from a civil war. The issue had been whether James VI, the infant son of Mary Queen of Scots, or his mother should reign, or rather which group of great men should govern in which name. Mary was a Catholic, and likely to be allied with Catholic power abroad. The war had finished with the King's side dominant, the side favoured by England. It was entirely understandable that the successful regent, the Earl of Morton, should flatter England by borrowing her legislation and then doing little to enforce it. It is true the Acts did name officials who were to see to enforcement. In burghs in both Acts these were the bailies and provosts; in franchises, stewards and bailies; in 'landward', that is rural, parishes, elders and 'headsmen' in the first Act, royal commissioners in the second. There is no parish officer known as 'headsman', and any specific meaning of elders applies to the Church's appointments. Royal Commissioners were appointed in the 1590s but it does not appear that the Acts led to organised response with any briskness on the landward side.[10]

But we can see activity in matters of poor relief which had no relationship to Acts of Parliament. *The First Book of Discipline*, which aimed at being the blueprint of the new Kirk, had declared 'Every several Kirk must provide for the poore within itself . . . We are not Patrons for stubborne and idle beggars . . . whom the Civil Magistrate ought to punish. But for the widow and fatherless, the aged, impotent or lamed . . . also for persons of honestie fallen into decay and poverty'.[11] Those parishes that had already assumed the structure there laid down had set up functioning kirk sessions of elders and ministers, creating the lowest of the hierarchy of courts by which the Church was to govern itself. In a few instances these can be seen as giving aid to the poor on Christian principles before the Act of 1574. For instance, in Canongate in 1564 twenty-eight people were persuaded to promise a weekly contribution for the poor. Not all fulfilled the promise but the burgh was able to set up a system of weekly distributions.[12] Here we see the use of deacons for the financial affairs of a parish, as laid down in the *First Book of Discipline*. In St Andrews, which like Canongate combined the authority of burgh and parish, there also seem to have been regular collections. In 1570 the session ruled that relief was to be available only to those who attended sermon and knew by heart the Lord's Prayer, the creed and the ten commandments. A month was allowed for the poor to memorise these. Couples living together had to be married. There were rulings against the letting of houses without permission of the bailies, crying for alms and begging at the gate.[13] Other places show small-scale activity. The *Gild Court Book of Dunfermline* indicates trickles of aid to the poor in the fifteenth century. In 1560 the court bought a cot for a 'puyr' bairn, and it paid on one occasion for bread for the poor.[14]

There were occasional larger movements of money. Dundee assigned the rents of its old priory to the poor. Aberdeen session used the disapproval of the Church for music to sell its organ for relief.[15] The boy King James VI made an annual birthday gift of cloth and money to as many boys as the years of his age. None of this was on a significant scale, or likely to get to those in real need. In 1578 there was a siege of Stirling castle, where the court was, by beggars:

being not onlie ane unpleasant and lamentabill spectacle, but sic a confusioun as alsweill his Hienes self as his nobilitie and utheris repairing to his presence ar grevouslie fascheit and inquietit throw want of ordour and universal provisions for the saidis puyr peopill, seing commonlie the strongest beggaris throw their importunitie gettis the almons, quhen the maist misterfull, seik and impotent creatouris ar owirsene and neglectit.

(The powerful word 'misterfull', or destitute, has disappeared from modern Scots.) The Privy Council made various suggestions, such as the transfer of the king's birthday generosity to 'poor aged honest folk' and set up a committee which recommended punishment of beggars and vagabonds, but this was not likely to remove the threat of people starving in a year of poor harvest.[16]

Some sort of delayed response to the Acts of the 1570s can be seen in the towns, but it was difficult for burgh councils to obey. The problem was that, in addition to the normal dislike of being expected to pay money, there was the novelty of the process. The demands of the crown had not yet made direct taxation a normal experience. Edinburgh made an effort to levy a rate in 1575, but it broke down and all that the council could do was to issue tokens licensing begging by those acknowledged as poor. In 1579 the city paid a surgeon for the medicaments used on the sick poor, but this money did not come from a rate. Another attempt at a rate in 1580 was defeated by the crafts which promised to care for their own members. (Not all of the poor would have belonged to a craft.) In the plague year of 1584–5 the city at last managed to extract a rate and by 1591 it had set up a list of accepted poor who were forbidden to beg.[17] The sick poor received medical aid from an unsalaried surgeon who was let off his municipal tax, but in the 1620s the city came to award him not only his expenses but also a fee.[18] St Andrews also gave medical aid before the end of the sixteenth century, and Glasgow was doing so in the 1620s.

Burghs were slow to respond to the demand for a stent. Glasgow did not raise one till 1638, St Andrews started one in 1597, Perth in 1599, Aberdeen in 1619, and Dundee and Stirling appear to have waited much longer.[19] There is no means of checking whether the level of taxation was adequate to the need. The insistence of Aberdeen that relief was dependent on attendance at church is likely to have meant ignoring some of the infirm. Some towns, for instance Elgin, acted through the kirk session, not the town council, and worked a regular system by the 1590s.[20]

Though the medical aid available at this period was not usually something that modern medical thought would support, it should not be simply dismissed. It could have a powerful psychological effect. Also there were some areas where it was valuable. There is a list of 1710 of treatments given to the poor in Edinburgh, which contains a leg amputation, and several months later there is a note on the supply of a wooden leg to the woman patient.[21]

There were two more statutes concerning the poor in the 1590s and one in 1600. These paid some attention to the method of enforcing the earlier Acts. But only with the borrowing of the institution of the Justice of the Peace in 1609 from England was there the beginning of some general civil government in rural areas, and this was still very fragile. The territories in which Justices could be competent were hemmed in by franchises. In any case the support of the poor was not within their remit. The Act of 1592 accepted the kirk session as the instrument of supervision of relief, and in that of 1597 the sessions were to be the administration. A later Act of 1600 not very sensibly threatened the sessions with a fine of twenty pounds Scots if they failed to act. Crippling the finances of the donor body was unlikely to improve the condition of the poor.[22]

The Church in the 1590s was still in the business of creating a parochial structure. The south-east was relatively well supplied with parish ministers, but elsewhere many parishes had only a 'reader', sharing a minister for the functions which required priestly status with two or three others. Aberdeenshire, for instance, was held to be richer in ministers than most shires, yet a quarter of a century after the Reformation date of 1560 only half of its parishes had the whole attention of a minister. Only the parishes of Old and New Aberdeen, from which kirk session registers survive, can for certain be seen as having the full Presbyterian system in the sixteenth century. That Aberdeenshire was not unusual is shown by studying other areas. The presbytery of Auchterarder's records, for instance, show that only four out of fourteen parishes had a full-time minister by 1590.[23] It is difficult to believe that a functioning kirk session could be created without steady pressure from a full-time minister. Even where a kirk session existed it was usually not the body envisioned by the *First Book of Discipline*, for the class of deacons, in charge of money matters, appears to have disappeared. Probably this was because parishes found it difficult enough to recruit suitable elders, and had to accept some illiterate. The near total absence of parish and presbytery records from the Highlands shows that the Church there had not yet received its basic structure. The state's sensible decision to hand Poor Law business to the only effective local government system has to be seen as fully functional only in the long term. So it will have been in the early decades of the seventeenth century that many lowland parishes were in a state to act. Lairds, mostly in the train of one or another great surnames, were not likely to show initiative on their own.

Various records show the Church taking on board the obligation of poor relief. In the visitation records of the diocese of Dunblane, the presbyteries were checking on the existence of some relief system, though not on its adequacy, in the early seventeenth century.[24] Dundonald (Ayrshire), a well-organised parish, had by the 1630s a long list of poor whom it was systematically sustaining. It had even got as far as to require those with their names on the list to agree to leave their possessions to the session, a useful mechanism for checking on the genuineness of destitution, which was not adopted in many places till the mid-eighteenth century.[25] The synod of Lothian and Tweeddale in 1594 was ordering ministers to organise poor relief. In the mid-seventeenth century its concern was more in repressing wandering beggars than in sustaining the poor: this is a demonstration of its assimilation to the concerns of government.[26]

The successful transfer of activity from lay control to the Church was the means eventually of making the Poor Law a reality in rural areas. There was, however, an important difference between what the statutes laid down and what the kirk sessions were prepared or able to do. The statutes expected that a parish would make a list of its poor, calculate the total money needed to relieve them and then raise this by stenting the members of the parish according to their resources. This would inevitably mean placing a considerable part of the cost on the landowner. In fact the parishes worked the other way round. They collected what money they could, set some aside for other parish needs, such as a fee for the session clerk, and then discovered how many of the poor could receive a dole. If a parish had a roll of established pensioners it might decide how much the pension could be irrespective of whether the sum given would keep a pensioner alive. (There was general agreement that a peck of oatmeal a week was enough for a fairly inactive pensioner to live on.) There would also be minor dribbles of money to people wandering through and in need. There was no likelihood of the parish levying a money rate on its landowners in normal times. It is not clear whether any rural parish thought that it was under obligation to obey a statute: an order from one of the higher courts of the Church was another matter. One of these might demand a special collection for a particular purpose, and the parishes would struggle to obey. The General Assembly, the highest court of the Church, was not, at this time, particularly concerned over the state of the poor.

The main agency of government that might have tried to get the statutes working more rapidly was the Privy Council, and its powers and concerns were both limited. Though it paid occasional attention to the provision of alms, for instance in 1585 it ordered the issue of low-value copper coins for alms giving,[27] its main concern was with the suppression of vagrants and beggars. It followed the line of the statute of 1600 which described these in terms calculated to make them appear objectionable to the right minded: 'leveing maist insolentlie and ungodlie, without marriage or baptisme of grite numbers of thair bairnes'. In a proclamation of 1617 the Council accused them of a 'wicked and ungodlie forme of living without marriage or baptisme'. In 1620 the comment was on their 'filthie and beastlie conversatioun'.[28] Remarks like these, presumably believed true, became a common accusation made by the upper class about this section of society. The Council was concerned that there was a threat to society from large bands of rough people and it also felt the nuisance of persistent begging. These were more important issues to it than the material state of the poor, about which its members knew very little. It objected, strongly and repeatedly, to vagrants on the principal streets of the larger towns, particularly Edinburgh and Canongate. In 1616, preparing for a visit of the king, it complained that 'hardlie can ony man of whatsoever qualitie walk upon the streits, nor yit stand and confer upoun the streitis nor under stairs, bot they are impeishit be nombers of beggaris'.[29] (Considering what was thrown onto the Edinburgh High Street every evening this remark shows a very selective fastidiousness.) In 1633, with another royal visit pending, the wording is different but the theme the same. Beggars 'by their shamefull exclamatiouns and crying so trouble and wearie the noble-men and others His Majesty's subjects walking upon the streets as they cannot conveniently attend thair lawfull affaires and business at the Counsell and Session'.[30]

In 1619 the Council particularly objected to beggars flocking to funerals and weddings, but the local poor did the same expecting a liberal distribution of alms. This security issue should not be seen entirely in vagabond terms. The 1621 Sumptuary Act, 'Anent Banquiting and apparell' shows nervousness at large assemblies of any class.[31]

The Council showed a particular hostility to gypsies, usually called 'Egyptians'. An Act of 1604 declared that any Egyptians found after 1 August would be liable to death: prison awaited any who sheltered them. This was reasserted in 1609. It brought into the open the progenitors of what was to become a famous gypsy lineage. One Moses Faa supplicated that the Act could not be aimed at 'honnest, lauchfull and trew personis'. He had separated his family from the 'thievish and infamous societie'. He claimed to have been born in Scotland. He had found surety for 1,000 pounds. His surety was David, Earl of Crawford: understandably the Council granted him permission to stay. It could be convenient for a great lord to have some muscular hangers-on who depended totally on him for their survival. Crawford had assured the Council that Moses had separated his family from 'the infamous society' of other Egyptians and that its members were 'honest, lawful and true'. But the concession to Moses did not stop the Council in 1611 launching a fresh attack on gypsies, including some Faas. In 1616, ordering all Egyptians to be banished, the Council admitted that various gentry were harbouring them. Judges and magistrates were ordered to convocate the lieges in arms, to apprehend, judge and execute.[32] The particular instance shows how uncertain were the definitions of vagrants, and how easily the rules could be manipulated by those with power. There was a fresh attack on gypsies in 1633, with penalties for landowners who did not act, and yet in 1634 there was the claim that groups of fifty or sixty were invading East Lothian, where the landowners had refused to act. Clearly, in the handling of vagrancy, though some executions are recorded, the Council's bark was much more severe than its bite.[33]

It is easy to see how vagabonds would be created by repressive legislation. A poor man without connections or employer would, if without work or holding, eventually have to go and search for work outside his own parish. He might band up with others in a similar condition. From then on he would be labelled as undesirable. His best prospects for survival lay in the burghs, but these were always anxious to keep out outsiders unless they came as reasonably well-heeled apprentices or servants. If the statutes on vagrancy were carried out, and for the most part they do not appear to have been, these men would acquire visible evidence of punishment as vagrants, as well as experience which would reduce any sense they might have of obligation to society. What actions had exactly taken place for instance in

Banff in 1636 to explain an entry in the burgh's accounts: 'To Willie
Wat, scurger, for outhalding the poor, L3.6.8'.[34]

The Council saw a value in manpower, and, though ready to
threaten death sentences, in practice preferred to make men useful.
In May 1620 a proclamation of the usual kind against sturdy and idle
beggars and masterless vagabonds stated that recidivists would be let
off the death penalty if they enlisted in the regiment Colonel Gray was
taking to Bohemia. Ten days later it was calling for those who had so
enlisted and promptly deserted to come out of hiding in Edinburgh
and its urban neighbourhood and be present for muster. Colonel Gray,
alleged to be a papist, embarked about 1,500 men. We do not know the
proportion of sturdy beggars among them.[35]

The interest in useful manpower later turned to its economic input.
In 1641 Parliament had conceived the idea of conscripting vagrants
into manufactories for eleven years of service, the first four to be
subsidised by the parish responsible, with one year at two shillings
Scots a day, enough for bread, and then three years at half that. No
particular arrangements were laid down for the costs of coercion and
control, except that discipline was not to extend to death or torture. A
vast overweight committee of thirty-six leading figures was set up to
carry out the Act, and no more is heard of it.[36]

In 1623 the concern of the Council changed. The harvest of 1622
had been a disaster. That oatmeal, the basic food of the country, was
seriously inadequate is shown by the near doubling of the annual grain
price in the only long-term local source we have.[37] The threat of crisis
poverty loomed. The Council had already forbidden the export of
victual and the 'forestalling' of grain, that is of buying it up wholesale
before it got to open market. In June the Council in an enlarged
meeting with gentry and bailies summoned commissioners from the
shires to meet in Edinburgh and make suggestions for the relief of the
poor and the employment of beggars. It produced two proclamations.
In June the first ordered every shire and burgh to hold a meeting of
office bearers, nobles and ministers to decide how much grain or
money was needed and how to raise money for purchases. For this
they were to tax 'the whole inhabitants' at a hundred merks for every
thousand pounds in stock under threat of prosecution and an excess
charge, to raise enough to support the labour force until the prospect
of the next harvest, at the beginning of September, provided work.
The shires were to report what had been done on 9 July. On 11 July,

presumably informed by replies, the Council ordered that all beggars and vagabonds were to be imprisoned and supplied by a further levy, a tax of between one and five shillings Scots according to means.

Proclamations such as these officially had the force of statutes, but what they ordered should have been done some six months earlier to be effective. Beggars, inevitably, were ordered to their 'own' parishes; 500 stone of copper was to be made into penny and twopenny pieces, for alms giving.[38]

The famine may well have been the most serious demographic crisis of the century. It is not possible to assess the level of deaths it produced: the only figures we have, which are startling, come from ports to which those faced with starvation would make their way, hoping for either work or food, and are therefore not representative.[39] But what we know of the unstructured system of Scottish government makes it no surprise that the crisis did not receive organised and effective response. The council soon complained of the sloth and negligence of those who ought to have acted, and of the 'preposterous pitie of the cuntrey people' who gave alms which they could not afford.[40]

The surviving replies to the Council suggest that some places could manage relief if outsiders could be kept away. The parish of Kilrenny (Fife) said that every gentleman was to sustain his own people. The shire of Midlothian took the same line, threatening to delate to the Council those who did not. It also pointed out that the Acts of Parliament could not be observed: the vagrant poor were too weakened to get to their own parishes. Also there were not enough men to act as constables and carry out the Acts. In Perthshire the poor were to get a peck of meal a week from their lairds. Dumfriesshire reported that no one was prepared to suppress 'puir straingers'.

Two replies are of particular note. That from Selkirkshire had a particular touch of despair. Much of the sheriffdom belonged to the crown and was worked by subtenants. If these men were forced to pay a tax, charity would dry up. There was a lack of work for labourers. Those put in prison as vagrants were likely to starve before trial.

The reply from East Lothian had none of this pathos. The shire took till November to answer and its reply was aggressive. The proposed scale of rating for supporting beggars 'keipis no proportiouns according to the diversity of menis rankis, rentis and estaittis'. The proclamation did not give adequate authority and the whole emergency scheme 'smellis of ane taxatioun'. Clearly no special effort for the poor was to come from the best farmland area of Scotland. The reply shows not only the surliness of the East Lothian landed class, but also the haphazard structure of legislation for the poor.[41]

It is not surprising that the programme made for the first Convention of Estates of Charles I's reign, called very soon after the king's succession in 1625, should have laid particular emphasis on the need for better administration of poor relief. The king had a strong sense of order and obedience, and clearly found the varied and inadequate administration of aid in Scotland a serious matter for reform. As it happened other issues were what the Convention concentrated on, so the matter lapsed.[42]

The political disturbances of the period of the Great Rebellion affected every part of government. In particular they forced on a totally new scale of taxation. Events created taxation but did nothing to make it popular.[43] Armies for the wars left families bereft of muscle power or reserves of food, men injured needed support, normal marketing systems were disrupted. For the effect of the revolutionary period on the Poor Law, the key years were those of the short period of Whig party dominance, 1647–51. For the first time in history the country was not dominated by the wishes and demands of the aristocracy and king, but by a mixed group of lesser landowners and ministers of religion. It was this party that passed the Poor Law Act of 1649.[44]

This was a thorough piece of legislation, worded by people who knew what they were about. The Privy Council or the Committee of Estates (a body created by the revolutionary events) was to send commissioners where needed to raise a stent in any parish. Kirk sessions were to fix a level of payment on the heritors of the parish – a ruling which made explicit the responsibility of these landowners. Beggars were to remain within their parish of birth, and there was to be no begging from door to door. If the parish of birth was not known, or acknowledged, the beggars were to be shared out between parishes on which the burden of the poor was slight. The 'slothful' were not to be supported, but work should be provided for beggars in their own parish. (This was the first clear acknowledgement that those out of work should receive support.) Presbyteries were to supervise the sessions in their work. There were some minor moral clauses not very likely to be acted upon: landowners' payments were to be higher for those who had treated their tenants harshly and the level of support was to differ between the pious and the vicious.

The important feature of the Act was the placing of responsibility for support clearly on landowners. Even so, it was not obeyed within its terms. Small contributions from tenantry and cotters (subtenants) remained the normal base of rural parish funding. When it was obviously inadequate for the level of need, landowners were expected to do as some had in 1623 and support the tenantry on their own land. The level of support would be left to them. This, for instance, was what happened in Yester (East Lothian). In December 1649 the minister had read the Act to the congregation and ordered the heritors to a meeting. The heritors adopted what was to become the usual method of frustrating the settling of a rate by not attending. A list of the poor was made up by the minister and elders, and divided by the baronies within the parish. Three months later the minister was still trying to persuade the barony owners to take on the support of their poor. Two of the three agreed, but one of these did not in fact act. Then in the late summer the parish was invaded and plundered by one or other of the armies that fought at Dunbar, and the minister was imprisoned. It was not for another two years that some sort of regular funding for the poor was achieved. This was organised by baronies, not by the congregation, and it is possible that one barony was not participating.[45]

This all seems some way from observance of the Act. But the Act has to be seen within its political context. The nobility had been disgraced by military failure and then counted out of politics by the Act of Classes. Many nobles had done public penance in their parish kirks for their political misdeeds. They were vulnerable in a way they had never been before. It would no longer be possible in future totally to ignore legal obligations to support the poor, though there was still plenty of room for failure to attend meetings, minimalist interpretations of the law, preposterous legal arguments, delays in decision-making and even greater delays in paying, and threats of other difficulties: by such means many landowners might get away with failure to pay.

The Act of 1649 marked the Kirk in charge of poor relief, even though the actual terms of the Act were not carried out. It had become clear that there was some sort of obligation on the part of landowners, in emergencies, either to give money for relief to the parish kirk session or to take over the support of the poor on their own land. It is clear from a vast number of parish records that this could not be taken for granted, and that pressure from minister and kirk sessions would usually be necessary to get landowners to fulfil their legal obligations. The Kirk would not only give out pensions to the old and infirm, but would also pay school fees for poor children, hire a wet-nurse for a motherless baby, give trifling funds to poor people on the road and contribute towards a surgeon's fee for a necessary operation.

The Act of 1649 was wiped out at the Restoration along with all other legislation of the Great Rebellion period by the Act Rescissory of 1661. It was not repeated. This did not matter. Its significance had lain in the period in which it had been passed and in which, partly at least, it had operated. The precedents established under it meant that there was a limit to the degree to which landowners could ignore their statutory role in relief. So long as the Kirk approved of support being given to the poor, there would be pressure on landowners to accept the idea of a rate in emergencies.

NOTES

1. See Robert Jütte, *Poverty and Deviance in Early Modern Europe* (Cambridge, 1994); Thomas Riis, *Aspects of Poverty in Early Modern Europe*, 3 Vols (Stuttgart, 1981–90); Brian Pullan, 'Support and redeem: charity and poor relief in Italian cities from the fourteenth to the seventeenth century', *Continuity and Change*, Vol. III (1988), pp. 177–208; Sandra Cavallo, *Charity and Power in Early Modern Italy* (Cambridge, 1995); Paul Slack, *Poverty and Policy in Tudor and Stuart England* (London, 1988).

2. Paul Slack, *Poverty and Policy*, ch. 8; Ole Peter Grell, 'The Protestant imperative of Christian care and neighbourly love', in Ole Peter Grell and Andrew Cunningham (eds), *Health Care and Poor Relief in Protestant Europe 1500–1700* (London, 1997), pp. 43–65.

3. H. Dingwall, *Late Seventeenth Century Edinburgh* (Aldershot, 1944), p. 250.

4. A. L. Beier, *Masterless Men: the Vagrancy Problem in England 1560–1640* (London, 1985), pp. 52–6.

5. *APS* III 88; 14. *Eliz.* I Cap. 5.

6. E. M. Leonard, *The Early History of English Poor Relief* (Cambridge, 1900); Marjorie K. McIntosh, 'The poor in late Medieval and Tudor England', *Continuity and Change*, Vol. III (1988) pp. 209–45.

7. W. S. Holdsworth, *A History of English Law*, Vol. X (London, 1938), pp. 256–95.

8. *APS* III 139.

9. For a view of the priorities possessed by the leaders of surnames see Keith M. Brown, 'A house divided: family and feud in Carrick under John Kennedy, Fifth Earl of Cassillis', *SHR* October 1996, vol. 75, pp. 168–86.

10. *RPCS* V p. 200.

11. J. K. Cameron (ed.), *The First Book of Discipline* (Edinburgh, 1972), p. 12 'The fifth head'.

12. Anna B. Calderwood, *Buik of the Kirk of the Canagait 1564–1567* (SRS, Edinburgh, 1961), pp. 5, 13, etc.

13. D. Hay Fleming (ed.), *Register of the Minister, Elders and Deacons of the Christian Congregation of St. Andrews* (SHS, 2 vols, Edinburgh, 1889–90), pp. 340, 408, 552.

14. Elizabeth P. D. Torrie (ed.), *Gild Court Book of Dunfermline, 1433–1597*, (SRS Edinburgh, 1986), pp. 42, 93, 149.

15. John Stewart (ed.), *Selections from the Kirk Session, Presbytery and Synod of Aberdeen* (Spalding Club, Aberdeen, 1846), p. 19.

16. *RPCS* III p. 137.

17. J. Goodare, 'Parliament and Society in Scotland 1560–1603 ch. 8 (Edinburgh Ph.D. thesis, 1989). I am particularly grateful to this author for correction of mistakes made by me.

18. Marguerite Wood (ed.), *Extracts from the Records of the Burgh of Edinburgh, 1620–42* (Edinburgh, 1936).

19. J. Goodare, 'Parliament and Society'.

20. W. Cramond (ed.), *Records of Elgin* vol. 2 (New Spalding Club, Aberdeen 1908), pp. 26, 47, 78. These samples show that the burgh was working some sort of relief in the 1590s.

21. Personal communication from Dr Helen Dingwall.

22. *APS* IV, 232.

23. Hew Scott, *Fasti Ecclesiae Scoticanae*, vol. VI (Edinburgh, 1926), pp. 1–274 for the Synod of Aberdeen: vol. IV (Edinburgh, 1923), pp. 257–88 for the presbytery of Auchterarder.

24. James Kirk (ed.), *Visitations of the Diocese of Dunblane 1586–1589* (SRS, Edinburgh, 1984), pp. 13, 15, 29, 33, 51.

25. H. Paton (ed.), *The Session Book of Dundonald 1602–1731* (Edinburgh, 1936), pp. 118, 263, 312, 398.

26. James Kirk (ed.), *The Records of the Synod of Lothian and Tweeddale* (Stair Society, Edinburgh, 1977), pp. 93, 106, 268, 292.

27. *RPCS* IV p. 317; *APS* IV p. 232.

28. *RPCS* VIII pp. 305, 372, 712.

29. *RPCS* X pp. 470–2.

30. *RPCS* 2nd series V p. 47 (1633).

31. *APS* IV 625.

32. *RPCS* IX p. 205, X pp. 132, 556, 559, 655.

33. *RPCS* new series V p. 402.

34. W. Cramond (ed.), *Annals of Banff*, vol. I (New Spalding Club, Aberdeen, 1841), p. 74.

35. David Calderwood, *The History of the Kirk of Scotland* (Wodrow Society, Edinburgh, 1842), vol. I, p. 253; *RPCS* XII p. 259.
36. *APS* V 411, 658.
37. A. J. S. Gibson and T. C. Smout, *Prices, Food and Wages in Scotland 1556–1780* (Cambridge, 1995), p. 84.
38. *RPCS* XIII pp. 129, 203–5, 238, 257–60, 287–90, 329, 803–4.
39. M. W. Flinn, Judith Gillespie, Nancy Hill, Ailsa Maxwell, Rosalind Mitchison, T. C. Smout, Duncan Anderson and Robin Lobban, *Scottish Population History from the Seventeenth Century to the 1930s* (Cambridge, 1977), pp. 116–26.
40. *RPCS* XIII pp. 287–91.
41. *RPCS* XIII pp. 805–40.
42. *APS* V 178b.
43. David Stevenson, 'The financing of the cause of the Covenants', *SHR* 51 (1972), pp. 89–123.
44. *APS* VI ii 220, 'Act anent the poor'.
45. SRO CH2/377/2.

CHAPTER 2

PROBLEMS AND ACHIEVEMENTS, 1650–1700

In lowland Scotland the Poor Law developed with what appears to have been general agreement in the three decades after the Act of 1649. Practice seems very similar in the different parishes which have left records. This is probably the result of the working of the presbyterian court system. Presbyteries met frequently and regularly and attendance by parish ministers was insisted on. Once the formal business was done there was opportunity for the sharing of problems and ideas. Synod meetings were more formal as well as rarer, and the General Assembly was supressed. Yet it is clear that the same interpretations of the law, the emphasis on some features of the statutes and the ignoring of others, prevailed in widely separate areas. But reliance on the documentation presents a bias. Some parishes were lacking in organisation. Few Highland parishes had a kirk session, nor had some in the Lowlands. For instance, Bunkle and Preston, in 1665 'could not be sure that it had ever had a kirk session register'.[1]

It became common for parishes to make a list of those in long-term dependence on aid, and to refer to the aid, given out perhaps monthly or quarterly, as pensions. This aid was normally not enough to live on, but for those who could not get about to beg and therefore needed full support, this would be given in kind or money. There seems to have been a general agreement that a peck of oatmeal a week was enough to live on, provided it was augmented by occasional supplies of clothing or fuel. The pensioners capable of walking were expected to ask for alms, and the statutory prohibitions about begging were ignored for them. Parishes took over the care of destitute orphans, a group not mentioned in the statutes, and, more grudgingly, foundlings. Since there was no certainty that an abandoned child had been born in the parish where it was found, once efforts to trace a parent had failed, the burden of support was often divided between neighbouring parishes. Parishes might pay the school fees of needy children and in some cases club together with other parishes to provide a bursary for a student at college. Sprouston (Roxburghshire) decided in November 1669 to pay half a merk quarterly to encourage poor people to put their children to the school. Parishes might also pay, in whole or part, for surgical treatment. Spott (East Lothian) in December 1691 paid three pounds to 'a poor lad that had his foot cut off in East Barns', and Guthrie (Angus) gave an extra 10 shillings Scots to Elspeth Emes 'to support already given her' to stay in Forfar 'under cure of the Cancer she had in her lippe'. In Yester (East Lothian) in 1695 2 pounds 8 shillings was spent on a 'rupture band' for an occasional but frequently aided parishioner. Another method of giving aid is shown in Bolton (East Lothian) in 1688 when the cost of setting a boy's broken thigh was met by private gifts from members of the session.

The concept of need seems to have been based on a compromise between the facts of the situation and the resources of the parish, not on any formal definition. But certain types of provision soon came to have a standard rate of support. Nine or ten pounds a quarter came to be the normal payment for the wet nursing of a twin or a motherless child, presumably based on the opportunity cost to the nurse. Payments for hazards to earning power seem to have varied. In Montrose in 1699 'a poor Carter' received 6 pounds to help him buy a horse, which would not be the full cost of replacement but merely help towards it. In Gordon (Berwickshire) in 1690 a man received the same amount towards a new horse, not from the Poor Box but from a special collection. Yester in 1663 gave 7 pounds 6 shillings to a man who 'through death of his beasts' was 'disabled to work for his livelihood'. The same parish refused to reimburse a man who had had a quantity of malt burnt. McPherson in his book, *The Kirk's Care of the Poor*, gives many instances of economic aid, but all for a later period than the seventeenth century. Parishes might help cripples to beg by contributing barrows on which they could be moved, or even stretchers in which they could be carried from house to house. In Fordyce (Banffshire) in 1666 a woman was carried about in a creel.[2]

Particular generosity appears to have been shown to the insane, who were not expected to do anything for their own support, not even to beg. The list of expenditure on one William Hay in Yester, shows this. He received a pension of 4 pounds a quarter, and a woman was appointed as his keeper. When the price of meal rose in 1695 an extra allowance was made. A milk cow was bought for him when his old one was sold, the session paying the difference, and in the autumn three pounds was spent on straw for it. He was kept in shoes and given new blankets and coverings. When his mother had died the principle landowner, Lord Tweeddale, stated to the minister concerning the tenancy 'God forbid that ever he should withdraw his Charitie from such an object . . . he should never doe it'. The session took care to record this statement in the register.

The funds of parishes came in the first instance from weekly collections made by the elders in their districts or at the church door on Sundays. It has generally been assumed that little coin was in circulation in late seventeenth-century Scotland, but the amounts that could be raised for special collections authorised by the Church could be considerable. These collections were called 'voluntary', but that word did not carry its normal meaning in church affairs; the Church would inquire if parishes did not contribute to collections which it had authorised. In 1684 in response to an appeal after the third occasion in which much of Kelso had been destroyed by fire, the minister of Yester gathered in 285 pounds from the parish. Of this, 186 pounds, 13 shillings and 4 pence came from the major landowners, the Earl of Tweeddale and his son, but some individual townships gave as much as 9 pounds. When things were going well, that the rural community had considerable wealth is shown by the fact that landowners might borrow from their own tenants.[3]

Parishes, recognising that special collections took the place of normal collections and so reduced parish funds, took to retaining a part of such special collections. Yester, for instance, in 1674 kept five pounds out of ten collected for two prisoners in Turkey, a cause to which it had given 62 pounds earlier in the year, and in 1678 kept 4 pounds 10 shillings out of 34 pounds 16 shillings from a special collection. Some of these special collections, which might be authorised by the Privy Council or the Synod, were for purely secular causes. Dunkeld presbytery responded in this period to collections for the repair of harbours such as that of Inverkeithing, the bridges of Almond and Dee and the brewery of Alloa. Chirnside (Berwickshire) in 1701 had collections for the harbours of Eyemouth and Kinghorn, and Sprouston in 1695 responded to the Privy Council's urging with 4 pounds 13 shillings towards Cullen harbour, hardly in this case a feature of use to its community.

Money also came from other sources. All the parish money was called 'the Poor's money' and put into the Poor Box. This definition did not stop it being used for other parish business, such as the purchase of communion cups or other equipment, the travelling expenses of ministers visiting during vacancies, the salaries of the parish's officer and session clerk, and the parish contribution to the salary of the clerks of the presbytery and Synod.

The keeping of coherent accounts by parishes was not yet well established. Sessions would appoint one or two elders as treasurers, but the accounts, such as they were, would be entered in the register, which was usually either compiled by the minister or by the session clerk from slips of paper written during the meetings. None of these men would have had any training in bookkeeping. Sometimes the financial record was a mixed list of outgoings and collections. Sometimes these would be in separate columns. Expenditure might be recorded simply as 'to the pensioners their pensions'. Money matters might be mixed up with other affairs such as the records of discipline, but sometimes they are recorded in a separate book, or the main register has been used in reverse. It is rare to find a list of the capital resources of a parish. For these reasons it is not practicable to attempt a figure of expenditure year by year by parishes on relief, or to estimate the proportion of resources transferred to the poor, but it is possible to identify very poor or relatively well-off parishes.

In parishes which kept a list of the 'regular' poor, the names of pensioners can be noted and pursued from list to list. People can be found on consecutive lists for several years, which suggests that even the small sums given out were effective in keeping the old and infirm or orphan children alive. But survival is not firm proof of the efficiency of the relief system, since charity of an informal nature was also assumed to be a Christian virtue. It could be that the Poor Law was merely organising on a coherent basis the aid that would have been informally available anyway. But it is a common feature of charitable giving that it is selective, and not all cases of need are usually met by it. Just as the Church provided a mechanism for the supply of aid to good causes or desirable economic developments, so it chanelled relief to people in need. But it is probable that there were cases of severe hardship which did not get aid or did not get enough, because the method of distribution in the poorer parishes was to count how much had come in during the last month, put aside part of it for unavoidable expenses, such as the salaries of officer and session clerk, and then see to what number of the acknowledged poor a small dole could be given.

Disaster striking an individual family or community, if it meant that more aid was needed than was likely to be available, would be met by a special collection, either simply within the parish or by enlisting the support of a higher church court, in a wider range of parishes. In February 1663 Sprouston session received an appeal from an individual, and the session 'finding him poor . . . appoyntit ye nixt day intimation out of pulpit for a contribution to be gathered', and in November the same parish, stimulated by a higher court, appointed a collection for the 'burning of the families in Ednam', for which 9 pounds 2 shillings Scots was collected.

The general expansion over time of aid to the poor shows in the generosity of the better off, and suggests that Poor Law development met a need in the givers as well as in the recipients. Yester in December 1674 recorded an anonymous gift of 20 pounds by someone on recovery from sickness. In the same parish in 1676 'one who desired his name concealed' gave 28 pounds, and ten years later there was another anonymous gift of 100 pounds which the parish used for the purchase of catechisms for all who could read. (This suggests that at this point there was no shortage of funds for the poor.) McPherson claims that gifts on recovery from illness or for the successful avoidance of danger were common in the north and gives among other examples the gift of 5 pounds 16 shillings in 1665 by an Elgin bailie for safe return from London.[4]

Most parishes for which records exist for this period had received one or more legacies. There was general recognition that this money should be used as a capital resource: indeed there was a ruling to this effect in the proclamation of the Privy Council of August 1692, but this ruling was unnecessary, merely a confirmation of practice. Yet the handling of capital posed difficult problems in the undeveloped state of the economy. The legal maximum rate of interest, brought down to 6 per cent in 1661, was too low for the Scottish economy. There was little in the way of safe enterprises in which to invest other than land. Landowners, whose pattern of spending varied considerably from year to year, were therefore the obvious destination for money, but it was wise to lend only to men whose lands lay in other parishes. Landowners often had close personal links with members of the legal profession; ministers and elders had not. A parish landowner could be of great assistance in litigation with outside borrowers, but the same powers could make it difficult to use the law against such a man. Lending to minor businesses, local craftsmen or merchants could mean that if repayment was enforced, the parish might find itself supporting the failed borrower. There were some other investment possibilities: Sprouston, for instance, lent its capital to Edinburgh, and was indignant when the city in 1695 decided to pay only 5 per cent interest. The parish's protest produced the response that the parish was free to go and find better: the city had other parishes ready to lend to it at the new rate. The minister of Dunbarney (Perthshire) had made a special visit to the city to assess its credit worthiness. Sprouston decided that it was best to let its money stay with Edinburgh.

That many parishes had by the 1670s come to work some approximation to various parts of the statutes about the poor did not mean that new statutes were productive, or that there was pressure to adopt the part of older statutes that demanded assessment of landowners, or that some sort of Poor Law extended to the whole of Scotland. Most highland parishes had not yet set up effective kirk sessions, and highland presbyteries were not powerful enough to exercise authority at parish level, so there was no Poor Law activity in most of the Highlands. The Scottish Parliament produced Acts in 1663 and 1672 in which was set out a possible link between the development of new industries and the existence of a labour surplus, in other words the proposal that vagabonds and beggars should be conscripted into a labour force for 'manufactories'.[5] The legislation shows a failure to grasp basic facts of economic life. It was skilled labour that new industries needed. Failed and infirm peasants would not make an effective labour force even if they were willing to try. We have no acceptable figures for the number of vagabonds or distressed peasantry on the roads. The estimate produced by Andrew Fletcher of Saltoun in 1698, and widely quoted by uncritical admirers of the man, of 100,000 at normal times, increasing to 200,000 in a dearth, is rubbish produced by the combination of innumeracy and upper-class distaste for the poor.[6] Certainly there appear to be more wandering people receiving small levels of help in the 1680s than in earlier periods, but this may reflect improved resources or enhanced willingness to give. But there were not enough people on the roads to amount to approximately a tenth of the nation. In defiance of the wording in many statutes and the rulings of baron courts, many kirk sessions aided the travelling poor and householders took them in.[7] When the kirk session of Bunkle asked a man why he had not had his proclamation of marriage made there he replied that he was too poor to have a constant residence but travelled from place to place for his maintenance. There was no suggestion that the parish would apply the Acts against vagrants against him.

Perhaps because the Parliaments which had produced the various Acts against vagrants and for support of the poor consisted of men with little practical knowledge of the problems of those far removed from them in status and resources, perhaps because legislators were interested in the rhetoric of legislators in other countries, perhaps because the courts of the Scottish Church were not prepared to allow secular legislation to determine their actions, the main features of the working system of poor relief in lowland Scotland after 1649 were not those ordered by statute. In particular the sharp division between the local 'poor, aged and impotent' and vagrants was not fully observed. 'Common beggars' were given small doles and allowed to go on their way. No rural parish would carry out the branding, imprisonment or forced apprenticeship laid down in various statutes.

Parishes did not openly break the law. In Yester the proclamation of the Privy Council of August 1692 demanding the sending back of all beggars to their 'own' parishes, after their presentation to a heritor who would list their names, and the imprisonment of any found around after the second Tuesday of September, led to a total cessation of doles to beggars for four months, but to no other action. Recognition of the proclamation and other rulings led, though, to local definitions. Begging by the poor was inescapable, since they could not be given enough to support themselves by parishes. A clear instance of the inadequacy of pensions is shown in Penninghame, October 1701, when Helen McTaggart was given 2 pounds instead of her usual 14 shillings because 'she cannot go around to receive charity'. Parishes might present the poor with the uniform of a blue gown, or issue badges to make it clear that those possessing these features were approved beggars. Some parishes took the view that the legislation did not apply so long as begging was confined within the parish, a view which received some support from the wording of statutes.

In a society where approximately a third of the gross agricultural

produce goes to meet rent demands, the obvious source of supple-
mentation of resource for the poor, when needed, must necessarily be
the landowners, usually known in Scotland as 'heritors'.[8] Of course
landowners who lived in the parish would contribute to collections,
and at marriages, baptisms and burials of their class there would be
general largesse to beggars.[9] The striking feature though of most
seventeenth-century session records is the absence of any suggestion
of assessment on land, the stent explicitly demanded in statutes from
1574 on. Stents are rarely proposed, except in the larger burghs, let
alone made effectual, yet the creation of a land tax, the 'cess' in the
Restoration period, meant that a valuation had been placed on all
estates, and the technical problems of levying a stent had disappeared.
The general lack of such a tax shows that the landowning class had
made it clear that it did not intend to see a new burden placed on rents.

But there were general burdens placed on the tenantry of some
parishes, and in such cases landowners might also have to contribute.
McPherson states that in Fintray (Aberdeenshire) in 1692 land had to
produce 3 pounds Scots a week or an equivalent in oatmeal.[10] At the
same date a levy was placed on land in Belhelvie (Aberdeenshire) and
in New Machar (Aberdeenshire) the landowners promised a regular
supply for the disabled. Gordon (Berwickshire) in the 1690s had a
stent laid on the peasantry: the greater tenants had to supply 15
shillings a quarter in money or the equivalent in oatmeal, the lesser 10
shillings, the cottars 4 or 2 shillings according to their holdings.

Spott (East Lothian) had in the 1680s some sort of agreed contribution from all, but in 1686 when the elders were expected to gather
it in they refused to act: they 'declared that the last time they met with
great difficulty and contempt . . . and that likely they would with more
now, the people generally still more and more withdrawing from the
church and that they judged it not worth their pains and very little for
the poors behoof to follow that course considering now the humours of
the people . . . whereupon it was thought fit to forbear it for a while'.
Two years later the elders were urging the minister to get the Justices
to give back to the parish for the poor the fines for scandalous cases:
the poor, they stated, were 'daylie Increasing and the ordinar collections daylie declyning through the contempt and separation of de-
faulters'. There was a covenanters' meeting house nearby in Dunbar
which was receiving the fees for marriage and baptism from those
'dishaunting the Church'. The problems of this parish show how

funds for relief were likely to be curtailed by religious division and by the overlap of civil and ecclesiastical jurisdictions.

In contrast to the preceding thirty years, the decade of the 1690s was a time of economic and social stress. The Revolution of 1689 led to the 'outing' of two-thirds of the Church's ministry and their replacement by men not contaminated by acceptance of episcopacy. In the south, where almost all the ministry was thrown out, the process was brisk and often accompanied by threats of violence. Groups of men went from parish to parish threatening or assaulting the minister. The process was given political approval by the self-appointed General Assembly. In the north, where there was stronger support for episcopacy, the process had to be done by church authorities, and this meant that the General Assembly could not act till death provided it with a vacant parish in which presbyterianism could be given a foothold, and from which the incumbents of the other parishes in the presbytery could be attacked. So in many cases the ministers in occupation at the Revolution could hold on for several years, though under threat. The loss of experienced ministers in some parishes, the uncertainty in others all meant that the Church was weakened by the Revolution and less able than before to carry out its social functions. In some parishes, for instance Kingarth (Bute), it had not yet been strong enough to compel heritors to carry out their statutory financial duties and was paying for church repair out of the Poor Box. Entries in session registers give other indications of the disturbance at parish level. In Blackford (Perthshire) no presbyterian minister was available till 1697: such a prolonged vacancy deprived the parish of the leadership it needed. In this case it also appears to have deprived the parish of its basic equipment, for all that it possessed at the induction of the new minister was a basin. In Chirnside (Berwickshire) the minister forced out left with the key to the Poor Box and the Register. The parish had also lost elders who did not agree with the new religious establishment. Those who remained had to obtain a sheriff's warrant to have the Box broken open. Similarly in Killearn (Dunbartonshire) the mortcloth, an important parish investment, had gone with the minister and was not regained till 1695. In Newtyle (Angus) almost open warfare existed between the mass of the parishioners who supported the outed minister, and the presbytery. Documents and money had been stolen. In May 1698 in an effort to oust the episcopal minister the presbytery had broken down the church door. The *Fasti* of the Church,[11] which does not lapse into impartiality over the schism, denies that any session existed, but the surviving register shows up the falsity of this claim. Peace was not re-established there till after the 1715 rising. The session of Auchtergaven (Perthshire) was being attacked as late as 1708 by Lord Nairne, a conspicuous Jacobite, doubtless for political reasons.[12]

The difficulties which the Church faced in carrying out its accepted social duties were enhanced by economic stress. The Revolution settlement involved Scotland in a war against France, to which the extra burden of hearth taxes and poll taxes bears witness. There was also a running sore of warfare in the Highlands whenever highland chiefs had enough spare grain to suport their followers in a campaign. Armies did not support their men once their usefulness was over. This meant that the roads carried a stream of semi-disabled soldiers and sailors. Session registers occasionally report the gift of aid to 'gentlewomen' or ministers, presumably made destitute by the Revolution. Yester (East Lothian) in 1694 gave three pounds each to a Mr Crastie and a Mr Brown, and Carriden (West Lothian) in 1698 gave four shillings to 'a poor broken Gentleman in time of prelacie', James Hornby. The surge of vagrants may, of course, owe something to increasing generosity. In June 1692 the Earl of Stair complained to the Privy Council about 'finding the beggars in Edinburgh very numerous and troublesome': he had asked the magistrates to take action about them but they had claimed that these were incomers from the neighbouring counties, and if turned out of the city would be a burden on these. A subcommittee of the Council was set up and it was this body which produced a proclamation in August 1692.[13]

That the Church had been weakened by the Revolution does not mean that its rival authority, the state, had been strengthened. Scottish ministries in the 1690s were amalgamations of the dominant noble families, but were under constant pressure from the leading English politicians who had better access to the king and represented a more powerful country. But lay government had acquired in the Restoration period instruments of local government that were eventually to be valuable. Since 1609 there had been Justices of the Peace, designed to imitate the same institution in England, but who, in Scotland, had badly defined spheres of action and had not yet established much authority. In an unusual Act of 1661 they had been ordered to appoint overseers for the poor, but there is no evidence that they did so at that time. In 1667 there were also set up the Commissioners of Supply. This body was recruited in every county from landowners on a wide spectrum: anyone with a hundred pounds Scots in rents qualified for appointment. Its function was to allot the cess or tax on rents, and hence a valuation. Other activities eventually accrued to this body, such as decisions about the allocation of superiorities on which the creation of bogus votes for county elections came to depend. The holding of county meetings, large gatherings of landowners, to express opinions on important matters (such as the proposal for a Scottish militia) was also organised by them, as was the selection of men to fulfil the county's share of conscripts in wartime. The low qualification made the body exceptionally representative, and its taxing function gave it authority. Two small local taxes were levied by the Commissioners: 'rogue money' to cover the cost of arresting and imprisoning suspect criminals; and 'road money', funds for repair of roads and bridges. Inevitably political authority followed taxing power, but for the most part this took place only in the eighteenth century.

Local power, like central, was temporarily weakened by the Revolution. In parts of Scotland no one would take the oath of allegiance to the new monarchy and therefore the offices of Justice and Commissioner were vacant. In 1696 the shortage of Commissioners in East Lothian was serious enough to merit discussion in the Privy Council. In the north-east it was much more serious and the central government had no instruments there.

The proclamation of August 1692[14] for the most part repeated previous statutory features. Beggars were to retire to their own parishes: parishes were to hold meetings on specific days, make lists of their own poor and estimate the cost of their support. They were to appoint overseers, and an officer to deliver the maintenance to the poor, who was also to see that 'stranger vagabonds' were expelled. The cost of supporting the poor was to lie half on householders, half on heritors. Fines of two hundred pounds were threatened for parishes which failed to act. Children under fifteen were to be bound as servants till the age of thirty and to be disciplined by their masters, 'life and torture excepted'. Vagabonds were to be imprisoned on bread and water for a month. Anyone found giving them alms was to be fined twenty shillings, and heritors who failed to act in dispatching beggars to their own parishes were to be fined twenty pounds. Correction houses 'hitherto neglected' (a rare recognition of the gap between statutory provision and fact) were to be built in the principal towns. Another proclamation followed in August 1693. It began by recognising that the previous one had been frustrated by uncertainty as to where beggars were to be located as a burden, and the general failure of magistrates and heritors to provide for them. The remedy was largely a repetition of the previous proclamation. Anyone found begging after the second Tuesday of September was to be imprisoned: heritors were to stent themselves, sheriffs were to prosecute persons or parishes which failed to act. There was, however, one new clause. Half the collections of the parish were to be handed over to the heritors for the poor. The council appears to have thought that it was the heritors rather than the kirk sessions who actively cared for the poor.

By now the statements on settlement were confused and were to become more so. In 1579 beggars had been ordered to remove to where they had been born or had passed seven years. In 1617 this had become three years, now it reverted to seven. It is a sign of the lack of serious thought on the relief system and its problems.

In January 1694 the Privy Council complained that good laws and proclamations were in many places not being observed, and called on sheriffs, the magistrates of royal burghs and Justices of the Peace to investigate and fine all those who had neglected their duty. A committee of the Council was set up to receive reports.[15]

Signs of the difficulties the economy was experiencing began to mount. The Council delayed the poll tax of 1695 because of the 'broken and uncertain' weather, but things did not improve. The unsuccessful Darien scheme of colonisation was mopping up resources needed elsewhere. The 'little ice age' as historians have called the late seventeenth century was about to produce the famine of the 1690s. Already in 1695 the harvest was poor, and grain prices exceeded those of the previous year by between 14 and 75 per cent. In 1696 they moved higher, till in some counties they were more than double the normal level. The white fishing of the north-east failed, sending fishermen into beggary, and the sheriff of Mearns pleaded for a further delay of the poll tax. The year 1697 saw a moderation of the weather and a normal harvest, but 1698 and 1699 were again harvest failures, which were particularly severe in the north. Biblical analogy has attached to this period of extreme hardship and loss of life the title of 'the seven ill years', an exaggeration, but four years of inadequate food supply was bad enough. The economy was still at the stage when lack of resources in the countryside meant unemployment there and in the towns. People who have not money enough for food have no money for other goods, so craftsmen also lacked resource. Normally the urban poor had more sources of relief than the rural: the incorporations and the town council would give aid. In Aberdeen, a city particularly badly hit, the whole marketing system broke down. The proportion of pauper burials to all burials rose from 30 per cent to 50 per cent. Significantly it fell to 20 per cent in 1700, for death had reduced the number of poor. Rural tenants could not afford to hire farm servants whom they would have to feed, so the young people of the cottar class were without work. The famine was probably not as severe as that of 1623 but, coming after a period in which the country had managed to support itself with something to spare, it was a devastating shock. It has been estimated that somewhere between 5 and 15 per cent of the population died from want and from the epidemics which accompany famine, but a gloomier picture has been drawn for the north-east of the death of some 40 per cent.[16] Figures on the scale of either estimate show that the Poor Law was not yet able to manage a crisis of this scale.

Yet a considerable number of the parishes of lowland Scotland were following their own accepted form of the Poor Law and trying to meet need. In the Highlands the few parishes which had attained a degree of presbyterian church organisation struggled ineffectually. It has been suggested that chieftainship in highland society meant that though clansmen were expected to sustain the chief and his followers with gifts and hospitality, there was a return service of feasting which meant that the chief was expected to support his men. The fighting strength of the clan would be sustained in hard times by whatever reserves the chief had, but it seems unlikely that any form of adequate help would extend to the wives and children of the men. In any case the highland economy normally depended on trading cattle for grain, and the grain prices of the Lowlands would not give Highlanders purchasing power for the 'Leith meal' of which the Gaelic poet Ian Lom wrote disparagingly. In 1696 Scotland exported 100,000 goat skins: this is an indicator of the pressures on the highland economy.[17]

For 1695 and 1696 proclamations of the Privy Council were replaced by Acts of Parliament, to much the same effect.[18] The Act of 1696 empowered the council to grant a commission to a group of persons to be supervisors and inspectors of the poor, but this does not appear to have been acted on. In the reprieve caused by the better harvest of 1697 the council produced a proclamation claiming that the poor were 'now competently provyded against by the plenty of victual': this marked a return to its normal efforts to control the export and import of grain. Export to France had been banned in March 1695 but allowed in December of that year. In March 1698, still in the euphoria resulting from the 1697 harvest, the council returned to proclamations about the poor. It approved the earlier proclamations and Acts of Parliament and reaffirmed the policy of providing for the poor by correction houses as laid out in the Act of 1672. These were to be built in a leading burgh in all lowland shires. Fourteen such burghs were mentioned. Elgin was to build one for Moray and Nairn combined, and Fife was to have four. Commissioners of Excise were to put the Act into execution and levy fines of up to 500 merks on all who failed to act, presumably on burgh authorities.[19]

The proclamation called on parishes to send their poor to these houses by 1 November. Even if the burghs had decided to obey orders and build such houses they would not have been ready for occupation by then, still less is it likely that a stock of materials on which the poor could work would have been laid in. In any case there is no sign of any such houses being built. The proclamation ended with the usual order for the ministers, elders and heritors of all parishes to meet and organise support of the poor.

In July 1699 the council was ordering a large committee to investigate 'what parishes have been most backward' in giving obedience to the proclamation about beggars, and to name them to the council so that they might be 'tryed or otherways punished for ane example to others'. In September the council recorded that further proclamations about correction houses had been put together but not published. The Lord Advocate was instructed to draw up a new order, which should include that all vagrant beggars were to return to their place of birth or of three years' settlement. The Commissioners of Supply were to be called into action by sheriffs and to report back by December.

This is the setting of the proclamation of 15 September, which in familiar terms called for parish meetings on the second Thursday of October to make arrangements about the poor, and to dispatch home all wandering beggars, and on burgh magistrates to build the correction houses, 'all of which . . . shall have a large close sufficiently inclosed, for keeping the said poor people that they be not necessitat to be always withindoors to the hurt and hazard of their health'. There were to be the usual penalties for inaction, and all in authority were to report back by 1 February. In addition in December the Lord Advocate was to make a special investigation of what had been done in the parishes of Fife and the Lothians.[20]

That is the story from the point of view of the central government. The Council had done what it could to get poor relief working. Less activity of a practical kind was shown by the central body of the Church. At various points in the crisis the General Assembly gave orders for a solemn fast to turn away divine wrath. But much of its output to the parishes took the form of the usual recommendations for special collections. One of these in the winter of 1695, which certainly burdened parishes in the early part of the famine, was for the Scottish church to be built at Königsberg. Parishes responded as best they could. For some reason the contribution in response to this gathered in by Chirnside (Berwickshire) was never delivered and was transferred to the local poor in 1699. Kemnay (Aberdeenshire) had an old collection made for French and Irish Protestants which the presbytery had failed to uplift, and part of this was used to help its own poor in December 1696. Spott (East Lothian) was called upon to give money for the harbour at Queensferry (hardly of local use) in November 1696, and other calls for funds went out as usual.

It is from the parish records that the performance of the relief system under stress has to be assessed: 229 parishes have left session registers for this period, that is approximately a quarter of all parishes and there are some other sources of information. In a famine of the scale of that of the 1690s the only effective remedy must be the shifting of purchasing power from the recipients of surplus production, that is the landowners, in some form to the poor. In how many parishes did this happen?

Besides the royal burghs of Edinburgh and Glasgow, which had some form of assessment, forty-six parishes can be found to have taken steps which tapped the reserves of their landowners, in other words enforced some sort of stent or assessment.[21] Performance appears to have been best in the Lothians. Taking assessed parishes as a percentage of those for which records survive, East Lothian achieved

56 per cent assessed, Midlothian 31 per cent and West Lothian 25 per cent. Other shires with a noticeable level are Fife, with 15 per cent, Lanarkshire 21 per cent, Perthshire 37 per cent (but not many parishes have left records here) and Ayrshire 17 per cent. Clearly response was mainly localised in the core area not far from Edinburgh, though a few parishes outside this also assessed, Ashkirk in Roxburghshire, Manor and Eddleston in Peeblesshire, Galashiels in Selkirkshire, Kettins in Angus, Longside and the city of New Aberdeen in Aberdeenshire, Drainie in Moray. The scanty registers of other parishes reveal no sign of assessment.

To anyone who has worked through the various volumes of the seventeenth-century registers of the Privy Council, there is a certain familiarity in the area in which assessment occurred. It is noticeably that in which the Council expected some level of obedience to its orders. Messages to these places not only penetrated but were often successful: there was not the block to action by the crown produced by the great feudal franchises.

Of course the other three-quarters of parishes which have not left records may contain some which did manage to assess their heritors. And there are some session registers which show assessment under discussion, but record no clear decision. In Glasford (Lanarkshire) and Livingstone (West Lothian) there was serious consideration of the orders of the Privy Council, and the Glasford register refers to a stent in 1699, but there are no signs that this included putting a burden on the landowners and the tenantry would not have enough to spare for the stenting of them to be an adequate source of relief. Two of the parishes noted as assessed have been found in sources other than session registers and others may come to light. But there tends to be some degree of correlation between the keeping of clear records and efficiency of performance, so it is likely that most areas with no surviving register were not effectively supporting their poor.

Methods of assessment were varied. The effects of wartime taxation and the Darien scheme had been to make specie scarce. The famine itself involved the export of coin for grain, so it is understandable that in some cases payment was in kind. In Kilwinning (Ayrshire), for instance, the lairds paid four pecks of meal a week; the minister one. In Lesmahagow (Lanarkshire) a stent of 10 shillings Scots for every hundred pound valued rent went on providing work, but a further peck of meal went in direct relief. In most cases the parish administered the relief, but some parishes left the individual estates to carry their own named poor. This was the case in Yester, Prestonkirk and Spott (East Lothian), Lasswade (Midlothian), Uphall (West Lothian), Galashiels (Selkirkshire), and Monzie and Blackford (Perthshire). In Pettinain (Lanarkshire) half the names on the list of poor were given to the heritors, the other half were carried by the session

The effective action of the Privy Council came in the proclamations of 1698 and 1699, particularly the latter. Several parishes turned to assessment in the spring of 1698: many more in October 1699. It may have been that by the autumn of 1699 desperation led to more powerful pressure on landowners, but the tenor of the local records shows intervention by the somewhat disorganised system of shire government. Sheriffs, Justices of the Peace and, most conspicuously, Commissioners of Supply sent orders to the parish ministers to call meetings of heritors and elders on the day ordered by the council. The members of these governing bodies were themselves landowners. In some cases their pressure can be clearly seen at the parish level. The high level of assessment in East Lothian almost certainly comes from the conspicuous position of the Tweeddale family as landowners and politicians. The first Marquess of Tweeddale was Lord Chancellor as well as the dominant landowner in two parishes; on his death in 1697 he was succeeded by his son, who was Lord Treasurer and sheriff of the county. Some other landowners were prime movers towards assessment; this was the case in Manor (Perthshire) and in Drainie (Moray), it was Gordon of Gordonstoun, owner of two-thirds of the parish who went into action in October 1699 to force the other landowner and the kirk session to fulfil the law by supporting the poor and repressing beggars. It was he, and not the minister, who called the required meeting.

Of course there were some parishes which could raise enough for relief without tapping the landowners. Bolton (East Lothian) was one. It supported its own poor and also paid money to tenants to enable them to employ shearers in harvest. Some of its capital was not lent out, but kept in a second Poor Box. Appealed to in 1696 by the minister of Yester, an adjacent parish which could not quickly get back the money it had on loan, it lent a hundred merks for six months at the legal rate of interest. Kinloch (Perthshire) declared 'the Letter of the Laws . . . impractical in this small parish'. Its population was probably under 400 and it managed without assessment.

Posession of wealth did not mean that it was readily accessible, as Yester found. Duffus (Moray) recorded its capital in November 1699 as 1,440 pounds Scots, but 400 merks was not to hand because it had been borrowed by the minister, who had since died. Another loan was to Lord Duffus, of 1,600 merks, and his lordship also later removed the session book. The absence of the book makes it difficult to decide what was done about the poor, but in a parish where a landowner could act so high-handedly, assessment was unlikely.

Landowners who did not intend to obey the instructions of the central and local government mostly used the simplest method of resistance, failure to attend any meeting called. A more sophisticated version of this was to have only a minor landowner attend who could argue that there was not enough property represented for a decision about assessment to be made. Records of heritors' and session meetings show a sharp difference between the attendance when such prestigious topics as the allocation of seats in church were made, or decisions about repair to the fabric of the church, and about assessment.

A particularly good example of the technique of non-attendance is to be found in South Leith (Midlothian). The sheriff made a particularly strong effort to get an effective meeting in October 1699. Through the Commissioners of Supply he named a particular heritor, Jasper Johnston, to chair the meeting, and ordered that a stent be levied for three years. The poor were either to be maintained by this or sent to the Edinburgh correction house. The sheriff wrote directly to Johnston. The session register records 'non of the heritors compeared except the Lord Balmerino's chamberlain', so Johnston 'concluded that they could not proceed in this affair at this time'.

Kirk session registers do not always contain explicit information about important matters: people thought there was little point in writing down what everybody knew. Also some sessions kept more than one book, and one of these might have been lost. So it is possible that other parishes than those noted raised an assessment. Certainly Jedburgh (Roxburghshire) was trying to get the heritors to raise money in this way from May 1698 to October 1699, and by that October had a list of the poor. Correspondingly among those that did use assessment there is room for doubt about what actually happened. Livingstone (West Lothian) in November 1699 ordered heritors and tenants to maintain the poor on each estate, but there are no clear signs that this was obeyed. With Spott (East Lothian), which eventually made a similar decision, the names of the poor continue to figure in lists of occasional doles by the session, which suggests failure by some estates to provide adequately. In Lasswade (Midlothian) in October 1699 at the meeting of heritors, elders and tenants about 'maintaining the poor in obedience to the Act of Council . . . they agreed that every Heritor with his tenants should maintain the poor in their bounds save some which the session was to maintain'. In the parallel volume of accounts for the parish the names of the poor disappear, showing that the decision was executed, but they are back again four months later. Still, even four months of assessment could enable a parish to get through the crisis. In a famine even a small amount of extra funding can make a great deal of difference to survival.

A reminder that support for the poor could be selective or partial comes from Perth. Here the landward side of the parish agreed to assess in January 1700. The town already had a number of particular pensioners, including a foundling girl. Anxious to provide for the widow of a burgess and not increase the burden on the townsmen, the session transfered the child's allotment to the widow; 'seeing that the Child being now come the length of five years and upward' it declared that 'she may travel and shift for herself at the begging'. In Monzie (Perthshire), in December 1698 those who attended the meeting made arrangements for the tenantry to pay 4 pecks of oatmeal a week and one estate agreed to give an equal amount, another to support its own poor, but since the session register records that 'none of the other heritors came or sent' there can be no certainty that the whole parish was assessed.

Pettinain (Lanarkshire), a parish put under pressure by both the sheriff and the Commissioners of Supply, agreed that both heritors and tenants should be assessed for thirty-six poor 'besides whoever will be sent from other places as belonging here', an unusual recognition that the burden might be greater than was apparent. Those tenants and householders who could not pay their share were to give 'meal and lodging'. Logie (Stirlingshire) also appears to have worked assessment in kind, with the added option of offering work. Payment in kind or some sort of billeting of the poor on households was the approach of Chirnside (Berwickshire). In July 1699 the parish agreed that tenants and heritors should pay 'according to the Cess roll' so that the poor would receive ten shillings Scots a week or 3 forpets of meal or a peck of beans 'as the payer thinks'. (Such allowances were too low for long-term survival.) If heritors would employ one of the poor they could pay in kind rather than by stent. The minister also agreed to support one of the poor. But in March 1700 comments show that this system was not working. Too many outsiders had flooded in, and the session and heritors decided that 'since we serve strangers our own poor make their best shift', in other words the poor were set at liberty to beg outside the parish. New Monkland also tried to get supply 'in a settled and orderly manner' by assessment, but either failed to set it up or had to abandon it early.

Study of the various session records shows that it was mostly only in the second wave of the famine after the lull of the harvest year of 1697 that parishes, under pressure from the Privy Council, seriously considered assessment. Yester, for instance, got through the early period by borrowing. Once real pressure by the Council began it was in no position to resist, with Tweeddale as its dominant heritor. But already one of the epidemics attendant on the famine had riven through the parish in 1696. Another followed in the autumn of 1699. Assessment did not deflect these epidemics. Disease was probably spread through the movements of the destitute who left their homes hoping to find either employment or food elsewhere, usually in the burghs. In September 1699 the register of Stirling notes that the parish had to bury seven persons 'dying on the streets'. Yester in 1699 had ten deaths of people able to pay for a mortcloth and thirty funerals partly or wholly charged to the parish. Spott, always niggardly in its allowances, shows the biggest increase above normal death registration in these years of any parish keeping a register of burials. As a result it found itself burdened with an unusually high number of orphans, in some cases the survivors of families so impoverished that there were no household goods that the parish could use towards the cost of their support. Yet the parish was not impecunious. At no point during the famine years had it less than 200 pounds Scots in hand, and the elders in the summer of 1698, complaining of the discomfort of collecting money at the kirk gate in 'cold, rainy and stormie weather', insisted on protecting their health by having nearly nineteen pounds spent on a porch.

There is a significant clause in the Act of 1696 which ordered the Privy Council to make the necessary Acts for employing the poor, recognition that lack of work could be an important effect of harvest failure. The proclamation of 1692 had already told heritors to put to work those capable of it, 'either within the parish' or 'in any adjacent manufactory'. But these attempts at using the labour of the destitute do not appear to have come to anything. There is one exception, the parish of Lesmahagow, as noted above. Recognition of agricultural unemployment can occasionally be found in the records. In Crichton (Midlothian) in 1699 John Spavine could not get his children, a boy and a girl, young adults, hired as servants: he would willingly have accepted work for them with no fee, since they would then be fed by their employer. The case came before the parish not as an issue of relief but of moral discipline, since he and his wife were sharing the only bed with them, and the session forced Spavine to move to a house with two beds. The main official classification of the destitute was to divide it between vagrants, to be repressed, and local poor, to be supplied.

The supply needed was clearly beyond the resources of many northern parishes, as is shown by the drop in population in Aberdeen-shire, now estimated at 21 per cent.[22] We can see levels of what was just manageable in some southern parishes. In Pettinain, if the population then stood near to what it was in 1755, some 11 per cent was on the regular pension list. In Yester some 30 per cent of households received help from the session at least once but mostly on several occasions in the famine years. In a society which laid stress on the seemliness with which the dead were handled many parishes had to economise on this service to the poor. Tingwald (Dumfries-shire) took to conducting burials in only a winding sheet; Douglas (Lanarkshire) in 1698 had a common coffin made for its numerous poor. Aberlady (East Lothian) and Carriden (West Lothian) turned from using coffins to having a bier on which to carry corpses to the kirkyard. There are stories of mass graves, and later of people who had simply disappeared with no trace. Still, there are records of minor kindnesses, such as the shilling Scots allowed in Sprouston (Rox-burghshire) for a poor woman's lyke wake.

The famine was the first large-scale test of the efficacy of the Poor Law. If a quarter of those parishes which have left records observed the law on assessment, then nearly three-quarters did not. (Some space must be left for doubtful cases.) Probably an even higher level of non-observance should be accepted for those for which we have no records. The sheriff of Haddington, Tweeddale, reported to the Privy Council that the heritors of Prestonpans and Tranent (adjacent East Lothian parishes) should be proceeded against by the Lord Advocate at 'his Lordship's first conveniency . . . for neglect of the Acts of Parliament and proclamations of the Privy Council about the poor'. These two parishes are among those with no registers for this period, so we do not know with what particular mechanism they evaded the law. In January 1700 the session of Sprouston resisting the attempt of a minor official in Jedburgh to extract a tip for his work for the Commissioners of Supply in 'seeing the acts made anent the poors mentiness put to operation' responded not only that the great number of the poor and the severity of their poverty made this impossible, but also that 'he has not put the acts into operation'.

NOTES

1. J. Hardy (ed.), *The Session Book of Bunkle and Preston 1665–1690* (Alnwick, 1900), p. 1.
2. J. M. McPherson, *The Kirk's Care of the Poor* (Aberdeen, 1940s), pp. 48–9. This book contains a vast wealth of detail about the working of the Old Poor Law in the north-east.
3. For loans made by the tenantry, see I. D. and K. A. Whyte, 'Debt and credit, poverty and prosperity, in a seventeenth-century Scottish rural community', in Rosalind Mitchison and Peter Roebuck (eds), *Economy and Society in Scotland and Ireland 1500–1939* (Edinburgh, 1988), pp. 70–80.
4. McPherson, *Kirk's Care*, p. 94.
5. *APS* VII 485, VIII 89–91.
6. Andrew Fletcher of Saltoun, *The Second Discourse Concerning the Affairs of Scotland Written in the Year 1698* (Edinburgh, 1698), pp. 24–5.
7. D. G. Barron (ed.), *The Baron Court Book of Urie 1604–1707* (SHS Edinburgh, 1892), p. 110, March 1695. Here housing beggars is listed with the offence of possessing stolen goods. See also C. B. Gunn (ed.), *Records of the Baron Court of Stitchill 1655–1807* (SHS Edinburgh, 1905), p. 135, 4 March 1698; 'Sir John Pringle of Stitchill Baronett, sittand in judgement dischairges all residents within the Barronny of Stitchill here after to resett harbour intertain or give alms any manner of way to any poor people whatsoever that goe from place to place . . . except those . . . listed as poor within the Barronny.' As an example of the Church's attitude there is the case in Penninghame, April 1737 when 'a poor begging man' died on his way from one house to another. The kirk session reproved the householder who sent him on after housing him for two nights for 'unchristian' and 'blame-able' conduct.
8. A heritor is a landowner whose estate is burdened with the obligation of supporting the parish church and minister.

9. For example, A. W. Cornelius Hallen (ed.), *The Account Book of Sir John Foulis of Ravelston 1671–1707*, (SHS, Edinburgh, 1894) p. 29, 2 April 1680 'to the beggers wn my sone adam was baptized 1.8.0. . . . to the poor at the church door 1.8.0.'

10. McPherson, *Kirk's Care*, p. 105.

11. Hew Scott, *Fasti Ecclesiae Scoticanae*, vol. 5 (Edinburgh, 1925), p. 272.

12. SRO CH2/106/2 April 1708. Register of the presbytery of Dunkeld.

13. Alexander Murray Dunlop, *The Law of Scotland Regarding the Poor* (Edinburgh, 1854), Appendix, pp. 169–73; J. Guthrie Smith, *A Digest of the Law of Scotland Relating to the Poor* (London, 1860), Appendix, pp. ix–xii.

14. Dunlop, *Law*, pp. 173–5. Smith, *Digest*, pp. xiii–xiv.

15. I am grateful to the staff of the SRO for access to the typescript of the as yet unpublished parts of the register of the Privy Council.

16. R. E. Tyson, 'Famine in Aberdeenshire, 1695–1699: anatomy of a crisis', in D. Stevenson (ed.), *From Lairds to Louns: Country and Burgh Life in Aberdeenshire, 1600–1800* (Edinburgh, 1986), pp. 32–52, and further communications.

17. T. C. Smout, 'Goat keeping in the old Highland economy', *Scottish Studies* (1965), pp. 188–91.

18. *APS* x 64.

19. Dunlop, *Law*, pp. 175–8; Smith, *Digest*, pp. xv–xvii.

20. Dunlop and Smith, the two standard legal works on the Scottish Poor Law give the earlier proclamations in full in their Appendices, but neither refers to that of 1699, which is to be found in the SRO's typescript.

21. The parishes, other than the main cities, which appear to have been assessed at some point in the famine period are: Colinton, Corstorphine, Cramond, Crichton, Currie, Lasswade, Stow and Temple in Midlothian, Garvald, Haddington, North Berwick, Ormiston, Prestonkirk, Whitekirk and Yester in East Lothian, Carriden and Uphall in West Lothian, Forgan, Kennoway, Kilconquhar and Kingsbarns in Fife, Blackford, Logie, Longforgan, Manor, Monzie, Perth and Tibbermuir in Perthshire, Kilmaurs and Kilwinning in Ayrshire, Galashiels in Selkirkshire, Drainie in Moray, Eddleston in Peeblesshire, Greenock in Renfrewshire, Kettins in Angus, and Longside in Aberdeenshire. The information comes from the KSRs except for Stow, for which see *NSA* vol. 1 (Edinburgh, 1845), p. 248, and for Greenock, see SRO CH8/178, 'List of the poor on Sir John Schaw's ground, June 1699'. I am grateful to Dr David Stevenson for this reference.

22. Tyson, 'Famine', p. 50.

CHAPTER 3

LAW AND UNCERTAINTY, 1700–1770

Legislation amending the Scottish Poor Law ceased for over a century with the Union of 1707, and after the abolition of the Scottish Privy Council in 1708 there were no further proclamations about the poor. In all there was very little in the way of statute law aimed at Scotland until the 1740s, and even then the concern of the British Parliament for Scotland was short lived. Little change issued from Parliament before 1770.

This does not mean that the situation was static. Changes in law were organised through cases in the Court of Session, and that court had a deliberate policy of enhancing the rights of landowners. As one of its judgments stated in 1744: 'It is the privilege of property that the proprietor can be put under no restraint'.[1] Most of the advocates and all the judges were landowners themselves. Their class benefited from Union, for it deflected the concern of the aristocracy to Westminster, and the physical presence of the aristocrats to London, the centre of power and preferment. The skimpy Scottish allowance of seats in the House of Commons did not enable the bulk of landed gentry to follow them there. It should not surprise that legal decisions followed the pattern already established in the handling of statutes by ignoring the specific legislation which ordered all parishes to raise funds by stenting their landowners.

Union led gradually to the strengthening of the system of justice and county government. In various ways the crown nibbled away at the feudal jurisdictions that still survived. These jurisdictions were not directly attacked till the Act of 1747 abolished them, but in one way or another sheriff courts, some of which were still in private hands, became more significant. The Commissioners of Supply came to occupy a more important position in county matters, administering conscription in the numerous wars of the eighteenth century, financing the expansion of road improvements, managing the occasionally important county meetings and carrying out the divisions of the valuation of feudal superiority on which were based the fictitious electoral votes for parliamentary elections. The Justices of the Peace, often the same men as the Commissioners, gained in status from this process and from the enhanced legalism of the day.

Strengthening the courts eventually meant the expansion of judicial activity into the area of the Poor Law, as can be seen in the major collection of significant cases from the eighteenth and early nineteenth centuries, W. Morison's *Dictionary of Decisions*.[2] Of the eighteenth-century cases on the Poor Law all but two come from after 1740. All are based in southern Scotland, mostly from south of the Forth-Clyde line and with several from the Borders. The issue in almost all is settlement, and between them they thrash out the uncertainty of the two definitions of three and of seven years' residence in favour of three years. The usual cause was a dispute between two parishes as to which was obliged to support a particular destitute person.[3] It is not surprising that there are no cases from the far north or from the Highlands, since in neither area was the Poor Law being operated as laid down, but the absence of cases from Angus, Aberdeenshire or Perthshire, all counties where there was an operative Poor Law, is interesting. The likely explanation of this is that issues of settlement were unlikely to lead to a legal process unless the parishes were assessed. Assessment, which would focus the attention of landowners, did not become common north of the Forth-Clyde line till late in the century. Morison's collection also includes some cases on Aliment, which declare the obligation of a child to support a parent in need, and of parents and grandparents to support children. Further samples of the legal opinion of the day can be gathered from smaller collections of cases, such as those of Sir James Fergusson of Kilkerran, Patrick Grant Lord Elchies or Henry Home, Lord Kames.[4]

From the cases alone the impression gathered is one of an effective Poor Law by which the poor of the parish were adequately cared for and under which the poor had a right to claim support. A very different picture is conveyed by the records of the kirk sessions. There is no mention of any right to support and it is clear that the success of any claim for aid was at the discretion of the session, a discretion deeply imbued with the Christian obligation of charity. In most cases support was only partial. The poor were expected either to earn or to beg for a large part of their needs. Children under the age of apprenticeship or service, which varied between nine and fourteen, usually received full support, and so did lunatics or people totally incapacitated. But there is no evidence in these records of the concept of rights, only of obligation. A good example of this comes from Tranent (East Lothian). In 1745 the parish, by then assessed, decided to have a spinning house in which the poor would live and work. In 1750 John Lamb, described as 'aged near 90' and his wife 'past 71' applied to go on the poor list; they were given sixpence sterling and told to apply for work at the spinning house. But as Lamb was to point out later the house had no materials and could offer no work. The parish therefore put him on its pension list, knocking off instead one Euphan Waters, over 50 and 'not so needful'. (Assessed parishes often tried to work to a fixed level of expenditure.) In 1756 Lamb died and the kin of his widow applied to the session for her to receive a pension, and for the few months of life remaining to her she received a shilling a week. For both her and Euphan Waters there was no suggestion of relief as a right.

The same absence of a right to relief is indicated by instances, not common, of parishes coupling relief with some form of discipline. In the 1690s there are cases in Dalmeny (Midlothian), Stranraer (Wigtownshire) and Cambuslang (Lanarkshire) of threats that aid would be curtailed if the recipient did not attend church, and in 1697 in Cambuslang it was ruled that children not attending school would not be supported. Rothesay (Bute) in 1721 allotted a pound Scots 'to buy shoes for Elspeth NcTaylour', 'and if she pawns them for drink she'll get no more'. Penninghame in 1702 cut the relief of a woman who did not attend church and Inveraray in 1706 threatened similar action. The clearest statement of a link between support and religion comes from the parish of Kiltearn (Ross). In 1697 the parish passed an Act 'anent the Distribution':

> whereas the Word of the Lord requires our Collection to be for the Saints, and what is given to such in Extremitie helps them to praise and glorifie God, and may have its owne influence on the rest of the poor of the parish (who ordinarlie are the Scumm and Refuse of the people) to set upon a Course of Reformation and may be more also for the Honour of religion and peace of our Consciences Therefore the Session unanimouslie appoints that the Collection, for hereafter, be for the supplie, first of all, of such as truelie fear the Lord, when reduced to straits and necessities and next of such as have endeavoured honestlie to gain a Livelihood to themselves, but have been blasted upon by providence, and failing these, of the Poor of the

Paroch that beg from Door to Door, but with this provisions that they get none of it but in time of great extremity and Dearth, to preserve their Lives . . .

In a similar but less dogmatic vein Peterculter (Aberdeenshire) in 1697 declared that 'the Poore are and shall be only accounted such as . . . have lived for some years . . . honestly and religiously without scandal . . . and not an idle life.' General statements of social policy are rare in the documents of executive agencies. I have not found statements of this kind after 1707, and it is possible that it was not common in easier times for parishes to take such restrictive lines over eligibility. But such statements are incompatible with the existence of a right to relief.

The discrepancy between the remarks of judges and the parish reality is comprehensible when a basic feature common to the legal cases is considered. They are all from parishes in which the heritors had been compelled to accept assessment. Compulsory assessment featured conspicuously in the founding statutes of the Poor Law, but the interpretation of the law by lawyers had come in the seventeenth century to mean that assessment was necessary only when the voluntary funds of a parish could not meet even the most restricted level of support for the poor. Parishes which were not assessed would periodically examine the available level of funds and allot pensions to the most needy cases which they knew about, and attempt by drastic cutting of the list of claimants to keep expenditure within the bounds of income. In other words the number accepted as poor was trimmed to fit resources. Assessed parishes, at least initially, worked the other way. The poor were listed, an estimate made of the likely level of voluntary funding and what was then seen as needed in addition was made the level to which assessment had to be geared. Bringing a legal case about settlement against an un-assessed parish was a waste of time, for the parish would not have the wherewithal to meet it. So the evidence provided by the cases has a bearing only on some parishes.

What the cases do show is that the law as accepted by lawyers was a highly selected set of rules derived from the statutes, and not the law as the founding statute and later amplifications and modifications set it out. As time wore on the selecting process gained authority from the legal principle of desuetude – the rule that statutes which had not been carried out lost authority. It thus became possible to justify the failure to assess as within the law, notwithstanding the wording of the statutes.

A further area of legal uncertainty hangs over the power of the instruments of county government, sheriffs, Justices of the Peace and Commissioners of Supply, to order parishes to give relief. In certain instances these bodies had assumed such powers, not always effectively, during the famine of the 1690s. Sheriff Calderwood's attempt with the Commissioners of Supply of Midlothian in October 1699 to make the heritors of South Leith carry out orders had failed, though the sheriff claimed to be acting 'by virtue of ane Act of Privy Counsell'. The advocate William Forbes in his 1707 treatise, *The Duty and Powers of Justices of the Peace in that Part of Great Britain called Scotland*, stated that the powers of the Justices included taxing parishes for the 'Maintenance of the Poor', within financial limits, and powers against both vagrants and those who 'reset' (housed) them, power to apprentice poor boys to sea service and the duty of appointing parish overseers. Certainly the powers of Justices over vagrants were considerable, though rarely exercised. But Justices of the Peace do not appear to have acted on the powers they were stated to have over treatment of the ordinary parish poor. Occasionally they might be appealed to by a parish to justify the removal of someone likely to establish settlement and without the means to sustain themselves, and occasionally they might order a parish to give support to an individual. Sheriffs also might order relief, and even state the quantity. But these practices were not frequent. The main way in which county government influenced, or attempted to influence, poor relief was in the form of county 'schemes'.

These schemes were very much a feature of the eighteenth century. There is a claim made in the 1830s that there had been a scheme for Berwickshire in 1705.[5] The statement was that an order issued by the sheriff and Justices of the Peace to the parishes to support their poor was recorded in the session register of Duns. Unfortunately the session registers of Duns for the relevant period and earlier have disappeared, so this claim cannot be verified. The first county scheme with surviving evidence, which was conveyed to the parishes and acted on by some of them, appears to be that for East Lothian in 1711. Pencaitland recorded the instructions in its session register on 9 September. The Justices of the Peace ordered the standard meeting of session and heritors to make out a list of the poor and demanded that the list be sent to them by 25 September. On 7 October the Justices produced an 'Act' ordering each parish to maintain its own poor and to hold the necessary meetings and agree the funds for this. Pencaitland's meeting took place and the session register recorded the list of the poor and the cost of their annual need, 163 pounds 8 shillings. The money likely to be available from the Poor Box would not be above 100 pounds, so 63 pounds 8 shillings would have to come from the heritors. A further Act by the Justices ordered the appointment of two constables at 6 shillings sterling a week. In all it was clear that the heritors would have to contribute 100 pounds 12 shillings. The Justices' instructions to the constables were that they were 'strictly' to observe the Act, to tour the parish twice a week and arrest all found begging, extract from these the facts about their settlement and cart them 'toward the Airth of the same', handing them over to the constables of the next parish, obtaining a receipt and keeping a record of such beggars. The tollbooth of the county town of Haddington was to be the place of incarceration of those who refused to give information. The names of those who had harboured the beggars were to be passed to the overseer that he might fine them.

This county scheme can also be found in the registers of Dunbar, Dirleton, Saltoun and Stenton, but action in these other parishes does not appear to have been as closely tied to the demands of the Justices as in Pencaitland. In Stenton the heritors held a meeting about the poor. The session, 'seeing some kirk sessions in the neighbourhood hes undertaken to maintain their poor for a year they would do all they could for relief of their own poor' so long as money held out. If necessary they would then apply to the heritors. In return they expected the heritors to employ constables 'for extirpating vagabonds'. At least for a short while there was assessment in this parish as there was in Pencaitland.

Dirleton also opted for a similar division of responsibility. The session held that its funds could support the poor without troubling the heritors 'with the provision, that if afterwards the Box should be found unable to maintain them' (the poor) 'and the present method laid down by the Justices be effectually prosecuted . . . then upon application by the Sessions the Heritors should consider the State of our poor and stent themselves and the Tennants and others living in their grounds'. Meanwhile the heritors were to pay salaries to three constables according to their valuation and to fine any of their number who let in vagrants.

Dunbar heritors displayed the established methods of resistance to county orders. They pointed out that most of the poor belonged to the burgh and not to the landward part of the parish: they could not settle any system of maintenance because most of the heritors were not at the meeting. A postponed meeting with representatives of the burgh also produced a high level of absenteeism. The session responded by allowing the poor on their list to 'goe through the paroch once a week to seek for supply', in other words to beg, till the heritors and burgh made provision. At the end of the year it was clear that the resistance of the heritors to assessment of any kind had won and there was no further talk of 'stenting'. In the remaining parish which acknowledged the county orders, Saltoun, all we know is that the instructions of the Justices were received.

There are session registers at this time for four other East Lothian parishes, and these make no mention of the scheme, not even to its desire to see vagabonds put down, always a more attractive aspect of the Poor Law to heritors than relief of the destitute. Given the nature of session registers it is not possible to say whether these parishes gave any obedience to the scheme, and it is also impossible to discern the response of those for which registers do not exist. Justice of the Peace records for this period have not survived. The level of obedience and its duration remain uncertain, but compared with later schemes this one appears to have had a good level of response.

Indications exist that a similar scheme was planned in the Border counties of Selkirkshire, Roxburghshire and Berwickshire.[6] The Justices of these counties discussed such action between 1711 and 1713, but it looks as if they were unable to get an adequate quorum to participate. Certainly an Act was drawn up and was discussed at meetings in 1712 and 1713. A small scrap of Justice of the Peace record in the papers of the Biel estate shows that Roxburghshire Justices had a subcommittee 'anent the poor, and servants' fees' from which a report was sent to the neighbouring counties.[7] In Lanarkshire, May 1711, the Justices of the Peace and the Commissioners of Supply issued an Act against vagabonds. All such were to be arrested and the sheriff would put the idle to work or service: those resisting would go to prison.[8] But this Act did not mention the support of the poor nor the stenting of heritors. It is not possible to see whether the impulse for action at the county level stretched further west, for there is a gap in the Dumfriesshire Commissioners of Supply records for the early eighteenth century.[9] There is, for somewhat later, a brief note of a Justice of the Peace

order for Wigtownshire in 1715 in which constables were told to
search for and arrest vagrants.[10]

There was a second period of activity by the county authorities from
the mid-1720s into the 1730s. The original impulse appears to have
come from the Church. Dalkeith and Edinburgh presbyteries took up
a recent Act of the General Assembly 'anent the Vagrant poor' in 1724
and decided that application should be made to Justices, Commissioners of Supply and the Magistrates and city Council of Edinburgh
'to apply the laws about Vagrants and to provide for the Needful poor'.
Edinburgh presbytery pointed out that regulations had to be worked
out between towns and their adjacent counties, and referred the matter
in an Overture to the Synod of Lothian and Tweeddale, recommending that the various presbyteries should take the matter up with lay
authorities. So Haddington and Dunbar presbyteries had applied to
the Justices who responded with an order to parishes, Edinburgh and
Dalkeith presbyteries were negotiating with the Midlothian Justices,
Linlithgow presbytery was in communication with other presbyteries.
In this buzz of activity the presbyteries of Peebles and Biggar
complained that there was a shortage of Justices of the Peace in
Peeblesshire, a point which might be the explanation for the county's
inactivity in 1711–13. The culmination of presbytery activity was an
Act of the General Assembly in 1724 calling on the church courts to
'use all Means' to get parishes to support their poor and to apply to lay
authorities to put into effect the laws against vagrants.

The activity of the church courts seems to have aroused the
sensibilities of the landowning class. Landowners had an inherent
anti-clericalism and the vision of a drive against vagrancy conducted
by the Church, even if it showed willingness to co-operate with lay
courts, was bound to arouse rivalry. It was in the Quarter Session
meetings of the Justices of any one county that action would be taken.
Unfortunately minutes of these meetings do not form a coherent
archive for the eighteenth century. For any one period there are two or
three counties supplying regular material. Material for no county
covers the whole century or even half of it. Scraps of these minutes
survive in private estate papers and supply small patches of information. Some parish records give information about Acts of the Justices,
and so sometimes do newspapers. For East Lothian we also have
posters for the scheme, issued in 1724, 1728 and 1731. Piecing together
such of these sources as I have managed to find, I can name various

counties which shared the desire to make the Poor Law more effective between 1724 and 1733: Ayrshire, Berwickshire, Dunbartonshire, Dumfriesshire, Fife, the three Lothians, Roxburghshire, the Stewartry of Kirkcudbright and Wigtownshire.[11] Silence on the part of other counties does not necessarily mean that they did not also share in the movement.

The most impressive of these schemes was that of Midlothian. In October 1724 the Justices took a look at representations from Dalkeith and Edinburgh presbyteries about 'regulation of the maintenance of the poor' and 'suppressing the abuse committed by vagrant and Sturdie Beggars',[12] and also at an Act of the Justices of East Lothian to similar effect, and set up a committee to consider the matter. In March this committee, which included a Judge of the Court of Session, met with the Lord President and another Judge, the magistrates of Edinburgh and some of the heritors of West Lothian. Letters were sent out to the parish ministers asking for information on the number of their poor and on the funds available for their support 'either arising from the Collections, Mortifications or other stock' (the omission of assessment is interesting). The answers showed that every parish in the shire was ready to maintain its own poor, so orders were issued that they should refrain from helping the poor of other parishes. This was backed up by the threat of a fine of twenty shillings Scots on any one who did so. In 1727 the committee was proposing that Justices pay a visit to each kirk session and compile a list of the parish poor, giving names, ages, etc. and of funds. The Justices should also write to the moderators of presbyteries to let them know what was being done, taking care to explain that there was 'no design of encroaching upon the management of the funds which are under the regulation of the Kirk Sessions'.

In 1731 the Midlothian Justices published their views on the topics of vagrancy and the poor which reveal certain fairly standard landowner attitudes. Vagrants are 'a great burden' and 'a reproach to the kingdom: for the most part live without all Law nor Rule Sacred or Civill'. 'A Numerous brood of such Persons are Daylie increasing who, if they were set to work and bred to trade and calling, the Countrie might not only be disburdened of them but they might in a short time and upon far less expence become usefull and profitable to the whole Kingdom.' The Justices reaffirmed the legal obligation of 'Vagabonds' 'to return to their own parishes of their birth or where they have resided for three years' to be supported and put to work there. Constables were to search these out and bring them to the Justices, who would confine them on bread and water in the Edinburgh Correction House for thirty days. The expense of this was to be met by a charge on each parish of five shillings on every hundred pound Scots of valued rent, half laid on the tenantry and half on heritors. Heritors and elders were to stent themselves at their next meeting. The order included in the definition of beggars 'actors of unlawful plays, Egyptians and others who pretend to power of charming . . . all persons having neither means nor master nor using any lawful merchandize . . . [and] all common Labourers being able in body Liveing idle'. The concept of involuntary unemployment was not yet grasped.

For the 'infirm poor' the orders of the Justices were as usual: heritors and elders were to meet, to make lists of those with settlement. Assessment was to be brought in and the money collected by overseers if 'the regular funds', in other words the parish's irregular voluntary resources, were not sufficient. All ministers were to report to the Quarter Sessions if their parish failed to carry out its legal duties and anyone giving houseroom or relief to vagabonds was to be fined five pound Scots for the Poor Box.

Reports on the level of parochial obedience came in through 1732. There were complaints that ministers had not made the announcements required on Sundays, that the roads to Edinburgh were not free of beggars as they would have been had the orders been obeyed, that various parishes had not levied assessment and that the planned meeting of Justices and the Edinburgh City Council had not occurred. A particular problem was caused by the disobedience of Dalkeith, and a special meeting between the Justices and the town's powerful patron, the Duke of Buccleuch, or his agent was suggested. The story cannot be carried further. At the end of November the topic disappears from the minutes of the Justices, and these are missing after October 1733.

Still, an impression of what was happening in response to the initiative of the Justices can be found in the registers of some of the parishes. It is clear that the sharp distinction drawn by the Justices between the poor and vagrants was not sustained by the parishes. For instance Saltoun, a well-organised parish and one in close relationship to the government through its principal landowner, Lord Milton, chief cabinet agent in Scotland, was giving financial aid occasionally to travelling beggars as well as to its own pensioners. Its register, available from 1729 to 1731, contains no reference to the county scheme.

The best documented of other counties at this time is the Stewartry of Kirkcudbright. Justice of the Peace minutes for 1728–85 survive, and can be supplemented by a pamphlet of 1820 which reprinted decisions made about the poor in 1730 and 1751.[13] The scheme of the 1720s had worked well at first, it was claimed, but two years after it was launched there were complaints of people being pestered with 'Tinkers and vagrants'. The Stewartry was divided into districts and local Justices were told to work with the heritors in these areas. In 1732 kirk sessions were ordered to name the most 'judicious, honest and intelligent yeomanry' as parish constables, but it was always difficult to get reliable men for this task. The reward of a shilling sterling for each arrest of a vagrant did not necessarily meet the opportunity cost of the work involved. Those who refused appointment might be fined by the Justices, but that did not encourage good performance. That the problem persisted is shown by the fact that in August 1772 there were still complaints to the Justices of 'mean and silly persons' in the office. The Justices were demanding that each parish supply four constables, which cannot have been a popular policy to the tenantry. In 1754 an alleged increase in vagrants was attributed to remissness on the part of head constables. These men would produce certificates to the Commissioners of Supply that they had made their rounds of inspection, but it was claimed that these were issued by heritors and ministers without proper checks. In 1772 fines of ten shillings Scots were placed on constables who had failed to arrest vagrants, so clearly the problems had persisted.

Assessment also produced problems. Parish heritors might vote for a stent, but later some would refuse to pay. In 1741 the Justices decided that the law which 'allowed' the stent implicitly implied that it could be enforced. In fact the Poor Law statutes did much more than simply allow a stent, but clearly selective interpretation was established. The Justices ordered that the names of those who did not pay be sent to them so that they could issue distress warrants. But in 1751 a meeting of the Justices, the Commissioners of Supply and heritors complained that assessment was a heavy tax 'imposed upon the whole nation by men possessed of very little property; since the small heritors together with the kirk sessions could always outvote the greater'. (The theme that taxation is more painful to the rich than to the poor is one found also in twentieth-century politics.)

The Justices took to releasing vagrants who promised in writing to leave the Stewartry. For this to be effective there had to be co-ordination with neighbouring counties. This may have been established, for in August 1751 the sheriffs of many counties had begun meeting together for 'the useful Imploying of Idle persons in Labour and Manufactures' and 'to execute the wholsom laws already made'.[14]

The Justices do not appear to have made inquiry whether the vagrants whom they exiled were merely unsuccessful chapmen. In 1772, for instance, one Robert Howence from Shropshire, with 'no particular trade' was arrested 'selling and exchanging buckles'. Since he was unable to read, status as a chapman is unlikely, but apparently no inquiry was made.

The Justice of the Peace records, fragmented though they are, show some unexpected problems which could arise in the matter of vagrancy and its definition. In 1767 the East Lothian Justices had used money gathered for the suppression of vagrants to pay for supporting a 'furious madman'.[15] Perhaps this was deemed improper expenditure, for in 1768, faced with one Helen Richardson, a woman who had occasional bouts of mania during which she walked through the county smashing windows (and window glass was still an upper-class privilege), the Justices looked around for someone to take over the duty of restraining her. Failing in this, they put her in Haddington gaol. A few years later they made complaint that the practice of putting lunatics in gaol and sustaining them on rogue money, the local tax for the pursuit and support of criminals, was 'turning the county gaol into a madhouse'. In 1774 a major county scheme there involved attempts to control movement by poor people. This led to representations by papermakers that their industry depended on a large number of poor women 'of mean Clothing . . . wandering through the Country in quest of linen raggs'.

The Selkirkshire Justices in June 1745 arrested a group of vagrants, one of whom stated that he was Prince Charles Edward, the rival heir to the throne. An agitated correspondence with Robert Dundas, the President of the Court of Session, ensued.[16] The Judges, backed by the Lord Advocate, did not want this man sent to Edinburgh for trial by the Justiciary Court: clearly the publicity resulting might be politically embarrassing. It was suggested that the man should be dealt with locally as an idle vagrant, or perhaps conscripted for the county's army quota, or after threat of a whipping he might 'voluntarily enact himself to Banishment'. It would be a good idea, before that, to have him looked at by someone who claimed to know the real prince by sight. What the episode reveals is that Justices had more powers for dealing with vagrants than they normally used.

Schemes such as those of the 1720s recurred in the 1750s and again in the 1770s. Indeed, that of the 1750s had been initiated in East Lothian in 1745 and postponed because of the Jacobite disturbance.[17] Roxburgh-shire appears to have made a move at about the same time, but this seems not to have got beyond a paper plan, the only trace of which is a report by the Clerk to the Justices in the evidence submitted to the Royal Commission in 1844 of an attempt in 1746 to get heritors assessed. The East Lothian plan was for a central county workhouse in Haddington capable of holding 300 inmates, who would be put to work on textiles. Funds of 300 pounds a year would be needed to support such a number. The money was to be contributed by the parishes, by valuation, and the parishes would then be entitled to send their poor to the workhouse, in numbers according to their contribution in cash. A governing body of major heritors would be chosen by the Michaelmas Head Court and supplemented by ministers and elders chosen by the presbyteries. The governing body of thirty-five would choose a master and mistress for the house. The diet was to be as in the Edinburgh Charity Workhouse, and the uniforms for inmates would be made in the house.

As might be expected with plans based on general assessment and regulated activity by the various parishes, much of this, including the large workhouse, never came to fruition. In the records of Tranent session and heritors we can see a parish getting ready for the new system by listing the poor and their capacity to work. The list included a man with only one arm put under the heading of 'able'. In 1750 the shire's Michaelmas Head Court complained that many parishes were not supporting their poor: the county was 'infested' with vagrants. The court ordered assessment: poor houses were to be set up while plans were still being made for the county workhouse. Begging was prohibited. But clearly the whole scheme was vitiated by inertia and unwillingness to hand over money.

Other counties with schemes at this time were Aberdeenshire, Ayrshire, Banffshire, Clackmannanshire, Dunbartonshire, Peebles-shire, Perthshire and Wigtownshire.[18] Special interest attaches to that of Aberdeenshire, for by the end of the century it had become the boast of the county that no parish there had ever been assessed, but Udny session recorded the Act of the Commissioners of Supply and by May 1752 was assessed.

It is interesting to speculate why the county authorities, particularly the Justices of the Peace, never succeeded in establishing the authority over parishes that Justices had in England. Indeed if our legal authorities are to be trusted, and one should be cautious in offering trust to such, Justice powers were declining from their condition as claimed by William Forbes. Gilbert Hutcheson in *A Treatise on the Offices of Justice of the Peace etc.* of 1806, while asserting the powers of Justices over vagrants, confined their right to act on the general poor to those aspects covered by the proclamation of 1694, in other words only when the parish had taken no action. George Tait in *A Summary of the Powers and Duties of a Justice of the Peace in Scotland* (1816) allows that Justices had sometimes intervened in parish affairs to order a specific level of allowance to a poor person, but, he says, 'seldom'. The right of sheriffs to intervene was eventually curtailed by the legal process *Paton* v. *Adamson* of 1772, in which the Court of Session stated that the level of support for an individual lay with the parish 'in first instance'.[19]

The Justices were, after all, only the more politically acceptable, distinguished and mature members of the county landowners, and it may be surprising that they should be defeated by the resistance of the less influential landowners who objected to the schemes because adequate support of the poor was likely to lead to assessment. Assessment would be a long-standing charge on an estate, and could be seen as damaging to property values. But resistance was not confined to landowners. There was a continuing strain of suspicion of landowing authority in the Church. Ministers, even of the Moderate persuasion, did not take kindly to orders from sheriffs or Justices to call meetings of heritors and elders or to compile a roll of the poor. But the presence and influence of landowners was built into the structure of the higher courts of the Church. It was not politic for ministers to complain in any but very general terms of unwarranted lay intervention.

At the parish level individual landowners could make difficulties for the management of the Poor Law. Sometimes difficulty was simply the result of ignorance of the law. In 1744 a landowner in Grange (Banffshire) put it to his lawyer that the maintaining of two foundlings for five years was a misapplication of relief funds. He received in reply that it was 'a most necessary application' and a brief essay on the basic features of the Poor Law. A similar attempt by a lawyer in 1808 went to the Court of Session before being defeated.[20] In 1775 a Mr Ogilvy, the factor of the Duke of Buccleuch, refused to pay assessment on the Duke's property in the parish of St Boswell's (Roxburghshire) on the grounds that the Duke's estate there had no tenants. His argument was that assessment was for 'the service and utility of the inhabitants', and no inhabitants on his Grace's lands, no utility. The estate also refused to pay its share of the schoolmaster's salary. The interest of the case is not the fact that the ducal position had no grounds in statute law but that the heritors had to take legal advice on whether the factor was in the right.[21]

Even when assessment had been agreed there could be difficulty in making heritors pay up. The argument that heritors not present at the meeting which accepted assessment could not be obliged to pay continued to be used well into the nineteenth century. Simple inertia could postpone payment for many years. At Innerwick (East Lothian) in 1766 the session revealed that it had heritors owing money for church repair since 1724, and that a particular heritor, David Smith, owed for assessment for the poor since 1750. The session had been forced to borrow to cover its needs, and though the overdue stent would not be increased by interest, the borrowings of the session were.[22]

The other main area of trouble between sessions and heritors lay in loans. If a parish had a mortification – a legacy – it was treated as capital and if possible invested – in other words lent. This custom was reinforced in the proclamation of 1692. But there were problems over investment. The safest place for it was land. But a landowner might fail to pay interest regularly, or to return the capital when it was required. Prosecution at law was possible, but cost money. The parish's own landowners could be helpful in such cases, for many of them had links with advocates and Judges. But they were of help only if the defaulting landowner's estate lay outwith the parish. Lending money to the landowners of the parish was unwise, for there were numerous ways in which they could make trouble for the minister and session. If a mortification was left to the session it was not rare for delivery to be delayed for some years by the family of the deceased. In the period of high prices following the disastrous harvest of 1740 the Earl of Hopeton summoned the elders of Dalmeny (Midlothian) to meet him to hear something of advantage for the poor. This was a gift of £50 from the late Marquess of Annandale, his brother-in-law, left to the poor of the parish and to be paid by the Marquess's heirs. So it carried one year's legal interest.[23] But the Marquess had died in 1730. Interest for one year only would seem to require some explanation.

The most important legal dispute concerning the eighteenth-century Poor Law arose in the East Lothian parish of Humbie, out of recurring bad relations between the church courts and the principal heritor, a Mr Hepburn. The quarrel spread in various issues over some thirty years and involved all the usual and some distinctly unusual grounds of friction between the Church and landowners. There was a loan of 3,900 merks Scots (£216.13/4 sterling) made by the parish, which had a considerable amount of capital, to Hepburn who failed to pay the interest for nine years and for which the security named proved inadequate. There was a demand by the presbytery that the heritors repair the manse, which was ignored for three years and then frustrated by Hepburn claiming that the manse's outhouses, including the kitchen, were his own property. There was a demand by the presbytery that Hepburn should satisfy ecclesiastical discipline for having murdered a servant as well as for fornication. There was a demand from Hepburn that a protégé of his, whom he had managed to insert as schoolmaster in one of the parish's schools, should automatically become precentor and session clerk. The session refused this demand because it had labelled the schoolmaster as guilty of drunkenness and cursing, and because in its view he he did not beat the boys enough. There had also been a conviction of the man for fornication at some point in the past.

In 1730 Hepburn raised a new issue of dispute and persuaded another heritor and some of the elders to join with him in attacking the minister, Mr Cuming, with a long list of failings both as an individual – not holding family worship, for instance – and as minister – failing to give receipts for money received, failure to visit the dying, absence on Sundays so that the parishioners, deprived of the entertainment of a sermon had recourse to the second best on offer, an alehouse, and many other derelictions. The case went up to the Synod which was obliged to take it very seriously. Evidence was collected from thirty-nine witnesses.[24]

Cuming was cleared on all counts, but not surprisingly bad relations continued and were made worse by a legacy to the session of 11,000 merks by a near relative of Hepburn's, and by a decision of the session not to lend the money within the parish. Finally in 1749, by now supported by four other heritors, mainly non-resident, Hepburn started a process in the Court of Session claiming in general terms that a parish's heritors should be consulted over any major financial decision by the session, and in particular that Cuming had not kept proper accounts of the poor's money or invested it to full advantage. In fact the accounts of Humbie parish are more clear and systematic than those of most parishes, though as with all parishes it is difficult to trace exactly what was being done with the capital. They are also better kept than most of those of small estates at this time. But behind the specific complaint lay a common opinion of propertied society, that those with small personal resources should not have control of large funds: men who did not own land were not accountable. If the money of a parish was badly managed the parish might have to adopt assessment, a policy particularly unattractive to non-resident heritors who could otherwise escape contributing to the poor.

The Court of Session, in an Outer House decision, that is by a single Judge, decided that the heritors had a right to see the session's accounts. The session had claimed that its money was an ecclesiastical good and so outside lay jurisdiction: the heritors had called this a 'popish' doctrine. Probably egged on by the anti-clericalism of their chosen advocate, Henry Home, later Lord Kames, the heritors went on to make a wider claim, that they had 'a natural right' to control all the money in the parish because if assessment resulted from misman-agement they were the 'only sufferers'.

This last point is simply untrue. If a parish ran short of funds the first sufferers were the poor themselves. If assessment was adopted, then the tenants had to pay half of the rate. Only if it was assumed that all the money circulating in a parish, from which collections and fines were made, belonged to the owners of the land, an extreme form of physiocrat theory, could the heritors' claim be sustained. Hepburn and his associates were encouraged to go for a wider victory, and a second Outer House decision led to an interlocutor (verdict) that the heritors of a parish had a joint control, with the session, of all parish funds.[25]

An interlocutor could be appealed to the full Bench of Judges in the Inner House. The matter was a serious enlargement of existing law, a fact recognised in complaints to the Commission of the General Assembly by the presbyteries of Perth and Dumbarton.[26] An appeal might have been successful. One at least of the Judges opposed the decision: Lord Elchies noted his disagreement in a commentary on cases, that 'neither by the nature of the thing, nor by the municipal laws of Scotland, nor by custom, had the heritors any case'.[27] But appeal was prevented by another legal process from a parish where relations between the Church and landowners were even worse than in Humbie.

This was Cambuslang (Lanarkshire), a parish with a minister bred in the Galloway interpretation of the covenanting tradition, and pushed into the benefice by the wishes of the parishioners over those of the patron. The leading landowner and some of the others adhered to the episcopal church, which prevented them benefiting from the normal way in which relations could be improved, membership of the session. Bad relations had come to a head because of the great revival of evangelical expression there in the spring of 1742. Preaching by the minister had had such an effect that by then he was holding daily services in the open air at which some 30,000 people were said to have attended. Although mass meetings of that period did not create the problems of litter and drug use which large gatherings today do, they still had effects on the environment and the workforce which were unattractive to property owners. Organised sewage disposal did not exist, pastures got trampled, fences were broken down, and the servant class encouraged in the expression of their religious experience at the expense of good working habits. One landowner stated that field preaching was a dishonour to religion, and another complained of the loss of work from 'gadding after conventicles'. Even the description of the evangelist George Whitefield, who shared in the preaching, that 'you could scarcely walk a yard, but you must tread upon some, either rejoicing in God for mercies received or crying out for more' hardly suggests a state of affairs attractive to the owner of the pastures where this was taking place.[28] And twelve years earlier the session had lent £30 to the most hostile of the local landowners, a Mr Hamilton of Westburn, on which interest had never been paid.

As at Humbie the case began as a simple demand to see the session's accounts. To prevent trouble the presbytery undertook to investigate these and found a cumulative error of ten shillings and fivepence halfpenny sterling. The complaint then made was that various payments made by the parish, such as fees paid to the synod and presbytery clerks, and more seriously the investment in equipment for the outdoor preaching, a mobile pulpit, called a tent, benches for communion, the hire of a field, constituted a misapplication of money dedicated to the support of the poor. The session's line in response was unwise, given the temper of the court, that what mattered was not whether its actions agreed 'with any Act of Privy Council or of our Scots Parliament but . . . with the Word of God'. Nor did it help its case by explaining that weaknesses in accounting came from the elders being 'all persons in low life illiterate countrymen' when confronting landowners who were convinced that none but themselves should handle any substantial amount of money. And the revival had made the session rich.[29]

While this case was proceeding through the legal track in leisurely fashion another hot issue blew up in the large and populous parish of St Ninians, adjacent to the royal burgh of Stirling. Here again was a rich session, for the minister had raised a large sum through a preaching trip to England. There were miscellaneous issues in the dispute. There were disputes over land which the session had bought and was using for a newly built church to replace one destroyed in the 1745 rebellion. Some heritors complained that the session failed to extract mortcloth fees from poorer families: the session had decided in 1746 not to charge at all for the use of the poor's mortcloth and sometimes to allow the use of a better one without charge. St Ninians was an assessed parish, the assessment covering about a third of the cost of relief. In spite of this minority role the landowners held that this reinforced their claim that they would be responsible for making up any deficiencies. The session, faced with a legal process, held that the costs of this would reduce the revenue of the poor. The arguments advanced give references to both the Humbie and the Cambuslang cases, showing the way in which the various cases supplied ideas for one another.

At some point the St Ninians heritors were allowed to see the session's registers and to the outrage of the session wrote in all of them 'This is one of the Books produced by the session clerk of St Ninian's to the general meeting of that parish to which their minutes of this day relate signed Arch. Stewart'. All levels of Church organisation took this as a claim to lay jurisdiction. There was some plain speaking in the Synod of Perth and Stirling, and normally Synods were of all the courts of the Church the most strongly under lay influence. The Synod declared that the insertion was a 'cause of general concern' and called upon the General Assembly not only to take up the issue of jurisdiction but also 'to think of some proper means to have all who reside in a parish and are so fond to manage the Poor's funds to contribute to the necessities of the Poor, especially those of opulent fortune who contribute little'.[30]

The Commissioners of the General Assembly pointed out to the Assembly that the result of the action at St Ninians could mean that 'People will withdraw their Charity at the Church Doors': it was alleged that this had already happened at Lauder (Berwickshire) where weekly collections had fallen from four or five shillings sterling to 'as many pence . . . All to the imminent loss of the Poor and Indigent'.[31] Implicit in this statement was the warning that such action could also be to the imminent loss of the heritors who would be faced with the need to assess.

The General Assembly responded to the overture of the Commission with an attempt at compromise. It sent a committee (it always worked through committees) to confer with the Judges to indicate that the Church might lodge an appeal, or even that pressure might be put on Parliament for legislation to ensure 'for the regular maintenance of the Poor in the Coming that all without Exception may contribute to their share proportionately'. This threat of general assessment came to nothing. This was the time when the lay members of the Assembly, which included several of the Judges, including the Lord President, were wrecking the attempts of the Assembly to secure an Act of Parliament increasing the stipends of ministers, which were levied on heritors.[32] But the Assembly on its own could at least assert the independence of church courts. It declared the entries into the books of St Ninians to be 'unwarrantable', ordered the parish to expunge them and warned the Procurator and Agent of the Church to be prepared to act in 'any Case of the like Nature'. Parishes, it declared, harassed in this way should get legal expenses from their Synod.

Meanwhile the quarrel of Cambuslang session with one persistent heritor wound its way by appeal to the Inner House and resulted in the decision in November 1752 that most of the expenditure made by the parish had been improper. It would no longer be legal for a parish to treat 'the poor's money' as an all purpose parish fund. In particular the fees of the clerks to higher courts and the hire of equipment for field preaching were disqualified. The hiring of seats for the communion was still seen as lawful, as was the salary of the session clerk, but otherwise what was called the poor's money must go to the poor. Also, of course, the use of parish money for litigation would not be sustainable at law. This point was made by the laird of Humbie to

Cuming, and explains the failure of that parish to appeal against the Outer House decision. The Cambuslang session had raised £5 in equal contributions from the eight members for its initial process, and the whole action had cost £28.14 shillings. An Inner House case, replete with 'replies' and 'duplies' and further pleadings would place a heavy burden on the elders.

It is difficult to believe that these legal processes were not inter-linked, not as a formal conspiracy but as the actions of individual landowners, conscious as a class of common interest, communicating with each other and sharply aware of how developments in the other parishes could be of use in their own. The Court of Session had already stretched the requirements against a minister of the law as to who paid for communion elements in a case in Strathmiglo in 1742. The Commission of the General Assembly reported that the minister of Cumbernauld was being pursued by his heritors with 'a vexatious Law suit' before the Commissary Court of Glasgow, which was demanding the delivery of all his session's books. Landowners were deliberately using their dominant position in the structure of justice to reduce the claim of the Church to autonomy. On a reduced scale it was a foretaste of the great struggle between the courts and the Church in the nineteenth century.

Some degree of concern over possible mismanagement of funds was understandable. General church purposes could so reduce the total fund that there was little for the poor. Abbey St Bathans, a poor Berwickshire parish, understandably put as its top priority for the poor's money the keeping of the parish coble in repair so that the two halves of the parish could be in touch across the Whitadder. Every few years the coble's keeper's neglect of his duties would mean that the boat was lost in a flash flood. The money available for the poor necessarily was reduced. In Edenkillie (Moray) in 1725 it was complained that the session owed eighteen pounds, thirteen shillings and fourpence in salaries 'and has no source but penalties and collections and so may be disabled to support the poor'.[33] But as the *Statistical Account* of the 1790s shows many parishes had devised means of raising money.[34]

The Humbie decision became part of the developing Poor Law of Scotland. Legal commentators accepted that landowners had legal control of all parish funds. In practice this meant that heritors expected to be called to any parish meeting that discussed investment. Presbyteries also tended to intervene in such matters, partly to prevent the lending of a parish's capital to a heritor who could not give adequate surety. It became desirable for parishes to keep financial and discipline affairs in different books, a policy also encouraged by presbyteries, though with limited success. The Cambuslang decision, by contrast, did not become recognised law. The disallowance of the fees of the clerks was soon recognised as impractical for the self-government of the Church. Lord Elchies had voted against it on this ground. His comment on the Humbie case was 'that neither by the nature of the thing, nor by the municipal law of Scotland, nor by custom, had the heritors any vote in the administration or distribution of the collections'.[35] Mr Cuming's successor as minister of Humbie, the Reverend Robert Dundas, made a stand on this point and insisted on paying the fees from the Poor Box, prepared if legal proceedings were taken to pay them out of his own pocket, but there was no trouble. (The Humbie heritors do not even seem to have inspected the parish books after their legal victory.) Session records in general continue to record the payment of the fees. In 1778 the heritors of Arngask (Fife) tried to resurrect the Cambuslang decision and brought a process in the sheriff court against the minister. The presbytery of Perth protested to the General Assembly, pointing out that the fees were essential to the government of the Church, and that the poor's money had been recognised in the *Second Book of Discipline*, 'the recognised basis of the Church's constitution', as intended for general 'use and utility' of the Church. The Assembly declared itself ready to pursue a process at public expence, and at this point the heritors appear to have realised that they had taken on more than they could cope with, and to have given way. Certainly there is no further trace of the issue in the General Assembly papers.

Miscellaneous expenses also continue to figure in parish accounts. Spare cash would go to providing New Testaments for parishioners. In 1778 Udny (Aberdeenshire) paid five shillings sterling for a mid-wife to examine the breasts of all unmarried women of the parish, to try to find out who was the mother of a foundling. In 1760 Ellon, also in Aberdeenshire, paid 24 shillings Scots to have taken to Aberdeen a woman suspected of infanticide. In the 1790s a minister advising one of the writers of the county reports for the Board of Agriculture wrote of the Cambuslang decision as invalid. It does not figure in the descriptions of the Poor Law made by nineteenth-century lawyers.[35]

Another issue between lay and clerical over Poor Law matters shows how damaging the rivalry between the two could be for the interests of the poor. A plan was made in 1739 to have a fund made for the poor of Stirling based on a regular subscription from the Church and a levy on the town. This was frustrated, deliberately, by Ebenezer Erskine, minister of the dissenting Associate Presbytery, who wrote, at enormous length with much repetition, how sincerely he wished to aid the poor but how impossible it was to associate with the established Church so long as it retained in office the five elders who had declined to be part of his dissenting kirk session. The poor were not Erskine's first priority. He was determined to defend the widest possible conception of the rights of the Church. Whatever the statute law might say, collecting money for the poor was the exclusive right of the ecclesiastical power. It was a sin for 'civil magistrates to exercise any act of Church government'. The voice of ecclesiastical intransigence in this episode foretells the dispute of the nineteenth century. As then, the main sufferers were the poor.[36]

Dissent, as it expanded in the later eighteenth century, was a source of restriction of funds for the poor. Collections in dissenting churches had as priority the sustaining of the dissenting ministry. In St Ninians in the 1780s, it was claimed that the dissenting churches made no contribution to the poor except for collections in the Relief Church on three days in the year.[37] The only unusual element in this arrangement was that poor relief received anything from organised dissent.

The obvious result of the legal disputes of mid-century was the increase in the accepted rights of landowners over the use of Church money, rights which for most of the time they did not wish to exercise. But there was a less advantageous element in the legal decisions. Clearly it was implied that the ultimate responsibility for poor relief lay with them.

NOTES

1. Henry Home, Lord Kames, *Remarkable Decisions of the Court of Session from the year 1736 to the year 1752* (Edinburgh, 1776), *Fairlie of Fairlie* v. *the Earl of Eglinton*.
2. M. Morison, *The Decisions of the Court of Session . . . digested under proper heads in the form of a dictionary* (Edinburgh, 1811), 42 vols, pp. 10, 551–96.
3. A typical example is *Heritors and Kirk Session of Coldstream* v. *the Heritors and Kirk Session of Hutton*, 6 December 1770, Morison, *Decisions*, p. 10,574.

4. James Fergusson, Lord Kilkerran, *Decisions of the Court of Session from the year 1738 to the year 1752* (Edinburgh, 1775); Patrick Grant, Lord Elchies, *Decisions of the Court of Session from the year 1733 to the year 1754 collected and digested in the form of a dictionary*, 2 vols (Edinburgh, 1813); Henry Home, as in note 1 and also *Select Decisions of the Court of Session, from the year 1752 to the year 1768* (Edinburgh, 1780).

5. George Turnbull, *Report on the Present State of Pauperism in Berwickshire* (Edinburgh, 1838), p. 8.

6. The papers in the SRO are miscatalogued as sheriff court records, SC 63/60/ 1. I owe this reference to John Ballantyne.

7. SRO GD6/117.

8. C. A. Malcolm, (ed.), *The Minutes of the Justices of the Peace for Lanarkshire, 1707–1723* (SHS, Edinburgh, 1931), pp. 116–17.

9. Dumfries Public Library, D1/1/2. Commissioners of Supply papers.

10. SRO GD72/629, Hay of Park papers.

11. For Ayrshire, T. Hamilton, *Poor Relief in South Ayrshire*, c, 4; for Berwickshire, Abbey St Bathans KSR, 1 September 1734; G. Turnbull, Pauperism in Berwickshire; for Dunbartonshire, SRO JP6/2/1, 6 May 1740; minutes of the Justices of the Peace; for Dumfriesshire, Dumfries Public Library, Commissioners of Supply papers D/1/3, 17 May 1726; for Fife, SRO Dysart KSR August 1731; for the Lothians, East Lothian, posters dated 1721, 1728 and 1731 catalogued under 'Haddingtoun' in the NLS; see also Oldhamstocks and Dirleton KSRs. For Midlothian SRO JP 4/2/1 14 April 1721: see also SRO Glencorse KSR 10 May 1731. For West Lothian see Midlothian Justice of the Peace Records: there are no signs in parish records. For Roxburghshire, J. Wilson, *Hawick; Its Old Memories* (Edinburgh, 1858), p. 136; for the Stewartry, SRO JP1/2/1, 3 March 1736, minutes of the Justices of the Peace; for Wigtownshire, H. Paton (ed.), *The Session Book of Penninghame*, vol. 2, 16 August 1730.

12. SRO JP4/2/1.

13. SRO JP1/2/1; Goldsmiths' Library, London, D. 120, Address by Sir Alex Gordon.

14. There is a note to this effect in the minutes of the Dunbartonshire Justices, SRO JP1/1/1.

15. SRO JP2/2/2.

16. SRO JP13/2/1. The letter from the Lord President is dated 23 June. The arrest appears to have been made some few days before the prince, on 22 June New Style, embarked and so launched the rising of 1745.

17. SRO Tranent KSR,

18. For Aberdeenshire, Udny KSR; for Banffshire, J. M. Macpherson, *Kirk's Care*, p. 206; for Clackmannanshire, SRO Perth and Stirling synod records, 1752; for Dunbartonshire, SRO JP 6/2/2; for East Lothian, SRO Tranent KSR and heritors' minutes, NLS Saltoun papers, box 192 (1750). SRO JP2/ 2/1 1752; for Peeblesshire, SRO Eddleston KSR 1752; for Perthshire, Blair Atholl MSS in Blair castle, 47 (8) 124, a letter of 7 August 1756 about the

scheme. I owe this reference to Dr Leah Leneman; for Roxburghshire, *PP* 1844, vol. xxii, p. 669, evidence of the clerk of the peace; for Wigtownshire, SRO JP 17/22/1, 1751 and also October 1757.

19. *Faculty Collections*, p. 73. Morison, *Dictionary*, p. 10,577.
20. EUL La III 746; Signet Library, Court of Session papers 480; 41–2 *Pollock v. Thomson*, 1808.
21. SRO GD 224/584/917. I owe this reference to Willie Orr.
22. SRO Newlands KSR, and GD/6/1208, Biel papers.
23. SRO Dalmeny KSR, 1741. When it was politically useful which it was not within a landowner's own parish, landowners could be very generous. The next Earl of Hopeton gave a hundred pounds sterling to the Edinburgh Charity Workhouse in February 1752, ECA Edinburgh Charity Workhouse minutes.
24. Much of this story is contained in a bundle of papers found in the tower of St Mary's, Haddington, during reconstruction in the 1970s and placed in the SRO with Haddington parish records, CH2/799/19. Further information comes from the Humbie KSR.
25. Morison, *Decisions*, p. 10,555. The decision was stressed in a biased comment of Lord Kames, the advocate of the heritors, in his *Remarkable Decisions*, pp. 250–1. See also the comment by Lord Kilkerran in his *Decisions*, p. 408, that the 'style' of the decision was 'more suitable for a statute than for an interlocutor'.
26. SRO CI I1/2/91.
27. P. Grant, *Decisions* (Edinburgh, 1818), vol. 2, *Notes*, p. 335.
28. Arthur Fawcett, *The Cambuslang Revival: the Scottish evangelical revival of the eighteenth century* (London, 1971).
29. Cambuslang KSR, 29 November 1749 and 23 February 1757; *Faculty Decisions 1752–6* (Edinburgh, 1760), 23 November, 1757.
30. NLS MS 9679. SRO CH1/2/94 f102. See also SRO CH1/1/50, General Assembly papers.
31. SRO CH1/2/94 f. 104ff. papers of the Commission of the General Assembly.
32. N. Morren, *Annals of the General Assembly of the Church of Scotland* (Edinburgh, 1838), vol. 2, pp. 190–6.
33. SRO Edenkillie (Moray) KSR. I owe this reference to Charles H. Morison.
34. See particularly the parishes of Angus, in vol. 13.
35. Elchies, *Decisions*, vol. II, Notes, p. 32. The decision is discounted in the Revd Robert Burns, *Historical Dissertations on the Law and Practice of Great Britian and particularly Scotland with regard to the poor* (Edinburgh, 1819), p. 98: 'the decision has been generally allowed to be erroneous, and uniform practice is against it'.
36. NLS MS 1506 ff. 15–17 (Delvine MSS). See also SRO GD/129/15/1482/, correspondence of Lord Grange.
37. NLS MS 9823.

CHAPTER 4

RESOURCES

The main base of the eighteenth-century Poor Law was voluntary contribution. There were numerous sources which came under this head, some more voluntary than others. Collections carried out by the elders, either at the church door or from house to house, were basic in all parishes where the Protestant Church was effectively set up. Collections might be weekly or monthly: weekly was the more common. They might be in money or in kind. In 1742 the session of Daviot (Aberdeenshire) distributed 12 bolls of meal and two pecks (a boll weighed approximately 140 pounds, a peck a sixteenth of this) among its poor, which probably represented a special donation by a landowner. In 1766 Dyce (Aberdeenshire) bought three bolls one firlot (four pecks) of meal, some of which went free to pensioners, the rest at a subsidised price to other needy folk. Lady Houston donated ten bolls of oatmeal every year from 1740 to 1749 to the poor of St Ninians (Stirlingshire). As the century wore on contributions in kind, except for large donations made by landowners in times of crisis, became rare.

There developed in Shetland a non-monetary form of relief, the boarding out of the poor with various families, for lengths of time related to the size of the landholding of the receiving families.[1] This continued in some parishes well into the nineteenth century. A similar method was used by some other parishes in the crisis of the 1690s, Kilmartin (Argyll), Largs (Ayrshire) and Greenock, and to have operated for a time in Chirnside (Berwickshire).

The pattern of collection and distribution was disturbed by the continuation of the practice of intervention by the higher courts of the Church, which would order special collections, or intervene to ensure fairness between parishes. For instance, in 1778 Dyce (Aberdeenshire) was ordered by the presbytery to send ten shillings sterling to the widow and children of a man in another parish who had recently lived in Dyce and whose cornyard had twice been burnt. A parish faced with exceptional need might suggest the application to a higher court for the ordering of a special collection. In 1755 Garioch presbytery promised John Sinklar of Meldrum, whose wife was bedridden, that either there would be a day's collection for him or a special recommendation to charity from the parish. But many such collections appear to have been arbitrary, simply orders to parishes to supply funds. The Church's courts would investigate afterwards if parishes or presbyteries had responded to the demand for a collection.

Some special collections could be held to have a bearing on local welfare. In 1728 the General Assembly passed an Act recommending voluntary collections for the recently founded Edinburgh Infirmary. This institution was to be available for the curable sick from the whole of Scotland, provided a subscription had been paid. Dalkeith presbytery received nine pounds Scots from Fala and Newton (Midlothian) to this institution, and recommended collections in other parishes. In 1731 the General Assembly repeated its Act, complaining that most parishes had sent nothing, and again in 1737, but with no great effect. Since the Infirmary had opened with only six beds, caution in contributing was understandable. The Edinburgh Surgeon's Hospital was also asking for a general collection at church doors. In 1739 the Synod of Lothian and Tweeddale ordered house collections for the Edinburgh Infirmary, but few parish records show any positive response till much later. The Aberdeen Infirmary, a later foundation, gained more ready support from its hinterland. The Synod of Aberdeen and Mearns ordered collections for it in 1733, and these became a regular feature in many parishes. Ellon collected 16 pounds in 1733 and 20 pounds in 1753; Udny contributed 4 pounds sterling, 2 shillings and twopence farthing in 1755. Northern parishes saw advantage in sending contributions which entitled them also to send patients.

Some of the 'recommended' or ordered 'voluntary' collections were too remote for parishes to respond. In 1740 the Synod of Perth and Stirling ordered a voluntary collection for the Edinburgh Orphan Hospital, a house into which it was possible to insert orphans from all parts of Scotland provided this could be done in the narrow admissions season and the children were of the right age. 'Voluntary' was a specialised word for the Church. The Synod later recorded a failure of contribution from the presbytery of Dunkeld, and ordered the representative of the presbytery to produce money at its next meeting. A further collection for the Edinburgh Infirmary ordered by the same Synod had generally done badly because of 'the severity of the season and straitning circumstances'. This was the time of the most severe weather experienced in the first half of the eighteenth century, producing shockingly inadequate harvests in the autumn of 1740. Yet the Synod continued to hound Dunkeld presbytery for its good cause, a worthy cause indeed but one from which benefit to the people of Dunkeld was unlikely, and Dunkeld continued to resist.

In the north of Scotland, where church collections were small and endowments rare, special collections, often to deal with devastation by fire, provided a means whereby disasters could be met. For instance, in 1760 Dyce gave six pounds to a man in Belhelvie who had suffered great loss by fire. Belhelvie itself used a parish level of collection and in August 1742 promised a whole Sunday's collection to the 'desperate case' of a man and his children 'all sick' and in June 1740 the same to a man with cancer of the lip. It accompanied the order with an appeal for 'enlarged charity'.

The amount a parish might receive in collections varied widely, and generalisations cannot be made. Parishes varied enormously in population and economic resource. In some areas money moved more readily than in others. The relative generosity of Border parishes, which became apparent in the 1740s, may relate to the close and early ties of this region to market forces,[2] and the parsimony of the north to the fact that in relative terms its economy was declining. Generosity has both the strength and the weakness of habit. Some spot figures can give an idea of the range of parish collections. Dyce, population of 383 in 1755, handled 36 shillings Scots a week in the 1760s. Penninghame (Wigtownshire), population 1,509, had collections averaging one pound, six and eightpence Scots, but half of the total raised came in at the communion service. Rothesay (Bute), population 2,222, averaged two pounds, eighteen and eightpence in 1733.

Weekly income, as shown in Penninghame, surged up sharply in communion week, and so did expenditure. Both the better off and the beggars of nearby parishes homed in on a communion, and alms were freely distributed. Little attention was paid to statutory prohibitions of payments to sturdy beggars on such occasions. KSRs show doles to people on the road as normal. In the 1730s Glencorse (Midlothian), where assessment was being set up, made small doles to several people who were obviously infirm, but also over a weekend supported a couple with four children on the move. They were probably looking for work but were liable to be classified as vagrants. A few months later the parish made a grant of three shillings to 'an old souldier travelling to Ireland' and six shillings to a family impoverished by sickness and now on their way north. Money also came to the poor at rites of passage of the upper class, but usually in direct distribution, not through kirk sessions. For instance, in St Ninians in 1758, 60 pounds Scots was distributed in the churchyard at the funeral of William Murray of Touchadam, and in 1750 Captain Campbell of Finab gave 24 pounds Scots at his mother's funeral.[3]

By the mid-eighteenth century many lowland parishes had acquired 'mortifications', legacies, and used them as a capital resource. Mostly these were in money from members of their own landowning families, but sometimes land or a house was given. It was often difficult for the parish to extract a legacy of money from the heirs of the deceased, and parishes might have to bring their complaints to the General Assembly. Even the Assembly's pressure does not appear to have extracted a legacy left to the parish of Kennethmont (Aberdeenshire) by Mr Leith of Leith Hall. In 1747 the presbyteries of Kirkcudbright and Dumfries asked the General Assembly to reimburse expenses caused by securing a legacy from James Blair of Fenwick to the poor of twenty-four parishes: clearly it would have been difficult for all these parishes to act individually. In 1746 the Assembly was trying to extract 500 merks and the interest on this sum due from Sir James Stewart of Bursay to the poor of Flotta and Burray (Shetland and Orkney), and in 1747 it was being asked by Dumbarton presbytery for support in securing a mortification.

Help by the Assembly was valuable, particularly since that body contained some distinguished lawyers among its membership, but its intercession was not always successful. In 1782 Perth session was claiming lands belonging to the local hospital which it managed for the poor and which had been lent to the town on an unusually favourable lease. The Assembly had to tell the town that past maladministration of resources could not be reversed.

Once legacies had been secured there were still problems for sessions. For the most part it was accepted that they were capital, not income, and were accounted for irregularly and on a different time scale from the reckoning of other sources of money, so it is difficult for much of the time to know how much a parish might have in reserve. In a crisis a parish might use up its capital stock in doles to the poor: this seems to have happened to a reclaimed loan of 50 merks in Belhelvie (Aberdeenshire) in 1742, when the Box was almost empty. But normally capital, it was thought, should be lent out at interest: the problem was to find secure debtors. In the markedly undeveloped Scotland of the early eighteenth century there were few safe outlets other than land, and the statutory rate of interest at 5 per cent did not help matters. Lending to landowners, often with securities from other landowners, was the usual form of investment, but lending to land-owners of the parish was unwise. Many parishes had had difficulty in getting loans returned in the famine of the 1690s. Dunbarney (Perth-shire) had to use litigation to get even part of a loan returned, and found that the surety, in land, had been sold. If a man who had stood surety died or went bankrupt, a session would normally try to terminate the loan. To regain capital it would often forgo interest. In any case it would not charge interest on unpaid interest. Misman-agement of capital sums was one of the accusations brought in the various legal processes of 1749–51, when it was asserted by the landed complainers that only men of property, who could be brought to book, should handle large sums, but the general impression gathered from session minutes is that such men were not particularly conscientious in their financial dealings. The trouble was that landowners could make life difficult for a session in many ways, and sessions therefore had an understandable unwillingness to sue them. Sometimes presbyteries might intervene to protect sessions from predatory and potentially insolvent landowners. Garioch presbytery (Aberdeenshire), for in-stance, insisted in the 1750s on vetting all loans to heritors.

A valuable source of money in most parishes, and one fairly regular, given the high death rate, was mortcloth revenue. The mortcloth was a sumptuous piece of velvet, often fringed with gold, a capital invest-ment by the session, which was draped over a coffin or a bier at a funeral, thereby doing something to redress the lack of ceremonial or comfort in funerals as organised by the Reformed Church. Parishes usually had several mortcloths, of different qualities, size and age, which were lent at a fee somewhere between 2 and 4 pounds Scots, and usually at a higher rate still if the deceased did not belong to the parish.

There was often a particular mortcloth for the poor, available at a low charge or free. Often there was a special one for a child. Tranent (East Lothian) even had a best and a second child's mortcloth. Families might not be able to afford any mortcloth, but this was rare for the burial of an adult: family prestige demanded display. For a 46-year-old day labourer in Tranent in 1760 the best mortcloth and the great bell (another item of expense) were used. For more distant funerals there might be a parish hearse – a splendid example from Bolton (East Lothian) survives in the Chambers Street Museum, Edinburgh. By contrast, some small babies were buried with no mortcloth, and a child in Tranent in 1779 had only a black apron on the coffin.[4] A suspected suicide there in 1774, buried outside the kirkyard, had no mortcloth. But most people earned the Poor Box some money by their method of leaving.

It was therefore important for a parish to have exclusive use of mortcloths. The process of gaining control of these objects can be seen in the attempts of Pencaitland session's offers in 1707 to various families which had possessed mortcloths since early in the seventeenth century. The session offered these families the best terms it could think of – free use of the parish's mortcloths for all heirs of the possessors and their families: the session was to maintain and replace the mortcloths where necessary, and would sustain the parish officer in his work of maintaining the cloths.

The complexity of rights in mortcloths is demonstrated in a bundle of manuscripts bound up together, stemming from the parish of St Ninians (Stirlingshire) in the late eighteenth century.[5] In 1660 many parishioners had subscribed to purchase a mortcloth, and they became known as the 'Portioners of the Mortcloth' with rights to its free use. The group decided that two-thirds of the fees gathered by other people's use of the mortcloth should go to a fund for its replacement. The issue which inevitably arose later was whether the rights of the portioners extended to replacement cloths. Then in the 1720s the heritors persuaded the session to allow the mortcloth fees to be used for the repair and expansion of the church. Expansion increased the number of church seats which could be rented to the advantage of the poor, but seems to have plunged the parish into long-standing disputes between heritors and ministers. In the mid-eighteenth century quarrel between session and heritors, the heritors accused the session of mismanagement of poor funds because the session had decided to allow free use of the mortcloth to the poor. The session held that it was not worth while pursuing poor people at law for fees, but the heritors claimed that the session's policy led to a calculable deficit from fees forgone. The claim to correctness over mortcloth revenue made by the heritors seems surprising since they had been using such revenue to carry out their obligation of church repair.

In burghs mortcloth ownership was complicated by the fact that many of the incorporations owned mortcloths and made use of them to assert the craft identity of their members, in the same way as craft emblems were used on gravestones. In 1750 Tranent took up the problem with its incorporations. If incorporations used their own mortcloths then, the session claimed, they ought either to pay a regular fee to the session, 50 pounds Scots was suggested, or support their own poor. The session clerk wrote to the craft deacons asking them how often they had used their mortcloths in the past. It was clearly not in the interests of the poor for the church to gain a monopoly over mortcloths if the incorporations were providing a significant element in the total relief system. The weavers replied twenty-four times for the small cloth and once for the big one in twenty years: the wrights claimed only a single use, a reply eliciting some scepticism. The session put pressure on some incorporations, notably the masons, to pay for the privilege of using their mortcloth, and a year later it decided to charge each incorporation at the level of the session's second mortcloth.

Other burghs reached different compromises with their incorporations. The Kelso skinners had a mortcloth fee of 2 pounds Scots, kept a common good for their members and dependants in need, but also made a subscription to the session.[6] Similarly the Mariners' Society of Ayr charged 3 pounds Scots for its best mortcloth, 36 shillings for the next, 18 shillings for an old cloth and 24 shillings for the child's, but also helped individual sailors and their families and gave 10 pounds Scots a year to the Ayr poorhouse.[7] This body also gave out money in casual doles to poor sailors, with special generosity to those captured by Turks or shipwrecked. A search through the records of other incorporations would doubtless show similar co-operation between the crafts and the parish.

Another source of funding, based on the desire of families for status, was the hire of church seats. The landed class felt very strongly about the possession of the more prestigious places in church, and some were even prepared to fight for them. The Privy Council had had to deal with a feud in seventeenth-century Largo (Fife) based on this issue.[8] In some parishes the heritors, who had financial responsibility for the church fabric, simply claimed the right to install seats; in others they might have a gallery. But in some churches the session was considered entitled to create and own seating, renting it out for a charge. The session might build a special loft for this purpose, a speculative venture which did not always produce a profit. Caputh (Perthshire) in 1755 was making a success of this method of fund raising, charging between 4 and 45 shillings Scots for various pews, and gaining over 11 pounds in the year.[9] In contrast the laird of Monymusk (Aberdeenshire) in 1792 claimed to himself the ownership of all the seats erected by the session, bringing to an abrupt end a profitable investment.[10] Eventually the session received a proportion of its capital expenditure. This parish was unusual in being all within the estate of Grant of Monymusk, a landowner who appears to have had an enhanced belief in the right of the landowner to all revenue on the estate.

There was a limit to the extent to which seats could be exploited as a source of revenue, for it was a matter of principle to the Church that the poorer part of society should not be barred from access to services. In 1752 Garioch presbytery was concerned because a landowner's factor in Meldrum (Aberdeenshire) had, on his own initiative, collected seat rents which he offered to the session. Session and presbytery were united in making it clear that there could be no charge on poor people's attendance. But the building of pews might come to mean that there was almost no room left for such people.

The numerous examples of parishes gaining by seat rents given by Macpherson suggests that this was particularly a feature of the north, for southern Scotland provides relatively few. Stirling had used the method of raising funds in the famine of the 1690s. Property rights may have been defined on a different basis there. But certainly seats were valued in the south, and by the end of the century were presenting a serious issue in parishes which had been experiencing population growth.

Another saleable commodity could be burial plots. A parish which did well on these was St Ninian's (Stirlingshire). There an ordinary plot went for 3 pound, 6 shillings and 8 pence, and in the 1720s the parish was netting 52 pounds a year, but since this was a permanent sale of rights, receipts declined. Still for the period for which this particular record survives the parish averaged 23 pounds a year.[11]

It looks as if what St Ninian's was selling was a right to land which had been bought with the profits of a trip by its minister to London where he raised funds for the replacement of the church destroyed in the 1745 rising. Distant preaching by effective ministers was a source of funds for the poor of some lucky parishes, though much of what was raised for St Ninian's was used to provide a salaried assistant to the minister. In the evangelical revival at Cambuslang in the 1740s the preaching by the Reverend William McCulloch outside the church brought in large sums.

A further source of 'voluntary' funds has a nature not entirely voluntary. This was fines for misbehaviour, particularly sexual mis-behaviour, but also the causing of scandal and lapses in Sunday observance. There was a standard level of 10 pounds Scots on most sexual offences, fixed soon after the Reformation. The rapid inflation and the coinage adulteration of the later sixteenth century reduced the cost of sinning in real terms, but it remained at a level which was useful. Young adult servants, the main offenders, could actually afford to pay their fines, and only occasionally had a session to reduce them on grounds of poverty.

There was also 'consignation money', a deposit which had to be made when the proclamation of a marriage was made. This sum, 10 pounds Scots in many cases, but sometimes much less, was held by the session and returned to the couple only when the wedding had not been followed by forbidden levels of jollification – 'penny wedding' was the name given to the prohibited party – and when a full calendar nine months had elapsed between the wedding and the birth of the first child.

Kirk session increasingly took the line that they were entitled to the goods of a pauper after death. Stirling discovered that a woman, put on the roll because she had claimed 'lack of subsistence', had died leaving substantial amounts of salt beef, mutton and money; stimulated by this event it required all future claimants to bequeath their goods to the session. St Andrews was early, 1597, in requiring paupers formally to assign their goods to the parish. It was not till 1751 that Ellon declared that 'if any of the poor refuse to dispone when called to they are to be struck out of the roll'. Also late in deciding to claim such goods was South Leith, which came to this action only after a dead pensioner had been found to possess 60 pounds. Most rural parishes simply stated or assumed that the property was theirs. As late as February 1816 Edenkillie (Moray) had trouble because it discovered that relatives were making off with the possessions of pensioners after death, and had to insist that all pensioners sign a promise of their possessions to the session 'at least to cover the expense of burial'.[12] The possessions appear to have been used not simply to cover basic burial expenses but also a wake, and the session accounts often do not record the value in full. Macpherson gives various examples of what traditional funeral practices meant.[13] For Tranent (East Lothian) in 1756 we have the relatively extensive list of the possessions of an elderly widow as taken by the parish: '2 Bedsteds, a Press, four Chists, two stools, three pairs of Blankets, One pair and a half of Sheets, a bed covering, a Bed Tyke, Pillows and a Bolster, a Pot and Crook, a Brace of Tongs, a Pint Stoup, two smoothing irons, a Lint and an out Wheel'. As a widow this woman had more plentiful possessions than would most single women, but the list still reminds us that many households in Scotland had not yet experienced Hoskins's domestic revolution.[14]

Where parents died and it was necessary for the parish to support the children the sessions appear to have had no hesitation in taking the goods. Between 1698 and 1701 Spott (East Lothian) found itself with three families of orphans, one a pair of totally destitute small girls, the others occupying houses still with some goods. The furnishings of the 'plenished house' in both cases were taken over and for one family of four helped the neighbours to take on care of some of the children, leaving the session responsible only for the youngest, 'a tender unthriving child who could not walk'.

Gifts in kind became rarer as the eighteenth century wore on, except for large donations of 'victual' (grain) from landowners who still received the bulk of their rents in kind. If and when a parish might decide to set up a poorhouse, gifts in kind to it were seen as appropriate and could take various forms. Inveresk (East Lothian) relied on the surgeons resident in the parish for medical services to the poorhouse which it had from 1752 to 1782. The Edinburgh Charity Workhouse, which opened in 1743, gave a favourable place in the queue for admission to those poor who would bring linen, blankets or furniture with them.[15] Small parish poorhouses may well have received gifts in kind which were not recorded by the session.

An item which in practice was a gift in kind, and not much desired, was bad money. There was strong pressure on everyone to be seen to contribute at the church service, and bad money was a way of not openly refusing. In 1699 Yester (East Lothian) was complaining of the number of 'Irish Babbies' given to the treasurer. In October 1740 the minister of Abbey St Bathans (Berwickshire) made a special visit to Edinburgh to change $18\frac{1}{2}$ pounds weight of bad coinage, and received for it 7 pounds 8 shillings, all useful in the aftermath of the disastrous harvest. When the presbytery of Garioch looked into the finances of the parish of Kinkell and Keithhall it found 65 pounds, 6 shillings good money and 40 pounds 7 and 4 pence bad. Stobo (Peeblesshire) in 1801 had collected 6 stone of bad halfpence, worth, it was dismayed to learn, a mere 9 pence sterling a stone. The problem of bad money is a reminder that the charitable basis of the Scottish Poor Law was sometimes more apparent than real.

In emergencies, periods of food shortage or severe dislocations of the labour market, parishes might receive gifts of considerable value from their landowners. These were conspicuous in the harvest failure of 1740, when many sessions record large gifts of grain or money. Of particular note are frequent references to large purchases by the county landowners of grain abroad, which was made available below cost price to the various sessions. A striking example is that of Midlothian, where the landowners raised £2,000 according to Sir John Clerk of Penicuik, and stored their purchases in a granary in Leith. It was offered to parishes below cost, but still at a price well above normal, so the parishes that bought it added their own further subsidy.

Details of generous response to this situation can be seen in the session register of Currie (Midlothian). The session recorded that it was 'deeply affected with the straitning circumstances of many families especially those of the Ordinary sort thro' the threatening scarcity and dearth' and unanimously resolved that 'they to the utmost of their power will provide for all indigent persons not only in the ordinary way of giving pensions and extraordinary allowances, but also by providing House-keepers with Meal at moderate price', and 'considering that by the good hand of God upon them they are provided with a considerable stock resolve not to spare the same while any family or a single person in the parish are in want'. The session set up a subcommittee to purchase from the store until in the following August it recorded that the market had fallen below the price of the subsidised grain.

Currie gives an unusually full description of the response to the crisis of 1740, but county gifts of a similar kind can be found in many areas. For instance, the Midlothian Justices of the Peace were sharing the cost of subsidised grain in Edinburgh with the City Council (after a serious grain riot). The Aberdeen Justices were making available subsidised grain and in Berwickshire the heritors imported 'a parcel of beans' as well as a large amount of barley.[16]

The study made by a researcher from the United States of this crisis shows that though Scotland was a country experiencing as sharp a rise in food prices as anywhere, mortality rose but not to a high degree. At least in the Lowlands it seems that the organisation of relief was able to cope with much of the stress. What could have been a famine was, instead, a season of considerable hardship, and much of this achievement was due to generosity by landowners.[17]

The obvious question from this crisis which must arise is why parishes did not adopt assessment. Some, of course, but not many, were already assessed. For those that were not, the setting up of a rate might have involved friction with the heritors, and would certainly have taken time. Unlike the crisis of the 1690s, the harvest failure was of a single year only, and perhaps the generous gifts of the heritors should be seen as a method of avoiding accepting assessment.

Landowners were almost always hostile to assessment. As a burden it was usually not heavy, and indeed it might be less than the contributions to relief made by those landowners who were resident. But as a regular charge on an estate it was not only seen as reducing its value, but also as a potential commitment to a later higher charge. An element of anticlericalism may have been involved. An assessed parish had its funds under the control of a joint committee of heritors and session, and would be administering a fund containing money raised by assessment, interest on capital stock and half the church collections which, by the proclamation of 1693 and later Act of Parliament, had to go to the poor.[18] In law this gave the heritors control of funds which were in origin both lay and ecclesiastical. But in practice the distribution of money was carried out by the session, who knew the conditions of the applicants for relief. Even deeply religious landowners disliked having any of their financial affairs controlled by the Church.

In spite of the efforts of landowners to prevent it, assessment spread after 1740. Parishes, usually in the south and south-east, would find that even in times of no particular economic stress, those poor whom they recognised needed collectively more in support than their voluntary sources could provide. Landowners might make generous gifts when there was an unmistakable crisis, but in what were felt as normal times might be less forthcoming, particularly if they did not live in the parish. And the pattern of intermarriage between land-owning families and the attraction of heiresses meant that increasingly families came to have estates in different parishes and live only in one. Also there was the pull to episcopalian dissent, which divorced some landowning families from the affairs of their parishes. As with all the dissenting bodies, voluntary contributions were needed to support the dissenting ministry, leaving relatively little for other good works. Even when landowners had not widespread estates, the economic oppor-tunities encouraged by Union and by economic and social change might take them from home. There were attractive positions and work in London and in other cities. When parishes found that they needed a sizable contribution to poor relief from their landowners, the only way to get it increasingly came to be by assessment. And if a parish laid on assessment in other than a crisis period, the odds were that it would not get rid of it. Half of assessment was, after all, paid by the middling rank of the parish, the tenants, and these people would not be able also to keep up voluntary contributions, or even if they could, would not feel obliged to do so.

It was not only the Episcopal Church that used its collection money for the ministry. There were other secessions, starting with the Original Secession, led by the Erskine brothers, which, after a period in which it managed to retain ecclesiastical stipends while denouncing the establishment, finally moved into complete independence in 1740. In 1764 a more significant schism followed in the creation of the Relief Church. This body drew strong support in urban and western Scot-land, and by the 1770s had formed a large number of congregations. The fissiparous nature of holier-than-thou presbyterianism was shown in the tendency of dissenting congregations to find further principles on which new divisions could take place. The effect of religious divisions was recorded gloomily by the the session clerk of St Ninians, which had lost half its congregation to Ebenezer Erskine. 'No part of the Collections has been hitherto allotted to the Maintenance of the poor by any of the Religious Societies . . . except three days of collection by the Relief Congregation . . . probably they may have some of their own Hearers to whom they occasionally give Charity . . .'.[19] This cautious statement was over-optimistic. In general the pension list of parishes was not a burden shared by dissent.

That dogma might seem more important to some than charity was earlier shown by the particular experience of Stirling in 1739, the time when the schism became established. The pending removal of Erskine from his charge led to much of the collection money being 'abstracted', in other words deflected from the parish treasurer, because Erskine and his followers disputed the status of the elders who made the collection. The sharp increase in destitution that resulted led to a plan of intervention by the town council. It was proposed that £18 should be raised, mostly from sixty well-off households, another £27 from other families, £8 from the town council and £12 from the collections. The church's share would be gathered in by burgh officials: the Magistrates, Dean of Guild and Convener would stand at the church door and receive money. The level of need was seen as static: the amount planned £65 a year. Erskine destroyed the plan, as is shown in Chapter 3, because he considered his quarrel with the established Church more important than the support of the poor.[20]

In all the miscellaneous sources of revenue there is rarely any mention of the role of kin in supporting those in need. Of course, the nature of the sources means that if kin were effectively supporting the poor, which might be expected in a society valuing kinship, the record would not concern itself with the fact. But in such a situation there would be cases where the kin could bring only inadequate or partial support, and so parish intervention would be needed.

Such cases are very rare. The kin of a mentally deranged man in Dundonald (Ayrshire) in 1637 had struck a bargain with the session to divide the cost of support. In Kennoway (Fife) in 1697, the session ordered its officer to give a fifth of his salary to his mother. Tranent (East Lothian) in 1750 dispatched a six-year-old boy to stay with his father (there was a legal obligation of support for parents and for parents and grandparents to support children). But Penninghame session (Wigtownshire) in 1704, when a woman's son in law had housed her for three years, did not consider it could compel a son of hers to reimburse him. In 1704 Pencaitland (East Lothian) sent an orphan to live with his uncle, who was 'in grand circumstances' in Dysart. More characteristic is a story from Spott (East Lothian), where the session in 1698 took over the care of two small girls, the survivors of a family destroyed by the famine. It recorded that they had no relations, yet, when in turn they became old enough to work, probably at the ripe age of ten, an aunt appeared from the outskirts of the parish and took them over. The rarity of remarks about kin support combines with other features to suggest that kinship links outwith the neighbourhood were not important to the working population of the Lowlands.

During parish vacancies landowners might help with poor relief without it being a new burden. In Udny (Aberdeenshire) in September 1770 there was a ministerial vacancy and a landowner offered the stipend for half a year which he was obliged to pay to the Church, for the poor. But in this case the factor of the principal landowner in the parish refused to pay and as this estate was responsible for two-thirds of the stipend, the session decided to sue.

Assessment was usually based on 'valued rent', a land valuation made in the 1660s and used for determining the obligation of heritors to county expenses and to the maintenance of the fabric of church and manse. As eighteenth-century agrarian changes led to 'improvement' and sent up the value of various estates, some parishes chose instead to distribute their burdens by the real rent. There was also the possibility of assessment by means and substance, that is by wealth in cash, income and movables, appropriate to a business community.

Once a parish accepted the necessity of assessment, there was a strong tendency, encouraged by the landowners, to keep it at a fixed and low level, say of 5 or 10 shillings for every 100 pounds of valued rent. It is common in OSA parish accounts that assessment brought in a specific sum, and the list of pensioners would be tailored to fit resources. The Poor Box would then be expected to prevent extra people falling into total destitution. The obverse of this can be seen in Sprouston (Roxburghshire) where the heritors at various times found that the Poor Box was well supplied and cancelled assessment for four, six or eight months. Assessment could be flexible, but often was not. From the point of view of the session the great advantage of assessment was that it forced the landowning class into decision making about the poor in a way that occasional generous gifts did not. Claims to the status of pensioner would be discussed in heritors' meetings and, though the provision of information and the delivery of cash rested with the session, heritors were bound to become informed about their parishioners.

The eighteenth century, at least up till the 1770s, was a period relatively untraumatic for the mass of the population. Certainly the savage winter of 1739 and the harvest failure of 1740 made for a very stressful two years: 1756 was another poor harvest, as was 1766. In the latter year the East Lothian Justices and landowners were urging parishes to buy up stocks of grain to sell at 2 pence a peck below market prices to those in need and, if necessary, to bring in assessment.[21] There was a slight but definite rise in grain prices from the 1730s, somewhat more marked after 1750 but not enough to cause difficulties over relief levels. Money wages were rising after 1750.[22]

The marked spread of assessment after 1740 in southern Scotland, particularly in the Border counties, has caused some debate. Comments in the early nineteenth century over assessment in the Borders attributed it to parishes having been contaminated by the bad practice of generous poor relief in neighbouring areas of England. This is not convincing as an argument. The Borders was an area of big estates, and landowners there were able to manage the burden of relief, but Scottish landowners were unlikely to impose financial burdens on their estates merely because English landowners had to pay them. We should look for an economic cause, and the feature which distinguishes this area of Scotland in the eighteenth century was depopulation. The Borders turned from mixed farming to pastoral, and such a change would necessarily produce a sharp drop in the demand for labour. This would particularly affect young adults, who would have to move elsewhere in search for employment. Migration of the young would eventually increase the burden of the old and unfit, and place higher burdens on the parishes.

Elsewhere in southern Scotland assessment spread, but not so generally as in the Borders. It became fairly common in the Lothians and around Stirling. This raises the question of whether there was an increase in the general level of poverty and destitution or an increase in the consciousness of the problem of poverty. There also may have been an increase in seasonal unemployment, particularly in ports where trading activity fell off sharply in the winter.

It has been held by many that the economy of Scotland was static and backward in the seventeenth and early eighteenth centuries but transformed in the last quarter of the eighteenth century. This is too crude an outline. Not all the new industries given government aid in the late seventeenth century were failures, and agriculture had benefited by state policy, though not enough to prevent the famine of the 1690s. Scotland may not have recovered the population lost in this disaster until the 1740s. It is in that decade that economic and population growth both become noticeable.

It is in the 1740s that many industries increased their output. Linen was the most important of these for it provided work, full time or part time, for large numbers of both sexes.[23] Increased work opportunities encouraged marriage, and the rate of population growth rose. Our first good figure for Scottish population is the 1.25 million of Webster's 1755 census. There are indications then that population growth was already well established. By the first government census of 1801 the growth rate was high: the population expanded by 12.5 per cent in the following ten years. It is possible that by then the growth was straining resources: certainly the high level of emigration suggests that resources and opportunities seemed inadequate. But in the late eighteenth century the pressure of population appears to have been economically beneficial. Rising grain prices encouraged landowners to reorganise their estates and gain higher productivity. Farming was planned to use labour more continuously. The effect of this was the disappearance of the cottar class. Those cottars fit and able became part of the labour force of the new, bigger farms, and their holdings part of the farms' land. Those who were too numerous for the farms moved into the nearby towns or villages to work at road making, carting or industry. The Scottish system of hiring fairs made it very clear when labour was superfluous to agricultural needs.

The absence of protest or demonstration over these changes suggests that for many the result was a higher standard of living, Certainly wages rose from their mid-century level. But employers may have become more selective in their choice of workers with a more mobile population available. There may well have been an increase in the seasonal nature of work. Transport labour might not be so much required in winter, fashion trades were always seasonal, building could not be done in bad weather, better organised agriculture might have little use for the work of women or the old. There had always been a section of the population living from hand to mouth, not receiving any regular resource but day by day surviving on what the various members brought in. Economic growth might make it more difficult for such families to support themselves. Certainly there seems to be a connection between the rapid growth of the economy and the increasing need to draw on the resource of assessment for the poor.

Made possible by these economic developments in the last twenty years of the century came the 'industrial revolution', the system of powered factory manufacture in large mills. This offered a wider choice of work for all ages, and higher wages for those who could take the discipline involved, but it enhanced the effects of the swings of the business cycle. Sudden slumps brought forward the stark problem of unemployment, and the workers in this new system did not have the residual rural activities of the burghs of the seventeenth century to enable them to survive. The inadequacies of the Poor Law became more apparent.

The Highlands and Western Isles also experienced population growth, partly as a result of the ending of clan warfare, but the effects were less beneficial than in the Lowlands. Highland landowners tried, as did those in the Lowlands, to expand income, but with less effect. They searched for a product which could use the labour force and be exported but, except in the form of manpower, failed. Highlanders went into the army or to the colonies or worked in the Lowland industries. The economic developments after 1750 provided jobs at a distance only, and were taken up on a temporary or permanent basis. There was little money circulating in the highland area and almost none of it went into poor relief. If the sick or poor got help in the Highlands it was mostly through the personal generosity of their neighbours.

A final question which must be asked about resources for the poor is whether the sums agreed to be raised or distributed actually went into the right pockets. It was very easy for heritors not to pay assessment till it was long overdue, and heritors' meetings did not exacerbate the resultant bad relations by charging interest on late payments. In Innerwick (East Lothian) in 1766 one landowner had owed sums for church repair since 1751.[24] His fellow heritors, conscious that they had had to pay at a higher level of assessment because of the shortfall, were still unwilling to take legal action against one of their own order. It was a common opinion in landed society that public money should not be in the hands of any other class because there was no surety in case of misappropriation. And it is true that there are occasional instances of embezzlement of the poor's money by members of the session. In the instances that have come to light this was regarded by the other members of the session as such a serious offence that it is unlikely that cases were ever covered up. And there are very few cases which were noted.

The longest standing abuse of funds which I have come across was in Penninghame (Stewartry). In September 1710 Cristen McKie had said to an elder 'Ye of the Session tak the poors money to keep your purses with on Saturday and Sunday and give it to the skybes of gentles'. Though it seems that she had been encouraged to make this and other subversive remarks by one of the elders who had doubts about what was going on, she and her husband were publicly rebuked in church, she on the stool of repentance. Twenty-two years later the treasurer, John McCaul died, and it was found that he had been lending out from the Poor Box on bonds, made out to him personally. Over 600 pounds had gone. The loans had been to local farmers, traders and craftsmen and, as McCaul was not a good chooser of financial risks, much of the money could not be recovered. The treasurer's son was prepared to make good the eventual loss, and the session spent much time in the next ten years chasing up small creditors and impounding stock as sureties. Eventually the loss was made good: nobody apologised to Cristen McKie.

What is unusual about this story is the length of time that systematic misappropriation went on for. All other cases that I have found were single or short-term events. In Dundonald (Ayrshire) in 1720 an elder was accused of similar unauthorised lending, but the matter was rapidly settled by his demotion from the eldership. In St Cuthbert's Edinburgh in 1743 the session clerk had either failed to make entries or had confused them, and lost the parish £14.13s. In Kineff (Mearns) heritors wanted to investigate the use of funds by the session, but were prevented by being told that they had no right to investigate.[25] This was before the Humbie and St Ninians cases had changed the law, but, in any case, the grievance they held was probably not about embezzlement but about using the funds in ways they did not like. There was a dispute in Keith (Banffshire) between the elders and the schoolmaster, who was also treasurer, in which it was alleged that the books had been altered. This ended up as a dispute between the session and the presbytery in the Court of Session.[26] In 1760 there was a story about a very small abstraction of money in Glasgow where an elder had failed to pass on the full weekly allowance to a woman and whose defence was that the poor were 'improper' witnesses: his case went up to the Commission of the General Assembly. The Poor Box of Crieff

(Perthshire) was found in 1700 to contain neither money nor papers and there were no indications as to what had happened to them. In 1760 the problem of what had happened to the poor's money in Burra (Shetland) went to the General Assembly. In 1737 a Dundee elder with an overdeveloped sense of the value of money was found to have been squirrelling it away from the collections for at least three months. He was sufficiently committed to the enterprise culture to try to strike a deal with the session so that it would supply him with a pension. In 1707 Dunkeld presbytery investigated an allegation of numerous serious faults made against the minister of Kirkmichael (Perthshire) which included the claim that he had embezzled some fines. What emerged, after a vast investigation at a major meeting of the public in Dunkeld cathedral, was that he had not yet succeeded in extracting them from the offenders: it seems obvious that the whole accusation had been a put-up job, probably based on political disagreement. In 1763 there was, it was asserted, a need for the minister of Kinkell and Keithhall (Aberdeenshire) to draw a distinction between the minister's funds and those of the Poor Box, which had been in his keeping.

These instances do not amount to much in the way of misbehaviour, or even of carelessness, and do not sustain the belief of heritors that unpropertied elders were unsuitable keepers of public money. There were, in the same range of parishes studied, far more occasions when landed gentry failed to hand over legacies promptly or to pay the interest on loans. But there is one serious case of embezzlement in which guilt, though never proven, seems probable – the case of John Jenkison, minister of Athelstaneford (East Lothian). In 1726 six elders raised a query about a loan made from the Poor Box to him when he took office at the start of the century: had it been repaid? There was no receipt. Moreover in 1726 the box, then kept in the manse, had been broken into. Worst of all, the figures of money provided by an elder had been altered in the session minutes, which the minister had written, sending up the discharge and down the charge. The elders took their concern to the presbytery, but both the presbytery, and later the Synod, refused to convict the minister of anything other than grossly negligent book-keeping. At this point the six elders resigned office, and twenty-nine householders asked the Commission of the General Assembly for an alternative minister to conduct the sacrament. The twenty-nine were rebuffed, but the resignation of the elders forced the presbytery to set up a committee drawn from other parishes to collect and distribute the poor's money, a considerable labour since these men were not intimate with the life of the parish. There was relief all round in February 1730 when Jenkison died, and the elders indicated their willingness to serve again.[27]

The fact that a discrepancy in the parish accounts of approximately 50 pounds Scots could go up as a case to the highest court of the Church, and cause inconvenience to the parishes of a whole presbytery, shows that the integrity of the poor's money, for all that it was also the general fund for all parish business, was of tremendous importance to all involved in parish affairs. It is a reflection of how large the duty of charity to the poor bulked in people's minds.

NOTES

1. Frances Shaw, *The Northern and Western Islands of Scotland* (Edinburgh, 1980), p. 201.
2. R. A. Dodgshon, *Land and Society in Early Scotland* (Oxford, 1981).
3. NLS MS 9823, f. 27. Papers connected with the parish of St Ninians.
4. SRO CH2/357/21. Tranent Bill of Mortality. For a rich vein of detail about mortcloths, see Anne Gordon, *Candie for the Foundling* (Edinburgh, 1992), pp. 496–526.
5. NLS MS 9823 ff. 128–34.
6. NLS MS 3083. Book of the Kelso skinners.
7. NLS MS 941. Records of the Mariners' Society of Ayr.
8. *RPCS* VIII, 1610. For the Lundie and Largo feud and others see pp. 83, 106–7, 145, 248, 531, 678.
9. New Register House, Edinburgh, OPR 337/4.
10. Macpherson, *Kirk's Care* (Aberdeen, 1940s), p. 84.
11. NLS MS 9823 ff. 25–6.
12. I owe the South Leith reference to Dr Leah Leneman and that for Edenkillie to Charles M. Morison.
13. Macpherson, *Kirk's Care*, pp. 68–79.
14. W. G. Hoskins has used the phrase 'the domestic revolution' to describe the change in housing and furnishings which took place in England in the sixteenth century, and somewhat later in Scotland. See his *Essays in Leicestershire History* (Liverpool, 1950).
15. ECA, Bay C shelf 14. Minutes of the Edinburgh Charity Workhouse, 14 April 1743.
16. For Midlothian, *Caledonian Mercury*, 24 November 1740, also Borthwick KSR, and John M. Gray (ed.), *Memoirs of Sir John Clerk of Penicuik* (SHS Edinburgh, 1892), p. 159: for Aberdeenshire, SRO JP26/2/1.
17. John D. Post, *Food Shortage Climate Variability and Epidemic Disease in pre-*

Industrial Europe (Ithaca, 1985). This study uses only limited source material for Scotland. Further research in parish records would certainly show effective action by both landowners and the Church in many areas, though of course not in all. For instance, the minister of Fearn (Ross) states in the *OSA* that people starved in 1740.

18. *APS* X Appendix 99b.
19. NLS MS 9823 f. 125.
20. NLS MS 1506 (Delvine MSS) ff. 15–17. SRO GD124/15/14 1–4. See also A. T. N. Muirhead 'A secession congregation in the community: the Stirling congregation of the Reverend Ebenezer Erskine 1731–1754', *Records of the Scottish Church History Society* (1986), vol. 22, pp. 211–24.
21. SRO JP2/2/1.
22. Valerie Morgan, 'Agricultural wage rates in late eighteenth century Scotland', *Economic History Review*, 2nd series, 24 (1971), pp. 181–201.
23. Figures for linen sold publicly are given in H. Hamilton, *An Economic History of Scotland in the Eighteenth Century* (Oxford, 1963), appendices iv and v; M. W. Flinn et al., *Scottish Population History* (Cambridge, 1977), part 5, parts 1 and 2; Rosalind Mitchison, 'Webster revisited. A re-examination of the 1755 census of Scotland', in T. M. Devine (ed.), *Improvement and Enlightenment* (Edinburgh, 1989), pp. 62–77; T. C. Smout, 'Where had the Scottish economy got to by the third quarter of the eighteenth century', in I. Hont and M. Ignatieff, *Wealth and Virtue* (Cambridge, 1983), pp. 45–72.
24. SRO GD6/1208, Biel papers, letter of 4 October 1766 from David Smith of Innerwick.
25. UEL La III 746 (1).
26. Pamphlet in NLS R 234 b 1 (1–30).
27. Rosalind Mitchison, 'The Athelstaneford Case', in *Transactions of the East Lothian Antiquarian and Field Naturalists' Society*, 23, 1996, pp. 45–7.

CHAPTER 5

THE POOR
AND THEIR SUPPORT

The most obvious feature of lists made by parishes of their poor is the preponderance of women over men. Counts made of this at different dates and for miscellaneous parishes show at least twice as many women named as men. Since often the entry of a name represents a household receiving relief, and normal prejudice in the session would think of a man as heading the household, the real ratio of female to male partly or wholly supported by relief would be nearer three or four to one than two to one.

Children would not be named in lists of poor if they had a living parent, but the name of such a parent may be followed by 'and three children' or 'and family'. Orphan children and foundlings would perhaps be handed over to a family with support, or to a woman already on a pension which would be increased to cope with the extra cost. Orphans were not rare. The expectation of life in the mid-eighteenth century was a little over thirty-seven years, and although a considerable element in keeping it low was high infant mortality,[1] loss of both adults in a family was not a rare event. Foundlings were markedly less common than orphans: it was unusual for a rural parish to be supporting more than one at a time, and many parishes were free of them. Approximately one child in every two thousand born was abandoned and so became a foundling if found while still alive. There is no indication in most parish records that foundlings were normally treated more meanly than other children supported by the parish. Both sets of children would receive general support, enough money for food, the payment of school fees at least till they could read and occasional payments for shoes and clothes. Those foundlings who can be traced through an unbroken series of session registers till they could be sent to work appear to have gone into service or apprenticeship at ages between ten and fifteen. New Aberdeen in 1738 decided to cease support of an eleven-year-old foundling boy, but since he was epileptic and nearly blind gave him some temporary aid. The suburban Edinburgh parish of St Cuthbert's recorded in 1721 the decision that support should cease at the age of nine, or earlier if 'of larger growth and stronger constitution', but this age limit does not appear to have been generally accepted. In 1762 the Canongate Charity Workhouse accepted a nine-year-old foundling boy.[2]

If the presence of children on relief was mainly a result of the natural features of birth and death, the preponderance of women seems to stem from artificial features of society, the conventions and assumptions about property and wages. Certainly in most societies where they are not semi-starved women live longer than men, and are not necessarily more infirm as they age. Women's weaker muscle structure and smaller frames made them less useful than men for some farming tasks, but there were many activities which did not need much muscle, and for which the smaller appetites of women made them economical workers. Women had less expectation of inheriting property than had men, were not considered as possible tenants except of very small holdings, were usually unqualified for work requiring the ability to write, and barred from being craft workers except under their fathers. In all occupations they could expect a lower wage than men. This wage discrepancy widened in the later eighteenth century.[3] All these features combined to mean that it was difficult for them on their own to build up resources for old age. The commonest full-time female occupation of spinning was particularly badly paid; it would earn between a penny halfpenny and twopence halfpenny sterling a day depending on the market, for work lasting about fourteen hours. The low nuptiality of the eighteenth century meant that many women were unlikely to marry, and were forced into this occupation as they grew frailer. It is noticeable in the lists of goods claimed by a session after a pauper's death that widows had homes more adequately furnished than had spinsters, but neither show much touch of luxury.

The pattern of untreatable disease in the eighteenth century meant a considerable risk of permanent physical impairment. Bovine tuberculosis, polio, smallpox and other infections could lead to physical handicaps for their survivors. So could simple undernourishment. There seems to have been little recognition of the possibility of accidents, and records show that falling under the wheels of a cart or down a mine shaft were not rare events. Drink as the main form of recreation increased the hazards to life or limb. Most parishes probably contained people expected to support themselves who today would be considered as eligible through infirmity for some sort of aid. Their earning power was bound to be low, and saving for further illness or old age impossible. And indeed until the creation of savings banks at the very end of the century there were no facilities for saving for the bulk of the population, other than concealing coins.

Parish records do not usually show the economic status of the recipients of relief but in one case, the parish of Dairsie (Fife), we have a list of the heads of householders in 1747, from a disputed Call, separated into categories of tenant, craftsman and cottar.[4] This can be brought into relation with successive lists of the parish poor in the 1740s and 1750s. Simply it shows that none of the tenants there was classified as poor. Yet occasionally elsewhere tenants can be found in parish poor lists: even millers, who were of all tenants the most privileged, secure in customers by the rules of thirlage, might lapse into poverty through incompetence, drink or disaster, but this was rare. The main block of the poor was made up of craftsmen, cottars and those in work with low pay such as day labourers, farm servants, parish schoolmasters; weavers, chapmen and small traders might also fall into destitution. There were also those crippled at birth or in childhood, the blind and the insane. Somewhat surprisingly those born deaf and consequently remaining dumb seem usually to have been able to find employment, though Pencaitland (East Lothian) in 1711 gave 20 pence as a single payment to a dumb man 'recommended by several ministers'. In many cases severe physical handicaps were not treated as grounds for full support; such sufferers would get a small pension, perhaps 6 pence a week, so long as they could get about at all, and be expected to supplement it either by work or begging.

Children supported or aided by the parish appear to have lived in conditions similar to those experienced by the children of the large class of cottars. The parish would have paid for their schooling and equipped them with clothes, shoes and, often, a New Testament when they went to work. Sometimes the parish would provide aftercare. In 1705 Pencaitland session bound John Redpath, an orphan, apprentice to a tailor. Nine months later it was reported that he was wholly destitute of clothes. Eventually the session bought cloth and paid for the making of two shirts for him, and in 1708 it followed this up with two more shirts, a waistcoat, a pair of hose and a pair of shoes, and told him that henceforth he had to provide for himself. He cannot have been much of an advertisement for the tailoring skills of his master. Auchtermuchty (Fife) in April 1780 was organising the making of three shirts for a boy approaching the end of a three-year apprenticeship to a tailor, which had cost the parish 30 pounds. The terms of the apprenticeship had stated that the tailor would make and mend the boy's clothes and, for extra pay, wash them, while the session was to provide the materials, but clearly these terms had not been observed. Eddleston (Peeblesshire) had two foundlings in the 1750s: the girl was clothed 'handsomely' when she went to service; the boy, whom the session had supported for at least eleven years, went to service in 1763 adequately equipped, but had to be further aided with two ells of harn in 1764 and in 1765 he was being looked after by the session while sick, with expenditure of 30 shillings on 'medicines for him in his distress' as well as being set up in clothes again. Edinburgh Charity Workhouse laid down in 1745 that it would take back into care children sent to service who became ill, and Dalkeith poor house records the same rule.[5]

. Tailoring was a frequent choice of trade for the apprenticing of orphans and foundlings. The workers in it were usually small men unsuited to heavy labour. Wages were low and consequently indentures were cheap. Ormiston (East Lothian) in the 1730s was handling a legacy from Adam Cockburn, its principal landowner, for the apprenticing of children and so was able to send them into more expensive trades, and had a boy apprenticed to a wright.

Parish concern for training included helping promising students to higher education in the universities. University education required the payment of fees for each course taken, and the students lived a spartan life in lodgings on a sack of oatmeal brought from home. The rigour extended for something over half the year. Even this standard of living was beyond the resources of most parishes to support for the four-year Arts course, and parishes would join together to give a bursary. Most of these students returned to rural life as meagrely paid parish schoolmasters, but there was always the chance of being taken on at a burgh school or even, with patronage, of adding a theological training and becoming a minister.

Parishes taking on the care of orphans usually took the household goods of the family and sold them to use the money for the children. Sometimes a neighbour might take on children if allowed the goods. Older people coming on relief usually held onto their possessions, but in most cases parishes came to claim the right to such goods after the pensioner's death. Edinburgh city regarded the possession of blankets or furniture as a high qualification for admission to its Charity Workhouse in its early days when the city was faced with spending £250 on bedding.[6] Small amounts of money often remained with pensioners, understandably since the parishes normally only partially supported their poor. That there were limits to what was acceptable for a pensioner to possess and still be regarded as poor is shown by an issue over two women pensioners in Cramond (Midlothian) in November 1741. One of these, Isabel Grieve, had enticed the grandson of the other, Isabel Ramsay, to search Ramsay's house and steal a guinea and three crowns from it. When the matter was discovered the session stopped both pensions, Grieve's 'to show . . . displeasure at her behaviour' and Ramsay's until 'she has great necessity'. Grieve was back on the pension list eleven months later. The other Isabel, who said she was keeping the money for her funeral, was not.

There was little difficulty in deciding whether children were or were not destitute, and the occupational structure accepted locally determined at what age they would be put to work. With older people and the various possible infirmities matters were not so obvious. Since it later became a dogma that the Scottish Poor Law did not support the able bodied, that disqualification has to be given more attention than it intrinsically merits. 'Able-bodied' is not a word in common use before the nineteenth century, though occasional instances can be found. Certainly an early statute had expressly excluded any who could earn from the scope of the Poor Law, but what that was intended to mean or accepted as meaning is not clear: unemployment (another anachronistic word) was occasionally seen as resulting not so much from laziness as from the state of the economy. In a legal process of 1749 'the poor' was taken to include 'those laid aside from Work'.[7] In any case the wording of statutes played a relatively small part in the interpretation of the Poor Law. In the crisis year of 1740 the Earl of Selkirk gave 20 bolls of oatmeal to the poor of Cramond expressly stipulating that it was not for the idle. Presumably he meant that it was for those often called 'the industrious poor', that is for people in work. There were many parishes which, in that year of high prices, gave aid to households normally independent, often by providing grain at a subsidized price. Selkirk's phrase might be intended to rule out the severely disabled pensioners but to allow in the large group of those whose support came from putting together miscellaneous resources brought in by the family economy, and one of these resources might be poor relief.

Since session registers do not mention disability unless it was severe, it is not possible to be certain that all adult recipients were not able-bodied. But the reasons given for aid often suggest recipients with some earning power but not enough for a crisis. For instance, Whitekirk (East Lothian) in the winter of 1740–1 gave aid twice to James Kindred, the first time 4 pounds to help him buy a horse, the second 3 pounds for his 'manifold infirmities in very straitened circumstances'. Yet there would have been little point in presenting him with a part of the price of a horse if he had not been capable of working with the animal.

Similar grants at varying levels are not rare. Ayr gave £1 in 1782 to a man who had borrowed another £2, the total sum which would enable him to replace the horse which had 'helped to subsist him and his family'. Saltoun gave the same amount for this in 1731, Spott (both East Lothian) 3 pounds in 1703; Currie (Midlothian) in 1718 gave 6 pounds Scots and Deskford (Moray) in 1774 put on a special collection for the same purpose.

Other cases exist where there seems reason to doubt that the recipient had any major infirmity. In Udny (Aberdeenshire) 3 pounds went to 'a poor man to build his house', and in Cambuslang (Lanarkshire) in 1753 a poor collier got 10 pounds for the same purpose. In that parish in 1750 a day labourer 'in a straitened Condition' received 8 pounds to pay a woman who cared for his child while he was at work, but since he claimed he could not on his own earn half her fee he may have been of reduced physical competence. The aid frequently allocated for nursing a child, a twin or a motherless babe, shows that the physical state of the father was not part of the qualification for relief.

House fires were another ground for help. In January 1706 Broughton (Peeblesshire) gave 2 pounds to a man in a neighbouring parish who had had his house burnt; Dyce (Aberdeenshire) in June 1778 sent 10 shillings to the widow and children of a man whose corn yard had twice been burnt. In March 1757 when a man's 'House, barn, Byre, Stable, Sheep Cote Corns and most of his Household plenishing were all with the Bed and Back Cloths of himself, Wife and Children . . . reduced to ashes, supposed by malicious burning', all the parish of Edenkillie (Moray) could offer was 3 shillings sterling and referral to the presbytery for a wider collection.[8]

The charity workhouses of Edinburgh, St Cuthbert's and Canongate, in the 1760s provide other examples of aid given to families apparently with an active earner. The workhouse was supported by promised contributions and the managing committee was prepared to prosecute those promisers who did not pay up, so the situation had a close resemblance to assessment.[9]

Though the founding statute of the Scottish Poor Law had broken away from its English model and not included orders for the provision of materials on which the poor could be set to work, this practice can all the same be found. Culross (then in Perthshire, now in Fife) in 1741 bought large quantities of lint to be worked on by 'such of the poor as are able to spin': by definition such could not be regarded as disabled. Similar actions can be found elsewhere. And of course the largesse given out at communion might well lead to the note in the 1752 accounts at Ellon of money given to 'sturdy beggars', 'two pounds two shillings Scots'.

Parishes did not usually apply formal qualifications for relief; what concerned them was whether someone was 'an object of charity'. This phrase was often shortened to the single word 'object'. It figures in this form in John Galt's *Last of the Lairds*, where the eponymous hero declares himself 'a verra object'.[10]

The standard of living of many cottar families was very low. Food supply might involve miscellaneous and irregular sources, so that it is not useful to think in terms of a level of income. Children would be taken from school once they could read and sent out to service as herds. Before that they might have contributed work in various stages of textile production, by carding wool, spinning, knitting or helping to warp a loom. Smallholdings would supply some part of food needs. Those in receipt of parish relief lived very little, if at all, worse, so there was a basic social unity in the poorer part of society. There was some form of visual discrimination in the seventeenth and early eighteenth centuries in many places, where parishes provided 'blue gowns' for their pensioners. These provided a social demarcation, at the same time as showing that begging by the wearers was approved. There were also badges which were used for the same purpose. These customs seem to have died out in the later eighteenth century.

The normal relaxations of austerity would be available for the poor as well as for the independent. The Poor Box of Chirnside (Berwickshire) in February 1776 paid 6 shillings and 6 pence sterling for a coffin for Alison Hunter, 4 shillings and 5 pence for a bottle of whisky for the wake, as well as 3 shillings and 11 pence for bread, cheese, pipes and tobacco and 6 pence for the invitations. Such entries are not common in session records, but their absence is probably because the goods of the deceased normally met these special expenses. In 1696 Currie (Midlothian) did not demand a refund when Alexander Waddell used the goods of his mother-in-law, a cow and some yarn, to pay for her 'funerals'. In Stobo (Peeblesshire), 1757, the daughter of a deceased pauper woman applied to the minister for the use of her effects for her 'funerals'; she had left 'a bed, chest and other small things'. A sheriff order allowed for a roup which brought in £1, the funeral cost 16/9 and a third of a penny.

Parishes offered help with medical or surgical expenses. There were few effective medical treatments available but this did not discourage doctors, who remained in happy ignorance of the statistical odds attached to particular treatments. In 1762 Kinglassie (Fife) was faced with a bill of £6.16, for treatment of a head injury to a weaver's son. The weaver said he could not pay without selling his loom and tools. Eventually it was argued down to £3.10/, of which the session paid £2. What treatment other than rest could have been applied is not clear. Auchtermuchty (Fife) paid 2 pounds, 19 shillings and 4 pence for medicines to a 'poor man' which did not prevent his death. We have no details of the treatment that cost Daviot (Aberdeenshire) £1.13 in 1764 for healing a man's leg, but, in general, surgery was more useful and occurs more frequently in accounts than medicine. Particularly beneficial were operations for stone in the bladder. Penninghame (Stewartry) paid 10 pounds for this in December 1724, and probably it was for a similar operation that Glencorse paid 3 shillings sterling in 1734, which was entered in the record as 'for a man troubled with gravel' to go to Edinburgh infirmary'. Amputations were the necessary way of preventing death after a wide range of injuries. Ecclesmachan (West Lothian) paid a guinea sterling in 1739 to have half a woman's foot cut off. Many northern parishes paid regular annual subscriptions to the Aberdeen infirmary so that they might send patients there. When Inveresk (East Lothian) was setting up a poor house in 1752, it noted with pleasure that there were two surgeons subscribing to poor relief in the parish, and proceeded to use their services without paying fees. When an independent surgeon offered his services in 1768 he was repulsed.

The response of a parish to a general economic crisis could be very generous, and this generosity was commonly sustained by gifts from the landowners. A conspicuous example is shown by Currie (Midlothian) in the harvest failure of 1740. In November of that year, when the failure of the crop was manifest, the minister and elders recorded that they 'did unanimously resolve that they to the utmost of their power will provide for all indigent persons'. The parish doubled the pensions of its regular poor and set up a committee to purchase grain from a store provided by the county's landowners who had spent £2,000 on importing grain. Similarly Sprouston (Roxburghshire) records large gifts of grain from its heritors, and later noted that the heritors of Berwickshire had imported a considerable quantity of beans for the poor. The Aberdeenshire Justices, less inclined to indiscriminate generosity, held a special meeting in April 1741 to ascertain the needs of the various parishes and to fix a moderate price for oatmeal. They had already forbidden the sending of grain out of the county, and were prepared to enforce the sale of a large reserve of grain held by the estate of Feteresso.[11] Several parishes in Lothian can be found subsidising their general population. In Borthwick (Midlothian) the heritors, elders and tenants agreed on a subsidy to all poor householders, and Edinburgh city was promised help by the Justices, Judges and nobility to enable it to sell grain at prime cost. In this case the city's generosity was sustained by a real fear of riot, and a similar threat may account for the actions of other towns. J. D. Post, in his examination of the response to the famine of 1740 across Europe, notes that Scotland experienced an exceptionally high rise in prices but had only a low increase in mortality.[12] He probably does not allow enough for the poor quality of mortality records, but it looks as if the relief system, partly through the functioning of the Poor Law and partly through the actions of landowners and the county authorities, worked effectively at least in the Lowlands.

Another bad year, though with less of a harvest shortfall, was 1756. By this time relief problems in the Lowlands had been accentuated by the annual flow of Highland harvest workers to the Lowlands. In a bad year such as this they would come south long before there was any likelihood of work. They concentrated on Edinburgh and Glasgow. In July 1757 Bathgate (West Lothian) purchased 20 bolls of oatmeal to sell to householders at 3 pence sterling a peck below the market price, though at 12 pence this was still high by normal years. The East Lothian Justices decided not to insist on their right to call on the peasantry for statute labour on the roads, unless it was paid for at 3 or 4 pence a day. In November they were threatening to prosecute parishes which failed to support their own poor. In another bad year,

1766, dearth led these Justices to produce a circular urging the parishes to buy up oatmeal and sell it at up to 4 pence sterling a peck below the market price so long as this stood above 11 pence, even if this meant adopting a stent.[13] An even more generous subsidy was offered by Dyce (Aberdeenshire) which spent nearly 60 pounds Scots selling grain at $7\frac{1}{2}$ pence to the needy and giving it away to those on the roll, but this offer was confined to only a few recipients.

Parishes often discouraged the settling in of impecunious outsiders. A typical example of this policy is the Act of Eddleston session (Peeblesshire) of May 1760, calling on the minister to

> Intimate Sabbath First from the Pulpit after Divine Worship that no Heretor nor Tenent nor Subtenent . . . shall receive into their Families or Cott Houses any person or persons Servants or cotters . . . who shall not apparently be Able to make a Reasonable and Lawfull provision for themselves and their Families Otherways to Dismiss them before three years that the Said Person or persons else may not become burdensome to the parish.

Eddleston was by then assessed, and this condition gave considerable authority to the landowners. In Sprouston (Roxburghshire) in 1752, also assessed, the heritors threatened legal proceedings against tenants letting houses to strangers without formal approval by the session: the session was recommended to make an annual investigation of house-lettings so as to spot 'Delinquents'.

Keeping people out was relatively easy in a well-organised parish, but removing people who had settled already was another matter. The word 'removal' covers different practical and legal events. It might mean the sending of people who had asked for relief to the parish where they had a legal settlement. Though instances of this can be found, it was not common. Instead the parish of settlement might be asked to send financial support. In April 1753 in Sprouston at the meeting of heritors and session, it was pointed out that Isobel Thorburne and her children had a legal settlement in Yetholm (Roxburghshire). Sprouston was willing to give her 5 shillings sterling a month while she applied to Yetholm, which she did. A year later it emerged that Yetholm would grant her only 3 shillings a month. With unusual generosity Sprouston decided to make this up to 5 shillings, and for the moment, because she was ill, to give her a further shilling.

The more difficult area of removal was the question of whether potential paupers who had not yet been in the parish long enough to claim settlement could be sent away. The legal authorities of the nineteenth century did not consider that this was within the powers of a mere parish. A.M. Dunlop, for instance, stated 'No one can be removed from a parish in which he has no settlement, merely on suspicion that he may become chargeable . . . so long as he does not beg', and Gilbert Hutcheson wrote that the 'English doctrine of removals is happily not known'. But the Reverend Robert Burns notes cases in which this had happened.[14] Certainly burghs considered that they could act against any kind of undesirable. Ayr session, for instance, in July 1771 'considering that the poor's funds of the place are overburdened' with 'the Spurious issue of Strumpets', set up a committee to discuss the matter with the town council and the house of correction, with the result that various women of 'bad character' and their children were referred to the council. In March 1782 it ordered a man to be prepared to support a woman who had come from Straiton and was 'like to be a burthen on the poors funds', presumably because he had given her house room. In 1751 Inveresk and Tranent, both burgh parishes in East Lothian, had a dispute over a widow and her children, and after the family had been shuttled between the two parishes, the respective kirk sessions had the sense to agree to set up two local gentlemen as arbitrators. The legal process of *Hutton* v. *Coldstream* in 1770 was over the issue of the removal of a potential pauper.[15] In 1759 the session of Straiton (Ayrshire) became worried that an elderly couple who had been known to beg, and had received occasional support from the session, might establish settlement, and applied to the Justices of the Peace for a warrant for the removal of the two before they had been in the parish three years. The warrant was not operated, though, because, at this point, three men of the parish made a bond, with witnesses, that should the couple become a burden they would provide support. The case is a reminder that at least in rural areas the Old Poor Law was never far removed from simple neighbourhood charity.

Study of the working of the Poor Law in this period and later is made difficult by vagueness and changes in terminology. Many people could be described as 'poor' without meaning that they would be entitled to relief. Indeed, the comment that 'the poor in Scotland are supported by the poor' made in the 1780s[16] brings out the dual meaning of the word 'poor'. The habit of middling and upper ranks to call the manual and labouring part of the population by this word becomes marked. A qualification often used is the addition of the word 'industrious'. The 'industrious poor' means either people in work or people normally in work but at present unemployed. An alternative phrase, the 'labouring poor' has the same ambiguity.

A category often dealt with sympathetically in relief schemes in continental Europe is the 'shamefaced poor'.[17] Apart from the numerous instances of genteel poverty after the Revolution of 1689, this category does not commonly appear in Scottish relief. For the most part Scottish parishes could attend only to basic needs. But there are, occasionally, cases of people aided who might be so described. A financial explanation laid out by New Aberdeen in 1768 has two entries that appear to refer to the shamefaced poor: £12 'to the Ministers for private Charity to indigent Persons of best rank at Each Sacrament' and £58 to 'indigent Persons of the Better Sort who are not on the Poor's Table at Each Sacrament'. The combined sums made up more than a quarter of the city's out relief expenditure. In 1700 Pencaitland (East Lothian) stressed that the sacrament collection should be distributed partly to householders 'who think shame to seek any charity'. In the abortive county scheme for Roxburghshire in 1712 there is mention of 'those persones who are described as honest parents and have led Creditable and Christian lyves But have fallen poor through misfortune and not by their owne ill manadgement'. Heritors were urged to be 'as cautious in exposing them as possible', and to be generous to such people and make distribution to them in secrecy. But this intent to prevent embarrassment assumed a level of funding from assessment which did not occur.

Limitations of funding restricted experimentation with a particular form of provision for the poor common in many countries, 'indoor relief', that is support available in a poorhouse or workhouse. There were various old foundations which had survived the Reformation; bede houses, hospitals and leper houses. Most of such accommodation, though not all, was for men. Many such institutions in northern Scotland are noted in Macpherson's book.[18] It had been the intention of the original foundation that bedesmen should reward the founder with prayers, but the theology of Calvinism forbade the use of prayers for the dead. The absence of duties and the level of resources made available by endowments to the bedesmen made them a privileged group among the poor. Given the usual assumption that a peck of oatmeal a week, approximately 8½ pounds, with some further help over fuel, would keep an adult alive, we can see that bedesmen did relatively well. Oatmeal varied in price within the range of normal harvests from 8 pence sterling a peck to 11 pence. That many pensioners would receive 6 pence a week or

2 shillings a month, or, for a family, up to 5 shillings a month, brings out the advantage experienced by bedesmen. In Cullen (Banffshire) a bede house for both sexes sustained the men on 2 pecks a week, the women on 1½ pecks, with each sex receiving a mart (a beast slaughtered in the autumn) and milk. At Tarves hospital (Aberdeenshire) the allowance for four men was for each 1 peck of meal and ½ peck of malt every week.

Another institution, which the central government had pressed for in the seventeenth century, was the correction house. Certainly that of Edinburgh, set up in 1632, seems to have been a response to pressure by the king, and that Aberdeen had one as early as 1636 also suggests response to crown demands.[19] A house of correction would be under the control of the town council. It would be used for vagrants, petty criminals and prostitutes: these were sent to it for a specific length of time and expected to be put to work. The sanction was a possible extension of the time of incarceration. But enforcement of the system required a stock of material, instruction and supervision, as well as arrangements for marketing the product. It was not a cheap solution for vagrancy, and in hard times may even have encouraged it.

Occasional scraps of evidence show the existence of these institutions in other towns. Glasgow had one by 1631. The papers of the Synod of Perth and Stirling refer to a Perth correction house in 1752. In 1725 the heritors of Tranent ordered vagrants to be sent to one in Haddington, but it may never have existed. Ayr was receiving beggars sent by rural parishes for incarceration in the 1720s, so presumably it had some secure housing. By contrast, the Stewartry Justices complained in 1728 of a lack of this; in 1730 they ordered that beggars be put to work in correction houses or be imprisoned, but made no mention as to where this could be done, and in 1732 they were ordering vagrants to the tolbooths of New Galloway and Dumfries which suggests that no correction house was as yet available. Later in the century these Justices adopted a policy of imprisoning vagrants and releasing them only on promise to leave the shire. It was still doing this in 1791 to a group of vagrants held in Kirkcudbright tolbooth. In general it looks as if only the larger burghs set up such houses and that there was little connection between such actions and the repeated statute demands in the seventeenth century. More probably it was local concerns and demands which led to them. It is difficult to ascertain at any period how many shires had them; still less is it possible to judge how adequate they were for the discouragement of vagrancy.

'Indoor relief' is inevitably more expensive than outdoor relief, even allowing for the receipt of money for the goods made by forced labour. Scotland could not follow the practice of some Catholic countries of reducing the cost by handing over institutions to be run by religious orders.[20] The poor houses and workhouses set up by parishes or by the central organisation of relief in Edinburgh and Glasgow ranged from the convenient housing of two widows together, probably not in a specially built house, to the major institution of the Edinburgh Charity Workhouse designed to hold 600–700 poor.[21]

A good example of a small poor house is that of Haddington (East Lothian) running in the 1750s on $2\frac{1}{2}$ pence of every pound of the parish's valued rent. It contained various orphans and some adults, and was run by an efficient woman who bought large quantities of cloth and used the juvenile labour to make clothes both for the inmates and to sell. A destitute schoolmaster was admitted in 1756 with the expectation that he would teach the children to read. Poorhouses such as this, holding people not able to care for themselves and not used for the accommodation of more able paupers, could be a reasonably economical way of meeting special needs.

Ayr poorhouse, opened in 1756, is well described by Hamilton.[22] It was sustained by varied sources: the incorporations, the burgh council, a rate on real property and the session's funds. We have the dietary, which, for a period when scurvy was accepted as inevitable in the old, was surprisingly well balanced and generous. Ale and milk were there for drinking on alternate days; potatoes, not yet established as the cheap food of the poor, occurred twice a week, as did meat and fish. The fish would be herring or salmon: in a moment of economy the governing council declared that since it was not possible to offer helpings of salmon of less than half a pound, this should be on the menu only when it did not cost more than 3 farthings a pound. Under the more stringent conditions of the 1780s meat and fish were reduced each to once a week.

Another comfortable and well-supplied poorhouse is to be found in Inveresk (East Lothian). This was set up in 1752, sustained by subscriptions and, from very early on, a complicated assessment over both the town and the landward part of the parish. It was expected that the support of forty inmates would cost £150 a year, an estimate which was realistic before the inflation at the end of the century. Much use was made of gifts in kind and in services, both in the construction of the house and in its management. Timber was offered for the building, and 2,000 bricks; two locally-based surgeons gave their skills to the inmates. Various types of work were laid on: textile production, brewing (for which instruction had to be given), tailoring, the planting of seed potatoes in the garden. But the original intention that the house should contain all the poor of the parish had to be abandoned. The homes of many of the poor were decrepit, insanitary and not weatherproof, but there were still some poor labelled 'too delicate' for the institution.

In any case there were also those only temporarily or partly in need. By 1763 it was noted that the parish was spending £40 a year on out relief; various of the better-off claimed that it was impossible to support both those in the house and those outside. The original aim of the poorhouse was thus destroyed.

The records of the poorhouse in Dalkeith (Midlothian), proposed in 1747 and opened in 1750, bring out clearly the problems of sanitation, discipline and work. In Inveresk there had been a complaint of 'nastiness' in the house; like other poorhouses it held a weekly wash of all linen on Mondays, and also had most of the house washed. In Dalkeith all infectious persons were to be washed on admission, and those described as 'nasty' were to be housed in a separate room. There was great difficulty in getting the older boys to work: they would find a way out of the house and jaunt about the town. As all were 'proper objects of charity' they had to be readmitted. In July 1751 the manager ordered 'the Boy Gregor', who had absented himself for three days, to be kept for the same length of time on bread and milk in the 'Prison Closet'. Troublesome inmates who spread malicious gossip or disorder might be thrown out, but would usually have to be readmitted. Once they had been named as 'an object of charity' it was not possible to discipline such people by withholding relief. While out of the house delinquents might sell their clothes, which properly belonged to the house, and then they would have to be re-equipped. Some paupers of business acumen were discovered to be selling the generous bread ration of the house to outsiders and stealing from the work stock.

The charity workhouses of the bigger cities faced the same problems in an enhanced form. Both Edinburgh and Glasgow by mid-eighteenth century had ceased to leave the support of the poor to the various urban parishes and had centralised it in a General Session. Paisley also came to this practice. This was a sensible recognition that people moved frequently from one urban parish to another.

New Aberdeen had a joint session for its three parishes in the eighteenth century, and in January 1768, after a year's debate, this body in conjunction with the managers of the workhouse, set up by the town council, put together an elaborate survey of its income, over £370 a year, including £5 from the dissenting churches, and set out how it was to be distributed: £150 was to go to the workhouse, which was to be run jointly with the town council in proportion to the contributions. By the nineteenth century it was clear that the town had become the main provider.[23]

Canongate was still separate from Edinburgh. Its charity workhouse opened in 1761 before the 'house of office' had been slated; since it was initially designed for only forty-eight inmates the sanitary problems were minor. Edinburgh's workhouse managers did not at first appreciate what a house planned for over 600 inmates could involve. For its first decade numbers were only some 500, but after a few months of use, in June 1743, its house of office was described as 'extremely Nauseous' as well as being placed much too near the main building for health. All large dormitories were bound to produce problems of cross infection. Many workhouses insisted on medical inspection of all incomers, but classification could be haphazard. Canongate in 1761 allowed in a woman said to be cured of the itch, but in the next year refused a woman with face cancer. Edinburgh St Cuthbert's, with a workhouse set up in 1760, allowed inmates to enter in their own clothes, but washed. It received many who had been discharged from the Infirmary as incurable.[24] It also had a large ward labelled with indifference to the feelings of the occupants as 'depraved'.

The list of qualifications for admission to the Edinburgh Charity Workhouse would probably have been applicable to other city workhouses.

The begging poor entitled to the Town's Charity.
Those who could bring blankets or furniture.
Orphans.
Burghers and their families.
Householders, residenters, servants.

The plans of 1752 for a poorhouse in Perth show the expansive generosity then common. There were to be 'Commodious apartments for all the really indigent, where they may be Lodg'd, Cloath'd and Fed in a Christian and Comfortable maner'. Work was to be available but for the aged and weak only 'the most Easie sort of Industrie'. The young would be 'taught to read and write (at least their own name)' while being given an education 'Calculated for the most Laborious Employments of Life'.[25]

Poorhouses and workhouses had to have paid staff, and it was not easy in the eighteenth century to find suitable people with high standards of performance. Edinburgh workhouse, when starting up, had the sense to employ as master the man who had been running the Glasgow workhouse. Governing bodies could be unwieldy institutions. That for Edinburgh contained ninety-six men, representing the various groupings of authority, and had a quorum of twenty-nine. St Cuthbert's had eighty-three directors, and even the smaller institution in Inveresk had forty-six. Edinburgh attempted to work through smaller inspection committees appointed for a short period of time, but even this arrangement did not make the development of expertise possible. There were potential economies in staffing. Glasgow, for instance, used the workhouse surgeon as dispenser at the Knox Hospital and Correction House, and as visitor to the sick poor.[26] Edinburgh suffered under a chaplain with subversive views: his sermons at the services, which all inmates had to attend, stressed too much, the committee thought, the common weaknesses of human nature of all classes. He had also allowed one Archibald Lees to purchase drugs and hand them over to various persons without the surgeon's authority with, it was held, fatal effects. Lees may have been a pauper working for the surgeon, for much of the in-house work was done by the inmates.[27]

The intractable problem was organising the work by the inmates. An enormous range of textile work was listed for Glasgow workhouse at its institution – weaving, warping, winding, heckling and lint buffing were merely part of the list. It was obviously particularly desirable that children should acquire some skills, including being able to read.[28]

It was not easy to devise an incentive so that children would put in long hours at boring tasks, which for those outside the house was to be found in the need to earn food. External businesses were, of course, expected to purchase the products of a workhouse, and in some cases the inmates were offered a proportion of the selling price, which encouraged attention to quality. In 1743 Edinburgh workhouse management allowed the workers 2 pence in every shilling of sales, but was not pleased when it found that its clerk was also giving drams to the spinners: strong drink was prohibited in the house. Allowance for work sold, used by several workhouses, disguised the uneconomic nature of much of the work done. It was also discriminatory, for no such reward was made to the women inmates who did the washing of the house, a heavy weekly load, cared for the sick and aided those in childbirth. This was not an issue likely to disturb the managers.

Work did little to reduce costs. The Glasgow poorhouse for the aged and infirm cost £4.7/per head per year: Dalkeith in 1752 estimated that the cost in Edinburgh was £3.3/and that its own was £4.17.7½ d the figure for Edinburgh probably held down by sending infants into the country. The different social mix of inmates could make for drastic differences in costs, but in general indoor relief was more expensive than outdoor, without counting the cost of providing the building.

Cost was one of the features that led to a cooling off of enthusiasm for institutional care. The period when poorhouses and workhouses seemed a good idea was from 1730 till 1770: after that disillusion reigned, though Dundee was considering setting up a poorhouse in the early months of 1773.[29] The cities could not close up their institutions because of the scale of the flood of destitution which would have been released, but smaller towns could. The house at Inveresk closed in 1782, and the reasons given would apply to many others. It had originally been expected that all those totally dependent on relief would be placed in it, but some were regarded as too delicate. Right at the start of its use there was a 'tender child' considered unsuitable. The house was funded by a mixture of assessment and promised voluntary contributions, but the latter component decreased. Once beggars were cleared off the streets there was less alms-giving, a fact which does much to explain the permanent financial crisis in which the Edinburgh Charity Workhouse existed. The minister of Inveresk, Alexander Carlyle, gave a long note to his parish report in the *Statistical Account* which listed, among other disadvantages, the constant corrupt attempts by the local business community to get the privileges of supplying its needs, a theme which could have been echoed by Canongate where one of the directors at the building of the house, asked to advise on timber purchases, said 'the one hand did not wash the other for nothing'.[30] The managers decided to do without his advice, but he remained on the governing board.

The Reverend John Macfarlan in his book on the Poor Law gives a general condemnation of poorhouses. They offered the same level of comfort to deserving and undeserving, and the level of expense was higher than that of 'the family of an industrious tradesman'. There were too many employees, whose wages sent up costs. He held that while the totally infirm should be cared for in hospitals or almshouses, the rest of the poor could be minimally supplied with bread, coal and clothes and left to look after themselves. In expressing a desire for a more austere level of care he was stating what was becoming a common view in the 1780s.[31] The practice of some English towns at this time of using the workhouse as a means of persuading people to manage without relief, the 'workhouse test', does not appear to have been generally adopted in Scotland. This was probably because so much relief in Scotland was of allowances below the subsistence level, which would make offering relief only within the house an expensive alternative. But there were occasional instances of it. In November 1751, Dalkeith, faced with the need to support a family, a woman, her daughter and two grandchildren, which the session felt was 'too great a Burden', decided to insist on indoor relief, so that the family might rethink the application.

It does not seem to have been normal policy to insist on the admittance of a family as a whole. In 1761, for instance, Canongate Charity Workhouse took on two children whose mother stated that she could not support them, and in the next year it received one boy from the six children of James Campbell. In 1749 we hear of a man who had placed his wife in the Edinburgh Charity Workhouse, but we hear of him only because he was being investigated by the session of South Leith for marrying another bigamously.[32] The concept of a family as dependants on an active male worker does not appear to have had currency, understandably, for family resources were often the result of input from every member.

Though a parish might demand of the poor in its flock that they should attend church if they expected supply, and in the case of poorhouse inmates, insist on this, it was by no means a general rule that relief and church attendance were linked, and occasional indicators show that relief was given to people who did not belong to the established Church. At intervals in the early part of the eighteenth century the General Assembly demanded information about the numbers, location and names of Roman Catholics, and at similar times such persons can be found in lists of the poor. Roman Catholicism was highly localised in the eighteenth century, but other forms of dissent, rents in the unity of presbyterianism, became more generally spread, and in the later decades presbyterian dissent produced considerable financial difficulties for the operation of relief. The dissenting churches needed the collection money to sustain their ministries and had little or none to spare for their poor. The result was that in parishes with large dissenting congregations a heavy burden was placed on the established Church. This was denounced at various times[33] but not mended, and the increase in the scale of dissent at the end of the century made it unlikely that the Church could continue to provide the main support of the poor.

Any account of the working practices of parishes is bound to be thin on material from the western Highlands and Islands. The Church of Scotland did not accept the idea that a large part of the country was not under its control in matters it claimed as religious, but certainly before 1746 there were areas where its control was merely nominal. Some clan chiefs, and consequently their clans, were of another confession, and for others the position might be uncertain.[34] In other areas disputes over patronage could prevent there being a resident minister, and if there was not a minister there would not be an effective kirk session. The Church made considerable efforts to find Gaelic speakers who could be trained as potential ministers, but did not do the same for the eldership, and there were few resident elders whose English was adequate for participation in the prebyterian church system. The very large size of some Highland parishes, which demonstrated the low level of resources, meant that ministers were likely to know little about their parishioners in the more remote settlements. We have coherent KSRs from only a few parts of the area. Argyll under its dukes is relatively well represented, and so are some parts of the eastern Highlands.

Even in areas well documented, it does not appear that poor relief was well supplied after 1746, and there was not much money about. Of course the Church may not have been the only source of welfare. Clan chiefs might offer hospitality to their clansmen or aid to their families, but not on any regular basis. Jacobite chiefs spent many years in exile after the rising of 1745, and so lost touch with their people. In the early nineteenth century many chiefs had got into financial difficulties and had to sell up. Highland land revenues did not go far in supporting standards of living appropriate to gentry. If landowners sold parts of their estates, there was no reason for the purchasers to feel obliged to support the tenantry by benevolence. There was no organised pressure for assessment, and the level of need in widespread estates would not be known. Annual doles to particularly severe instances of destitution might be a few shillings a year. Parishes saw no reason to pay for those of their people who had fallen into poverty while working in the Lowlands. Large numbers of Highlanders in the later eighteenth century took to temporary migration, going south to find work and returning only when their own crops were ready. By so doing they relieved their own communities of the burden of their appetites and created a pattern of mobility and acquired some fluency in English which might lead to more permanent migration. Economic developments in the south of Scotland could use Highland labour, but did not extend its welfare to the labourers if this could be avoided. For the most part the travelling Highlanders stayed out of the factories but took other types of work. Highland population continued to rise until the 1840s, but the Highland economy could not support the people it bred.

NOTES

1. Rosalind Mitchison, 'Webster revisited: a re-examination of the 1755 "census" of Scotland', in T. M. Devine (ed.), *Improvement and Enlightenment* (Edinburgh, 1989), pp. 62–77.
2. Aberdeen St Nicholas KSR August 1758. I owe this reference to Dr Leah Leneman. ECA Canongate Charity Workhouse Minutes, 1 June 1762.
3. Valerie Morgan, 'Agricultural wage rates in late eighteenth century Scotland', *Economic History Review*, 2nd series, xxiv, 1971, pp. 181–201.
4. SRO CH/1/2/87 f. 169.
5. ECA Edinburgh Charity Workhouse Minutes, June 1745.
6. *Ibid*. April 1743, Categories for admission.
7. *APS* VII 311b (1661): 'no person be receaved who are anie way able to gain their oune liveing'.
8. I owe this last example to Charles Morison.
9. ECA Canongate Charity Workhouse Minutes and St Cuthbert's Charity Workhouse Minutes.
10. John Galt, *The Last of the Lairds* (Edinburgh, 1829), ch. xxxi.
11. SRO JP 16/2/1. For the Midlothian subscription see John M. Gray (ed.), *Memoirs of Sir John Clerk of Penicuik* (SHS Edinburgh, 1992), p. 159.
12. John D. Post, *Food Shortage, Climatic Variability and Epidemic Disease in Pre-Industrial Europe* (Ithaca, NY, 1985), ch. 6. See also *Caledonian Mercury* 4 and 24 November 1740.
13. SRO JP/4/2/1, May 1757 and January 1766.
14. A. M. Dunlop, *Treatise on the Law of Scotland relating to the Poor* (Edinburgh, 1854); G. Hutcheson, *Treatise on the Office of Justice of the*

Peace, Constable and Commissioner of Supply etc. (Edinburgh, 1806); Reverend Robert Burns, *Historical Dissertations on the Law and Practice of Great Britain and particularly of Scotland in regard to the Poor* (Edinburgh, 1819).

15. Morison, *Dictionary of Decisions*, p. 10,574.

16. This phrase is used by James Anderson of Monkshill, farmer, editor and economist, in a letter to Jeremy Bentham, 18 July 1781, describing what he claimed to be the main features of the Scottish Poor Law. The description minimises the obligations placed on landowners, invents some features, and seems to have been solicited by a desire of Bentham's to see the English Poor Law reduced in scope. Anderson's words are 'The poor are supported by the Poor, I mean by Tradesmen, Mechanics, Labourers, Servants etc.' I. R. Christie, (ed.) *Correspondence of Jeremy Bentham*, vol. iii (London, 1971), p. 36.

17. For the shamefaced poor see Stuart Woolf, *The Poor in Western Europe in the Eighteenth and Nineteenth Centuries* (London, 1986); Brian Pullan, 'Catholics and the Poor in Early Modern Europe', *Transactions of the Royal Historical Society*, 5th series, 26 (1976), pp. 25–34. I owe the Aberdeen reference to Dr Leah Leneman.

18. J. Macpherson, *The Kirk's Care*, pp. 163–75.

19. Marguerite Wood (ed.), *Extracts from the Records of the Burgh of Edinburgh*, 1626–41 (Edinburgh, 1936), p. 107.

20. The Spanish *inclusa* and the French *hôpital général* are examples of this.

21. *OSA* vol. VII p. 611, Wiston and Robertson (Lanarkshire). *Extracts from the Records of the Burgh of Glasgow* (Glasgow, 1881), vol. 2, 1630–62, pp. 28, 33–4, 42–3.

22. T. Hamilton, *Poor Relief in South Ayrshire* (Edinburgh, 1945), ch. 5.

23. New Aberdeen KSR for January 1768. I owe this reference to Dr Leah Leneman.

24. The minutes of Canongate and St Cuthbert's Charity Workhouses are in ECA.

25. SRO CH2/449/10, Perth and Stirling Synod papers, 1752.

26. Robert Renwick (ed.), *Extracts from the Records of the Burgh of Glasgow*, vol. 6 (Glasgow, 1940), p. 488, October 1756.

27. ECA Edinburgh Charity Workhouse Minutes, vol. 2, 1750 and August 1752.

28. There is a full description of the work intended for Glasgow's workhouse by its charitable founder in *Glasgow Burgh Records*, vol. vi, p. 267, 1,747.

29. I owe this reference to Dr Leah Leneman.

30. *OSA* II pp. 318–21; ECA Canongate Charity Workhouse, vol. 1.

31. John Macfarlan, *Enquiries Concerning the Poor* (Edinburgh, 1782), p. 410.

32. ECA Canongate Charity Workhouse Minutes, vol. I.

33. James Headrick, *General View of the Agriculture . . . of Angus* (Edinburgh, 1813), p. 549.

34. Rosalind Mitchison, 'Religion and Glencoe', *SHR*, vol. LIV (1975), pp. 114–16.

CHAPTER 6

CHANGING DOGMAS

By the 1770s the Poor Law seems to have secured an important role in keeping people alive within the community in most of Scotland, and was doing so at relatively low cost. In parishes which were already working what had become accepted as the law at the beginning of the eighteenth century the performance does not appear to have changed. But by now many more parishes were taking the business of relief seriously and, with economic development and a higher level of monetisation, it had become easier for a parish to have funds to distribute. Highland parishes were not in a position to support those in need, but in many cases the kirk sessions made small doles to the most pressing cases, showing a recognition of the Kirk's obligation to the poor. The rapid economic growth of the third quarter of the century put money into a lot of pockets, but the expansion of trade and manufactures put a larger section of the population at the mercy of unemployment through market fluctuations.[1] Some inadequate harvests produced high grain prices, while the levels at which the Corn Laws arranged subsidies for export or import became anachronistic through the slow but steady upward movement of prices after 1750, and this put some households in want. There was a very poor harvest in 1756, and in the 1770s several less severe events led to meal riots in the towns. The disastrous failure of crops in 1782 was coped with effectively in the Highlands as well as in the Lowlands by a mixture of effort and aid from both landowners and the central government, but it pushed some permanently into debt. The 1790s, even before the outbreak of the long wars, produced pressures which show that Britain was ceasing to be self-sufficient in grain. The Poor Law was going to have many opportunities to show that it could be effective.

By the 1770s the law can be seen as established. There had been important additions to case law. *Paton* v. *Adamson* (1772) had removed the sheriff from ordering relief in first instance, though he retained an appeal jurisdiction. *Hutton* v. *Coldstream* (1770) had defined the qualification for settlement on a basis different from the statutes and had established that paupers could bring cases in the courts free of costs.[2] There had been a long run of cases referring to the rights of the poor, and the widespread acceptance by parishes of the duty of aiding the poor at some level of subsistence made this more than simply theoretical.

The 1770s saw a fresh outbreak of county schemes for relief of the poor and control of vagrants and there appear to have been attempts to reduce vagrancy by the Justices of the Peace in Aberdeenshire and East Lothian in 1775–6. The schemes may owe something to the high prices of 1772–3. Schemes can be traced in Argyll, Ayrshire, Dumfriesshire, East Lothian, Fife, Midlothian, Perthshire, Roxburghshire, the Stewartry of Kirkcudbright and Stirlingshire,[3] and systematic examination of parish records would probably show schemes in other shires south of the Tay, since for Argyll, Berwickshire, Fife and Stirlingshire it is only at the parish level that I have found evidence of schemes. It is however clear from the Justice of the Peace records for the county of Kinross that that county did not have a scheme. The most elaborate, perhaps pretentious, schemes are those for East Lothian and Perthshire.

In the East Lothian 'Police Scheme' the Justices emphasised that the existing laws requiring heritors and farmers to arrest vagrants, imprison them for eight days and then dispatch them to their own parish, or at least to their county, ought to be enforced. The scheme supported this by a 'voluntary' association of heritors and tenants, with contributions of up to 5/ each to pay the cost of the arrests and to reimburse anyone who had suffered theft from the vagrants. Parishes were to be grouped together and landowners and tenants meet together with the rest of their group. All parishes were to appoint constables, and for these 150 copies of instructions were printed. Constables were to receive 1 shilling (sterling was by now the currency in thought and use) for each arrest and 6 pence a mile for taking those arrested to gaol.

On various dates the Justices noted the failure of parishes to send representatives to meetings, their slowness in raising money and appointing constables, and in January 1778 the Justices' minutes report 'the failure of the late Police scheme'.

The Perthshire scheme, which runs to many pages of documentation, involved more detail. Great effort was made to gather in funds. In particular non-resident heritors were to be asked to contribute. Every parish was to have at least one constable, to make out lists of the poor and decide the amount of money needed for their support, and appoint an officer to collect funds. Clearly some sort of assessment was envisaged for many parishes. It was pointed out that it would be inappropriate to use Rogue Money for the arrest of vagrants. Finally a new Act was produced in October 1775 which covered, among other matters, the licensing of public houses and, either in the parishes or in some nearby manufactory, the creation of work for those able to work.

The crop of schemes shows attempts at large-scale organisation and also of collaboration with the higher courts of the Church. The Justices of the Stewartry were working with the presbytery of Ayr, and those of Perthshire included in their documentation a memorial from the Synod of Perth and Stirling which assured the Justices of the full co-operation of the clergy in any plan for the support of the 'really Necessitous but neglected Poor' who suffered as much as anyone from the burden of vagrancy.

It is not surprising that the schemes did not produce an effective reduction in vagrancy, a guaranteed support for the poor and a general uniformity of qualifications and aid. Eighteenth-century Britain was not accustomed to the exercise of executive authority in internal affairs. In Scotland there had been no such authority since the Privy Council had been abolished in 1708 and the Justices had not developed the administrative powers exercised by their English counterparts. Indeed county authorities had been warned off intervention in Poor Law matters by the decision of *Paton* v. *Adamson* that in the first instance the duty of support lay with the parish. Schemes of local government which required activity, organisation and expense were unlikely to be put into action generally unless imposed by a central authority, and at least in Scotland, not necessarily even then.

That the schemes appear to have pushed some parishes into raising funds by assessment in the Border areas is of interest because already this was an area where assessment was common. In the famine of the 1690s few Border parishes had achieved assessment: of twenty-five parishes which have left session registers adequate for detail in Dumfriesshire, Berwickshire, Selkirkshire, Roxburghshire and Peeblesshire, only four can be seen to have used assessment. Yet by the

1790s almost every parish at least in Berwickshire, Roxburghshire and Selkirkshire was assessed. Later critics of the whole system of relief attributed this to an unfortunate infection from the English system of poor rates, but failed to note that, if this was the case, it had taken a long time from the union of the Crowns for the infection to manifest itself. Such an explanation is inherently improbable: the matter is discussed in Chapter 4. In the early nineteenth century, however, there was a borrowing from England. The Royal Commission of 1844 has examples of doctors working on both sides of the Border who commented freely on the low level of assistance given in Scottish parishes compared with English. Such men probably had already made their views known locally.[4]

For the spread of assessment in the Lothians, an explanation may lie in the relatively high level of urbanisation of the Forth basin evident even in the seventeenth century.[5] It was a region deeply involved in trade, not only the trade of Leith but also of numerous smaller ports. There was also a commitment to mining and to miscellaneous industries. These features made it more susceptible to wider economic fluctuations than was the rest of Scotland, and the frequency of war in the eighteenth century affected shipping in the narrow seas, often suddenly. This explanation is, however, thrown in doubt by the fact that none of the parishes on the Fife coast, even those complaining in the *OSA* of a high level of poor, adopted assessment in the eighteenth century.

The absence of assessment in some areas may have been the result of a relatively generous level of legacies. The *OSA* makes it clear that in Angus by the 1790s almost every parish had a comfortable amount of capital from these, in striking contrast to the neighbouring county of Mearns. Perhaps the lairdly families of Angus had prospered in the seventeenth century from the fertile acres of the shire and put their profits to a use not easily achieved elsewhere.

That county organisation was able in the eighteenth century to cope in a crisis of food shortage without resort to assessment was shown in the 1740 harvest failure. For the even more serious shortfall of 1782, we have the record of the decisions made by the landowners of Aberdeenshire, who estimated carefully the shortfall and set out a plan for how it was to be met.[6] The plan relied on the labouring and farming population tightening their belts, on the consumption of reserves, on the early anticipation of the next harvest and on the banning of brewing and distilling, but these economies still left the need for a large-scale purchase and importation of grain at the expence of the landowners. The fund for this was raised by 'Voluntary Assessment', that is by the voluntary payment of a sum calculated on the valued rent of estates. In the event, the peace treaty which ended the War of American Independence left the government with surplus cereal stores, and Henry Dundas, a member of the government, was able to secure their use as emergency supplies to northern parishes in the spring of 1783. Both these approaches lay outwith the Poor Law, and showed that the governing class could respond effectively in an emergency.

Yet it is at this time, the early 1780s, that opposition to the whole concept of poor relief becomes vocal. An interesting example of this is in a letter sent to Jeremy Bentham by James Anderson of Monkshill in Aberdeenshire. Anderson was the instigator of the Aberdeenshire meeting about the crop failure, a self-made man, described by Bentham as 'quite one of us', a phrase acknowledging a clique, who had married into the gentry and kept himself busy by a combination of writing and farming. It was in these self-supporting middle ranks that particularly strong resistance to the support of the poor was to be found in the nineteenth century. Anderson described the Scottish Poor Law to Bentham as an institution almost entirely sustained by 'gratuitous' funds, a system 'much preferable to the mode adopted in England' as more economical and judicious. Few sessions, he stated 'gave more, and many less, than the price of a peck of oatmeal . . . in a week'. The burden of real poverty was low; only ten persons in a thousand were 'really poor'. His description of the Scottish Poor Law makes no mention of assessment: it recognised that landowners, though not belonging to the established Church, for the most part made no contribution to relief: with approval he stated that the poor were supported by the poor.[7]

Anderson's farm was in a poor part of Aberdeenshire, the Garioch, but he had passed his early life in the south-east and so might have been expected to recognise that assessment, though not practised in Aberdeenshire, was widespread elsewhere. He was later to write a pamphlet on the Scottish Poor Law. Though this does not survive, we have almost certainly his later description in a 'letter' to a periodical he edited and largely wrote, signed by one of his frequently used pseudonyms.[8] In this he made some unusual statements about the

Poor Law and its history. He remarks firmly 'the nation at large were at all times perfectly satisfied that the *real* poor were abundantly cared for', a statement difficult to reconcile with seventeenth-century comment. Later he states the belief as general that 'there is no country on the globe where the poor are more suitably provided for, or enjoy a greater proportion of happiness'. One important statement which might support this is his recognition that there was a considerable gap between practice and the law as laid down by statute. But on statute law he had some highly individual claims. 'No money can be *legally* issued from the poor's funds . . . unless legal proof can be brought that public intimation has been given from the pulpit . . . a full fortnight before the time of distribution'. His anti-assessment stand produced some new arguments: it would be inquisitorial to make the burden proportional to means. In any case the statute of 1661 allowed assessment only for dealing with sturdy beggars: the local indigent poor were to be supported only by alms. In many cases, therefore, rates had no legal justification. The whole paper is an ingenious attempt to whittle away the law, but the absence of quotation from it in other works or newspapers suggests that it had little influence.

Anderson's cannot be taken as an accepted view of the Poor Law and in particular it differs markedly from the description given somewhat confusedly by a parish minister at the same date, the Reverend John Macfarlan, minister of the Canongate, in his *Inquiries Concerning the Poor* (Edinburgh, 1782). Macfarlan, who might as a landowner have wished to play down the element of assessment, stresses the similarities between the English and the Scottish systems, with the difference that the English system had become expensive, and as a result the poor rates were 'enormous'. He disapproved of poor-houses and workhouses: these were expensive, costing more for a family's support than the income of an average labourer, and producing very little profitable work. It was by scrupulous inquiry into all claims for relief, and knowledge of potential claimants that costs could be kept down. Support for the 'undeserving' poor should be minimal, but the 'deserving poor', by which he meant the frail and sick, should get twice as much. Even so the condition of those not in work should be less comfortable than that of the working population. If this procedure (which sounds intrusive to the modern ear) were followed, rates could be reduced and in many places abolished. But Macfarlan recognised that, in his opinion, many claims were made by 'worthless people' asserting that unemployment had caused them to beg; but in some cases this complaint had real cause. Unemployment was an obvious risk in a commercial and industrial society, but rural society could also suffer from lack of work, for instance in a hard frost, and savings could soon be exhausted. Support for at least a short period might be needed, though Macfarlan held that want of employment was a less frequent cause of poverty than sloth, dissipation and vice. Still, Macfarlan held that begging was acceptable in small communities where everyone was known. He accepted that rates might be necessary where heritors were absent.

In the 1770s letters objecting to rate-based relief or to repressive actions over begging appear in the Edinburgh press, but the weight of correspondence still favoured charitable giving. In 1776 generous gifts to the Edinburgh Charity Workhouse by the Duke of Buccleuch and the Earl of Hyndford were reported in the *Caledonian Mercury* as evidence of public spirit.[9] In 1774 this paper had also noted the failure of subscribers to pay their assessment to the workhouse. In the 1780s the topic of the Poor Law became more controversial. There is a letter in the *Caledonian Mercury* referring to assessment as an 'odious and oppressive tax' which echoes the remarks of the East Lothian gentry in 1623. Another writer criticised poorhouses as leading strongly towards 'invitation to idleness'. Comments were clearly influenced by views on the level of poor rates in England. The Poor Law there was claimed as 'almost equally pernicious to those who pay, and those who receive', 'gross oppression to the wealthy and industrious', 'an enticement to idleness and debauchery' to the indigent labourer. It seems unlikely that much debauchery could take place on weekly allowances in Scotland which, as Anderson had pointed out, were frequently below the price of a peck of oatmeal, but some degree of irrationality is understandable in Edinburgh which received an undue proportion of the beggar population of the whole of Scotland in times of crisis. The concept of the city as a centre of Enlightenment receives something of a setback when, as in 1784, there was a demand for the public flogging of beggars.[10]

Horror at the prospect of poor rates on the English scale, voiced surprisingly by lawyers who might have been expected to be looking forward to Poor Law litigation on the English scale, received fresh ammunition in the 1780s from Joseph Townsend's *Dissertation on the Poor Laws.* Townsend, an English rector, had travelled abroad, had some claims to be considered a scientist, and, like Anderson, had a record of miscellaneous articles, on health, geology, the old Testament, the principles of government, etc. His view of the English Poor Law was that it took money from those who could hardly spare it to give to the profligate. Pre-empting Malthus, he stated that the size of the population was regulated by the quantity of food: interference with the natural system was bound to produce unemployment. Only hunger would spur the poor to labour, so to prevent hunger by relief bordered on insanity. In Scotland, which he had visited, he claimed there was 'no legal provision for the poor', an interesting example of selective perception. His remedy for England's problems was to reduce the standard of living of the labouring class – no tea, sugar, spices, nor expensive luxuries such as shoes and stockings until a high earning power had been achieved. His image of the future included gradual reduction of rates, workshops for the training of children, the change of the use of horses, with their appetites for corn, to oxen in agriculture, no relief for anyone who was not a member of a friendly society, and so on. Eventually the poor would be supported solely by charitable gifts, but even these should be limited. In spite of the recommendation of charity in Matthew: 25, it was not desirable for the Christian Church to be indiscriminate and blind.[11]

The denial of a Scottish Poor Law is surprising since in the parish reports of the *OSA*, written not long after Townsend's book, there is evidence of some sort of a relief system in every parish which gave a full report. Only occasionally does a minister omit the topic of the poor, and when one does he is clearly taking little trouble over any part of his contribution. Even in the far west island of Barra, where the Protestant population was so small that it was not considered necessary to demand a church from the heritor, the minister was handling a legacy and giving some small aid to forty or fifty people. Highland ministers in their reports tend to stress the role of charitable giving, both by neighbours and by landowners. It is unlikely that this was on a scale that would prevent real hardship. The enormous area covered by some Highland parishes would inevitably lead to pockets of population too remote to be communicated with, and suffering there would not be known. And we have occasional outside evidence of hardship in the Highlands. Thomas Pennant, for instance, in his tour of 1772 was horrified to see that the people of the Small Isles were actually starving.[12]

The small sums given in relief in the Highlands were not useless. In a pre-industrial economy many households did not have a regular income but pieced together support from the various activities of the members of the family as well as the product of a smallholding. Harvest wages which included food might be an important element. To such a family a dole of 3 shillings or 3 shillings and 6 pence, which was the annual relief allowance in the Arran parish of Kilmuir, would not be derisory: it might fill a gap in earnings. But it would not prevent real hardship in a bad year.

Macfarlan notes that the inability of Highland parishes to maintain their poor was the reason for the failure of the county schemes set up in Perthshire, particularly that of 1756. Study of the *OSA* gives the impression of a strong geographical gradient in the number of complaints about beggars from outwith the parish: the destitute leaked from the north and west to beg in the more affluent south and east. Highland parish efforts at relief were based on too low a level of resource to be adequate.[13]

Comparison of the levels of accepted poor in the *OSA* reports does not show the Highland area as unduly burdened. No Highland county comes out with such a low percentage of poor as some Lowland counties – Stirlingshire at 0.86 was remarkably low, but Fife with 1.2 and Berwickshire at 1.5 were under half the level of most Highland counties. But Sutherland and Caithness, with respectively 3.3 and 3.1, were not very different from Peeblesshire 3.3, and Selkirkshire at 3.2. Aberdeenshire, Perthshire and Inverness all lay between 2 and 3. The only county with a high level of pensioners was Ross at 4.4.

But these figures may not be meaningful. The decision of whether to admit some petitioner to the roll was made by the parish kirk session on what it regarded as severe poverty, and in an area where the bulk of the population was very poor, the standard for need would be low. Though the court system of presbyterianism provided opportunities for ministers to exchange ideas and information, it was not a mechanism for setting fixed standards. Variation in the concept of need is clear in the level of allowance granted. Poor relief in the Highlands was only one aspect of the general impoverishment of the region. The relatively late date at which effective presbyterian church government was established there meant that relatively few parishes had received legacies to help out, in contrast to some well-endowed lowland parishes.

Highland ministers were well aware of the reality of the need they could not meet. In the Lowlands, where the economy was not in crisis, ministers could afford to have doubts about the system they worked. As opposing views, one can set those of the minister of Selkirk, the Reverend Thomas Robertson, against those of the Reverend Alexander Carlyle of Inveresk (East Lothian). Robertson would have agreed with Townsend on the undesirably high expectations of the labouring classes, whose level of daily wages (10 pence to 1 shilling for men, 6 pence to 8 pence for women) was

> inadequate to their expenses, when they are in health and makes them a constant Burden to the public, whenever any misfortune happens to them. Such a mode of living is but a miserable preparation for the cares of matrimony and the burden of a family. In that state the rustic beau sinks into a peevish and complaining churl. The gaily attired shepherdess becomes a prey to stupid insensibility and sloth.

Robertson observed young people refusing to support their parents and 'in the prime of life, indulging themselves in every species of debauchery common to their rank of life'. Parishes were compelled to set up assessment, as had all in Selkirkshire. 'Poor-rates, without a system of management not yet practised in the country parishes, is unfriendly to the cause of virtue in general and to the best interests of those they are intended to serve.' Though the claim that much in the way of debauchery could be indulged in on 1 shilling sterling a day seems overstressed, the view that it was inappropriate for the labourers to have any luxuries was one commonly held by their social superiors, who frequently expressed disapproval of their drinking tea or wearing cotton clothes.

Robertson was writing before the hardening of social and political attitudes which followed on the start of the war with revolutionary France in 1793 and is clearly marked in the later volumes of the old edition of the *OSA*. Carlyle, in his contribution in one of the later volumes, was openly differing from the current opinion. On rates he wrote 'the arguments arising from the *danger . . . of erasing the sense of shame* of dependence on the poor's funds from the minds of the indigent, or of *blunting the feelings of compassion* in the hearts of their relations . . . would have been considered as the suggestions of avarice'. This was his view of the past policy of his parish. He described how the parish was trying to make assessment effective on industrial plants, and discussed a system of friendly society insurance used in Portmoak (Kinross-shire), for which the minister, the Reverend Andrew Grant, was an enthusiast. Grant wanted such an institution made compulsory on the lower orders and was strongly against the assessment of landowners. Carlyle's view was that any system by which the better off subscribed only by a voluntary assessment was not sustainable: 'no contribution remains long just and equal' was his comment. The elements in the debate over poor relief which was to go on for the next forty years were set out in these opinions.[14]

Three new sources of funds for the poor had arrived by the end of the century. Two are mentioned in the *OSA*, friendly societies and voluntary assessment: the third arrived later, savings banks. There is also evidence of the increased use of organised and specific charities. The first friendly societies consisted of groups of men, often working in some specific craft, paying regular sums into a common purse, often quarterly, with the expectation of financial help in time of sickness or a pension to a widow. There might be two or three such societies in a parish, or alternatively men in some craft might belong to a society in a neighbouring parish. A common scale of payment was 1 shilling or 1 shilling and 6 pence sterling a quarter with support given at 2 shillings and 6 pence a week in illness.

The weakness of friendly societies, which did not stop them being popular investments throughout the nineteenth century, was that there was no adequate actuarial base for their scale of payments. The ability of any one society to survive depended on its ability to continue to attract young and healthy members, and to avoid being rendered peripheral by the shift in profitable skills. Some less open form of mutual saving existed in trade unionism, which, though illegal, was well established in some industries, notably mining. Since there was an effective natural society on which the finances were based, these could extract themselves from bankruptcy by special levies or sudden changes of rules.[15]

A questionnaire launched at all parishes by Thomas Kennedy of Dunure, later MP, in 1815, gives some sense of the spread of friendly societies and savings banks: 160 Lowland ministers answered his enquiry. The population was not then so brainwashed by opinion polls as to see any special merit in sticking to the questions asked but seventy-four of the replies state that their parish had one or more friendly societies, fifty-two that they had not. On savings banks, which some called parish banks, thirty-one had one and eighty-six had not.[16] In a number of cases the minister stated that his flock could join friendly societies in neighbouring parishes. There is some evidence that friendly societies could stave off assessment when collections and voluntary funds were proving inadequate, so approval of them united ministers and landowners. Savings banks came to be mainly a resource for domestic servants; the analysis we have from the *OSA* of the relation between labourers' wages and outgoings shows that there was little room for savings by any family with children.[17]

The responses to Kennedy were in many cases informed by a horror of assessment, which the clergy appear to have absorbed from the landed class. For instance, the minister of Bathgate called assessment 'oppression on landowners and tenants'. A particularly effective demonstration of this attitude is to be found in Old Deer (Aberdeenshire) where Mr John Burnett had, at the end of the eighteenth century, left his estate, a substantial one, to provide a fund for annual distribution to the parishes of the Synod of Aberdeen, except for those in the presbytery of Fordyce, to aid poor relief, provided the parish had never been assessed. Part of the legacy was also for the poor on his own estate, but this was to revert to his heirs if ever the parish adopted assessment. Such parishes might receive a bonus of £30 or £40 once in a while, a very real boon to a hard-pressed poor fund. The effect of this legacy has been to distort the historical judgement of ministers: parishes which by their own records can be seen to have adopted assessment for a short while were claimed in the *NSA* and in the reports of the General Assembly as never assessed.[18]

One of the techniques for avoiding was to use a form of 'voluntary assessment'. This is an ambiguous phrase, and its meaning was changing in the early nineteenth century. Given the current practice in parishes, all assessment had an element of the voluntary in it: landowners, whatever the law might say, could only with difficulty be forced to levy it, though repeated badgering by sessions and the clear inability of the parish to support the needy without it might make landowners feel under compulsion. County schemes could push landowners into agreeing to be rated according to valued rent to support a head constable, as in Mearns, or a workhouse, as in

Aberdeenshire. In 1774 Inveresk (East Lothian) had decided to base its relief on a voluntary agreement, which involved promises of specific support to the tune of £208 from the heritors, the burgh of Mussel-burgh, the village of Inveresk, the kirk session and even the Episcopal Church, which promised £5 a year. The parish was prepared to prosecute any of these bodies failing to pay up, but in 1778, 'finding that the voluntary contribution diminished every year' it reverted to a full legal assessment. Some element in the mixed agreement was probably in favour of this for it to have been possible.

At the end of the eighteenth century a new form of 'voluntary assessment' emerged. Landowners, including the non-resident ones, would agree to raise a specific sum with shares calculated on the valued rent, and would run the parish Poor Law by a joint committee with the session, as if legally assessed. The advantage of this arrangement to them was that since it was not a full legal assessment it did not affect the value of their estates. It was merely an agreement from which at any moment an individual could withdraw by refusing to pay his share. The disadvantages were two. One was that such a withdrawal would destroy the arrangement and, usually, compel the parish to impose a regular assessment. The recognition of this fact might restrain the irresponsible from destroying the system. The other disadvantage was that the tenantry could not be legally compelled to pay half of the sum levied, though they could be bullied into it.

The system was cosmetic, but it had its attraction. Hamilton locates the first example for Ayrshire in 1799 when parish meetings were called to consider action in a year of high price, and subscriptions were promised. In Straiton (Ayrshire) the heritors were ready to contribute by valuation rather than see the session use up its capital reserves, and in several other parishes a similar agreement was made.[19] There was some sense in this approach to a single crisis year. In Dailly (Fife) a similar arrangement was made in 1816 and the heritors continued to fill the gap in relief needs by their valued rent until the 1840s. In various Ayrshire parishes it was the initial step by which the heritors became eventually the main source of funds.

According to an account in the Peeblesshire parish of Newlands, that county's landowners decided in 1818 to abandon legal assessment for voluntary assessment, which, it was felt, would keep in check the growth of pauperism. There were some difficulties in carrying out this system, most notably in Newlands: some heritors, in particular Lord

Wemyss, thought that assessment should be based not on the valued rent of the later seventeenth century, but on the current real rent. This issue and other difficulties led to the obtaining of a legal opinion, which contained elements of surprise. The lawyer stated that if there had been a meeting to adopt voluntary assessment those present who had not objected could be forced to pay their share, and the half share which the landowners had been expecting to pass to their tenants could not be enforced unless these agreed.[20] The existing ignorance on this last point suggests that in most cases the tenants were burdened without any attempt to obtain consent.

In 1779 there occurred an important signal of economic change: the first large-scale workshop dependent on an outside power source, to which the title 'factory' was later given, was set up in Scotland. Even by the end of the century the number of such factories, cotton mills, was small. They were confined to the process of spinning; the use of water power had not yet spread to other processes. A mill used a concentrated labour force of several hundred. Set in the country to gain access to water, it would probably have to provide housing and dormitory accommodation for this, and fluctuations in the demand for its products could produce hardship on a new scale. Much of the labour came from children and adolescents. New Lanark, for instance, one of the most famous industrial units, had 70 per cent of its population aged under twenty, and of this labour force 400 were 'pauper apprentices', that is children sold to it by urban poorhouses.[21] Some Scottish parishes also sent orphans to English mills. These children spent up to fifteen hours a day in the mill, of which one and a half were meal breaks. Such labour may have been no more lengthy than it had been in the past for apprentices to individual craftsmen, but it now began at a younger age and involved more constant labour, for work was set at the pace of the machine. It also involved life constantly in a crowd. New Lanark became the largest single industrial complex in Britain. It housed its 400 children in six dormitories and imposed a rigorous standard of cleanliness on the workforce to prevent outbreaks of infectious disease. Probably no child was as neglected as some had been under the older system if working for wretchedly poor craftsmen, but the weight of regulation on every aspect of life was repressive. In the early nineteenth century Robert Owen took over New Lanark and managed to raise the age at which children started work to ten, but there was still little liberty and the hours were lengthened by his educational provision.

Yet it was employment and, hence, support to many, particularly widows with large families. A correspondence in the KSR of South Queensferry (West Lothian) shows the attraction of New Lanark for such families. Archibald McIntyre had left his family there early in 1815 while he searched for work. He came back to find his wife dead and his six children, all under eleven, creating a crisis for the small financial resources of the parish. He took the family to New Lanark where he remarried and had another child. The crisis for his home parish was renewed in 1817 when he died, leaving a widow and seven children, all legally the financial responsibility of South Queensferry. The two oldest children were already part of the mill's labour force and the third would soon be old enough. The South Queensferry session reluctantly recognised that it would be cheaper to agree to a pension to the widow of 8 shillings sterling a week, rather than face the return of the whole family to South Queensferry where there was no demand for child labour.

Factory production was at first to be found in only a few spots, but it was soon to take over the textile industries altogether in the nineteenth century, and to change, by the social divisions it enhanced and the scale of other lines of work, the economic and social world. In particular it created an economy more liable to the swings of the business cycle, and so to surges of unemployment. It destroyed the value of established skills and the fact that new skills were created did not help hand spinners or handloom weavers. There has long been debate among historians over whether real wages rose or fell in the early years of the nineteenth century, but most of this has been focused simply on the wage packet, not on the numbers it had to support. The rapid increase in population between 1790 and 1820 seems to have been largely due to a rise in nuptiality and fertility: families were larger, which meant that an adult's wage packet had to feed more people. When, through a hiccup in the marketing system or a general slump, that packet disappeared there was an increased need of outside support.

New forms of support for some of the poor were developing. Voluntary assessment was near to the creation of a voluntary charitable society, and its spread may have been helped by the fact that such institutions were becoming more common and providing an important part of the fabric of social life, giving aid to specific types of need and also giving women of the middle-class opportunities to develop their talents for organisation. They also provided outlets for the social philosophies of particular groups. Already in the eighteenth century there had been a few such societies: Glasgow had, for instance, the North Parish Washing Green Society, set up in 1797, which rented out laundry facilities and used the profits charitably. Societies also existed to provide company and aid to particular incoming groups: the most conspicuous of these was the Highland Society, founded in 1727. Dundee in 1797 had started up the Society for the Relief of the Indigent Sick in the Town and Suburbs. To our age when even short titles are replaced with acronyms, the verbosity of some of the societies' titles is surprising, witness the Edinburgh Society for the Suppression of Begging or for the Relief of Occasional Distress and for the Encouragement of Industry among the Poor. Some enterprises were borrowed from England. The idea of savings banks was English and a society for the suppression of beggars, based on Bath, was widely copied.[22]

The economic changes of this period were bound to cause stress and hardship. This effect was increased by the dislocations of war. The war which had opened with revolutionary France in 1793 had been expected to be short, but soon engulfed most of Europe and showed no signs of ending. A short interval of peace was established in 1801 but did not last. War by then was against the military skill and imperialism of Napoleon, and did not end till 1815. Of course war produced unemployment even though it also enhanced demand for certain types of manpower. A financial crisis was averted in 1793 but in 1797 the country ran out of gold for business. Paper currency led to inflation. Population growth had by now made Britain dependent on some proportion of imported grain, and war made importing expensive. After 1806 the trade war between Britain and the French empire led to sharp fluctuations in the tracks and cost of trade. Though much of the Scottish rural labour force was protected from the most conspicuous effects of inflation because wages were paid mainly in grain, high prices made for restrictions on other needed purchases. The degree of inflation can be seen in the changes in the annual 'fiars prices', the prices named each year in every county for the conversion of obligations between grain and money. The fiar for Stirlingshire oatmeal averaged 7 pounds Scots a boll in the 1770s: in the distress year of 1782 it stood at 11 pounds 8 shillings, but then fell back to 9 pounds. In 1795 it reached 12 pounds, in 1799 18 pounds, in 1800 24 pounds, later to fall to 15 pounds.[23] The industrial world suffered from uncertainties in exports and imports. New Lanark was closed altogether for four months after the United States placed an embargo on cotton supply to Britain. In this case Robert Owen the manager continued to pay wages but smaller units of production could not afford this generosity.[24]

Governments and policy-makers of this period were not used, as are those of the late twentieth century, to the concept of inflation and lacked mechanisms, either intellectual or practical, for coping with it. The price of food in 1800 was seen as a disaster, and the year was long remembered as one of crisis, in which famine had been only just averted. Parishes were encouraged by the county authorities to meet the needs of the poor. There was already in rural England a model of how poor relief could be used, the so-called Speenhamland system, adopted by the Justices of Berkshire in a recent hard year. this meant using poor relief as an enhancement of income to those in work, on a scale calculated by the size of the worker's family and the price of bread. This system had been borrowed by many other rural areas, with encouragement by the government. The wheat-growing counties of southern England suffered from low wages and had little industrial employment. The impoverished labourers there could not easily transfer to the industrial north.

'Speenhamlanding', that is the use of rate-based poor relief funds to supplement the wages of those in work, can be found in rural Scotland in the early 1800s. Sometimes the funds were based on special subscriptions. Kirkoswald (Ayrshire) divided the 'industrious poor', that is those in work, into three classes: those earning less than 1 shilling sterling a day, those earning between 1 shilling and one and fourpence, and those with higher wages. The parish had bought oatmeal and made it available at between 1 shilling and 1 shilling and 6 pence a peck to the three groups. A similar classification of the working class was made in Prestonkirk, now East Linton (East Lothian) for all earning less than 2 shillings sterling a day with specific quantities of subsidised oatmeal and barley meal allowed for families of various sizes. The lowest earners were 'single women, widows, those who are unable or cannot pursue work as labourers and tradesmen, whose wages are at or below one and fourpence a day'. On the quantities of subsidised food allowed the households of such workers would have had to spend 80 per cent of income on food to obtain a diet adequate in calories. Such a pattern of expenditure is appropriate to severe poverty, but it allowed them to live.[25]

Speenhamlanding can be found for a few years in many areas in southern Scotland. Sometimes the support came in the form of subsidised meal, sometimes in money. It was particularly common in East Lothian and Berwickshire and in the area round Stirling.[26] It did not always command unanimous support among ratepayers, and in particular in Duns (Berwickshire) opposition led to an important legal process, the case of *Pollock* v. *Darling 1804*.[27] A tenant farmer, John Darling, had refused to pay rates in support of those he held to be little worse off than he himself. The wording of the pleading, which was successful for the parish, is a valuable indication of the mental climate of the day. 'Inability to earn subsistence is the true and only distress which it is the object of a poors' law to relieve . . . Shall not assistance be afforded to the honest and industrious man who works diligently and yet is unable, from the circumstances of the time, to secure himself and his family from want?' A majority of the Judges agreed, and rebutted the claim by Darling's lawyer that the gap between wages and need was 'merely an accidental and temporary feature'.

Edinburgh city, as already mentioned, faced a similar crisis over 'the labouring poor' in 1809, when inelastic wages for those in work and high unemployment led to distress. It raised a 'voluntary' fund with considerable pressure put on the better off and the business community to contribute. Only the banks refused. The elders of the Church distributed the results in money and coal tickets.[28] The fund was a cautious recognition not of the fact that wages had not kept up with food prices but of the reality of unemployment. The voluntary base of the fund shows a retreat from the generous impulse of the judges in *Pollock* v. *Darling*.

In 1816 the explosion of a volcano in the East Indies created chill summers and harvest failures all over the northern hemisphere.[29] Scottish parishes faced a crisis in poor relief similar, though not as intense, to that of 1800–1, enhanced by high unemployment caused by the dislocation and deflation after the wartime high prices. Yet hardly any parish can be found using the Speenhamland solution to its problems. Towns set up soup kitchens. Montrose raised a special subscription for 'the industrious poor', and Edinburgh still had the fund and organisation surviving from 1809. Some parishes dug into capital funds. Two can be found raising money on assessment to create work, Crichton (Midlothian) and St Vigeans (Angus), but they are exceptional. Altogether the evidence shows an unwillingness to adopt the Speenhamland way out.[30]

The most likely source of the change in intellectual climate over the poor is the publication by the Reverend T. R. Malthus of the second edition of his *Essay on the Principles of Population* in 1803. The first mention of it that I have found in a Scottish journal is of some years later. Malthus was not a concise writer and it took some time for his opinions to be absorbed. His chilling message was that the relief of poverty and the prevention of starvation merely meant the postponement of the moment when food supply failed to meet human needs. 'The man born into a world already full', he stated, 'if he cannot get subsistence from his parents, on whom he has a just demand, and if society does not want his labour, has no claim of *right* to the smallest portion of food . . . At nature's mighty feast there is no vacant cover for him'.[31] There was no right to relief because there was no guarantee that adequate supply would exist: by contrast prudent delay of marriage until a man could be sure of his ability to support a family would mean that in the long run there would be no need for relief.

Eventually Malthus hoped that the Poor Law would disappear. The early nineteenth century looked on property as a given right, but such obligations on it as were represented by the Poor Law were artificial. There were others than Malthus attacking poor relief; in particular many felt it undesirable that the English Poor Law went a considerable way towards giving the unemployed as comfortable a situation in life as many employed labourers. Malthus's significance was that he gave a strong argument in terms of the intellectually fashionable political economy for the general attack on systems of relief. The main object of this attack was the English Poor Law. In Scotland his significance lay in the way in which he brought God's intentions into the case against the Poor Law.

NOTES

1. T. C. Smout, 'Where had the Scottish Economy got to by the third quarter of the Eighteenth century?', in I. Hont and M. Ignatieff, *Wealth and Virtue* (Cambridge, 1983), pp. 45–73.
2. W. Morison, *Dictionary of Decisions*, pp. 10,577 and 10,591.
3. Traces of various schemes, mainly those of the 1770s, can be found in miscellaneous places. For Argyll, in collaboration with the Synod, *OSA* vol. VIII, pp. 90–1, Dunoon, and pp. 412–13 Strachur and Strathellan.

Ayrshire, 1771 in collaboration with presbyteries, T. Hamilton, *Poor Relief in South Ayrshire*, ch. 4. Dumfriesshire, *OSA* IV p. 46 Canonbie and p. 365 Langholm. See also the Stewartry Justice of the Peace records, SRO JP1/2/1 August 1772 for collaboration between the two counties. East Lothian SRO JP2/2/2, December 1773 June 1778. Fife, Wemyss KSR, March 1777 quotes the sheriff's order for suppressing vagrants and keeping the poor from begging. Midlothian, *Caledonian Mercury* 5 February 1773. Perthshire, SRO JP20/2/2 for 1773, *OSA* XII Caputh, p. 205 and Kincardine, pp. 553–4, for 1775. For an earlier scheme combining control of begging with repression of crime, see the Blair Atholl muniments. I owe this reference to Dr Leah Leneman. Roxburghshire, SRO JP14/2/6, April 1773. An earlier scheme of 1746 is mentioned in the evidence given to the Royal Commission of 1844 by the clerk to the Justices of the Peace, *PP* 1844 XXII p. 669. Stewartry of Kirkcudbright, JP1/2/1, 1772. Stirlingshire, *OSA* IX St Ninians and also NLS MS 9823 'Scheme for the better Regulation and Maintenance of the Poor in the county of Stirling'. The Border counties were already working relief effectively and did not need schemes.

4. For instance *PP* 1844 *XX* p. 691–2, Dr James Douglas and surgeon John Stewart, both of Kelso.

5. Michael Lynch, 'Urbanisation and urban networks in seventeenth-century Scotland: some further thoughts', *Scottish Economic and Social History*, xii, 1992, pp. 24 41.

6. T. C. Smout, 'Famine and Famine Relief in Scotland', in L. M. Cullen and T. C. Smout, *Comparative Aspects of Scottish and Irish Economic and Social History* (Edinburgh, 1976), pp. 21–31.

7. L. S. Spriggs, (ed.), *The Letters of Jeremy Bentham*, vol. II (London, 1968), p. 494 and I. R. Christie (ed.) ibid. vol. III, pp. 18–39.

8. C. F. Mullett 'A village Aristotle and the harmony of interests', *Journal of British Studies*, VIII (1968–9), pp. 94–118. See also his short-lived journal of the 1790s, *The Bee*, 15, p. 275; 18 (1793), pp. 9–28, 204, 358–83.

9. *Caledonian Mercury*, 24 January, 20 and 27 March, 17 December 1774. I owe these references to John Dwyer.

10. *Caledonian Mercury*, 18 and 20 February 1786, 7 February 15 March, 26 April 1784.

11. Joseph Townsend, *A Dissertation on the Poor Laws by a Well-Wisher to Mankind* (London, 1786).

12. Thomas Pennant, *A Tour in Scotland and Voyage to the Hebrides, MDCCLXXII* (London, 1777), vol. I, p. 311.

13. J. Macfarlan, *Inquiries Concerning the Poor* (Edinburgh, 1782), p. 459.

14. *OSA* vol. III, pp. 716–17 Selkirk, and vol. II pp. 318–21 Inveresk.

15. C. Whatley, 'The fettering bonds of brotherhood', *Social History*, 12, 1987, pp. 139–54.

16. The returns to Kennedy's questionnaire are in the keeping of Lord Moncrieff of Tullybole at Tullybole Castle, where, by the kindness of

Lord Moncrieff and the late Lady Moncrieff, I have been able to consult them.

17. M. Goldie, 'The standard of living of the Scottish farm labourers in selected areas at the time of the first two *Statistical Accounts*, 1790–1845', Edinburgh M.Sc. thesis, 1971.

18. E.g. Udny (Aberdeenshire).

19. T. Hamilton, *South Ayrshire*, pp. 111–17; SRO CH2/543/6, Newlands KSR, 1832.

20. EUL MS La III 753–4.

21. *OSA* vol. VII, pp. 460–7; Margaret Cole, *Robert Owen of New Lanark* (London, 1953), p. 48; J. Butt, *Robert Owen, Prince of Cotton Spinners* (Newton Abbott, 1971), pp. 103, 158; Ian Donnachie and George Hewitt, *Historic New Lanark* (Edinburgh, 1993), pp. 40–9.

22. Olive Checkland, *Philanthropy in Victorian Scotland* (Edinburgh, 1980); EUL MS La III 753–4.

23. Stirlinghshire and other fiars prices are to be found in M. W. Flinn et al., *Scottish Population History* (Cambridge, 1977), Appendix B.

24. M. Cole, *Robert Owen*, p. 61.

25. Hamilton, *South Ayrshire*, p. 93; *Caledonian Mercury*, 15 December 1800.

26. G. M. Birnie, 'Tradition and Transition: the Scottish Poor Law, Harvest Failures and the Industrious Poor, 1799–1801'. M.A. thesis 1976, Department of Economic and Social History, Edinburgh University, 1976, ch. 5.

27. *Faculty Decisions*, vol. 13, pp. 294–8; Morison, *Dictionary of Decisions*, p. 10,591.

28. ECA, p. 72 of catalogue 'Fish supper', Committee for the Relief of the Labouring Poor, 1809–10.

29. J. D. Post, 'Famine mortality and epidemic disease in the process of modernisation', *Economic History Review*, 2nd series, 1976, pp. 14–37.

30. June Irving, 'The Scottish Poor Law's Response to the 1816 Harvest Failure', M.A. thesis, Department of Economic and Social History, Edinburgh University, 1982.

31. T. R. Malthus, *An Essay on the Principles of Population* (London, 1803), pp. 531–8.

CHAPTER 7

POST-WAR
DISCOMFORT AND DEBATE

In 1815 Thomas Kennedy of Dunure, a young Whig lawyer and landowner, soon to be a Member of Parliament, sent out a questionnaire to the ministers of the established Church in Scotland. The document asked about the funds available for the support of the poor from 1790 to 1815; the share in them of assessment and of 'voluntary contributions' (a phrase which seems to mean 'voluntary assessment'); the date at which assessment started, if it had; the numbers of poor incapable of earning; the numbers receiving partial or occasional support; and whether, and since when, there were savings banks or friendly societies in the parish. At the end of the document there was a request for 'general facts' about the poor and the Poor Law.

Kennedy was fairly naive as a politician. As he admitted in a letter to Lord Minto, a leading Whig peer, he expected that the returns would show an increasing burden of poor rates which would stimulate a parliamentary inquiry and legislation, and this would lead to cutting back expenditure on the poor.[1] The questionnaire, by its wording, invited answers which would show a massive recent increase in the scale of relief and the level of assessment. It was in tune with a growing emphasis of the evangelical revival on personal independence. Evangelical thought was abandoning the Calvinist emphasis on the congregation as a unit of the true Church, and stressing instead individual responsibility. Landowners approved of both friendly societies and savings banks as institutions which were likely to reduce the demand for any transfer of wealth from rich to poor, but to the evangelicals, while savings banks were admirable institutions, for an individual's savings were expanded only by interest marginally enhanced by legislation, friendly societies might pay out to a man more than he had invested, and so could lead to the weakening of the sense of self-support.

The responses to the questionnaire ended up in the hands of Sir Henry Moncreiff Wellwood, a leading evangelical divine and an eminent Whig. There are 160 of them, and this is probably all that were made, for, to get a complete or near complete response to a questionnaire, there would have had to be some reward or some pressure from the General Assemby.[2] Some ministers refused to give detailed information, holding that the research involved, not to mention the arithmetic, was more suited to the status of parish clerk than minister. Only twenty-seven gave the full range of cost and numbers of poor for the whole period asked. These were mainly rural parishes, with relatively high representation from central Scotland and Aberdeenshire. From this self-selected sample it can be seen that the monetary cost of poor relief had almost exactly doubled between 1790 and 1815: it had risen to three times the 1790 level in the severe dearth of 1800. But the years after 1797 form a period of debased currency. Britain left the gold standard in that year and did not get back to it till 1821. The true cost of relief for the intervening years has to be calculated in kind. The most respected measure of the price of grain for this period is the middle fiar of East Lothian. If the expenditure of these parishes is adjusted by this, the cost of relief in 1800 had risen by 40 per cent above the 1790 level; thereafter it fluctuated between that level and 20 per cent below, ending in 1815 just below the level of 1790. This adjustment is appropriate for the two main groups involved in the politics of rural relief, for landowners in this period were able to adjust their rents to the inflationary situation and ministers' stipends were calculated in grain. In real terms the cost of relief had not gone up.

It would not be realistic to expect the general public of 1815 to think in terms of inflation: it had been difficult to get Parliament in the bullion debate of 1810 to recognise that such a thing existed. What the public did appreciate was the discomfort of the immediate post-war period. The release of a large body of men from the armed forces and the shifts in demand for goods consequent on peace led to high unemployment. Deflationary policy increased this. The fear of the landed interest of competition from abroad led to the banning of imported grain until the home price was very high by pre-war standards. Yet even with this artificial heightening of food costs, landowners were finding it necessary to reduce rents. High rents had been sustained for a generation and become built into the expectations on which the structure of legal settlements for the dependent members of landed families were based, so that when rents were reduced the landowner, in many cases, experienced a much more drastic reduction in the residual income on which he had to live than that of the estate as a whole. It is understandable that there was considerable pressure from landowners for reduction of one of the burdens on those estates that were assessed, poor relief. And in this period of general discomfort there came the harvest failure of 1816 which affected the whole northern hemisphere, and which led to increased demands for relief.

Deflation, dislocation, the arguments of evangelical Christianity and of political economists all combined to make for a major attack on the English Poor Laws. There was a flurry of pamphlets expounding the evils of such laws. It was pointed out that they laid a heavy burden on farmers, encouraged idleness and dissipation and, at the same time, did not improve the standard of living of labourers because they encouraged early marriage. It was generally believed that the Speenhamland allowance system of supplementing wages with relief was in widespread use. Historians working on this topic have shown that this system had never spread to the more industrialised parts of England, and that even in the agricultural south-east where there was a surplus of labour, it survived mainly as a payment to large families.[3] In Scotland, where something similar had been set up in many parishes in 1800, by 1816 it had almost totally disappeared. Investigation into a wide span of parish records shows no sign of it.[4] The support of the poor in the harvest year of 1816 was met by stretching out the normal resources.

The pressures of expressed opinion forced the topic of poor relief to be frequently raised in Parliament.[5] A big debate in 1816 led to the setting up of a Commons select committee, chaired by Sturges Bourne, which set out to collect evidence, mostly opinions, and report. The House of Lords also set up a committee.

Kennedy had got himself elected to the General Assembly in 1815 as a carpetbagging elder for Rothesay. In 1817 the House of Lords committee wrote to the Assembly for information on the cost of the Poor Law in Scotland.[6]

From the great comparative burthen of the poor rates in many parts of England and Wales it is evident that the management of the poor in Scotland must have been conducted upon a different principle and therefore whatever information can be furnished to the Committee upon the general system upon which the different parishes have acted will be extremely useful was the somewhat confused message.

The General Assembly made its usual response of a committee: this had sixteen members, mixing ministers and elders, and among these were both Kennedy and Sir Henry Moncreiff Wellwood. At the end of May, as the Assembly finished its normal work, a further letter arrived, this time from Sturges Bourne. The Assembly passed this to its committee, adding a further seventeen committee members, enough to make it thoroughly cumbersome.

The committee did not wish to miss an opportunity for expression, and did not wish to wait for next year's Assembly for material. The Kennedy responses, though they had not yet been systematically worked through, could be used for a report. The Sturges Bourne request had been received on 29 May, and on 19 June a short report, based ostensibly on the Kennedy material, was dispatched.[7] It is not clear whether Moncreiff Wellwood or Kennedy was responsible. The committee went on to circulate its own questionnaire to the parishes, to which, eventually, it claimed to have received approximately 700 replies, representing a wide spectrum of Scotland. These have not come to light.

Kennedy's material had thus unexpectedly been given a wide audience. The report brought out what was to become the standard historical theme on the Scottish Poor Law. 'The Scotch have uniformly proceeded on the principle, that every individual is bound to provide for himself by his own labour, as long as he is able to do so, and that his parish is only bound to make up that portion of the necessaries of life, which he cannot earn or obtain by other lawful means.' By 'other lawful' means it meant the charity of kin and neighbours. The report claimed there had been 200 replies to the questionnaire but that so far only half of these had been digested. (Given the limited numeracy of many Church of Scotland ministers, this does not necessarily mean that the body of 160 replies which now exist is incomplete.) Among the replies, it stated, there was 'a great proportion' of country parishes which had adopted legal assessment but had afterwards abandoned it for voluntary contributions. Regular assessments 'have very generally been observed to produce an influx of Paupers from other parishes, who in three years . . . can acquire a legal settlement if during that time they have supported themselves'. 'In almost all country parishes using assessment this has been found to increase progressively.' Such was the message.

The report was obviously made in a hurry, but this does not fully explain the gap between some of its statements and the content of the returns. The imprecise wording of the original questionnaire is partly responsible for some of the obscurities of the report. In neither is it clear whether 'voluntary contributions' means occasional gifts or voluntary assessment. Apart from the fact that a number of parishes had taken on some sort of assessment in the crisis years of 1800–1 or 1813–14, and then dropped it, only one, Dunblane, claimed in the returns to have abandoned a long-standing legal assessment for voluntary. In this parish an influx of settlers had been reported: these of course were not paupers because they could support themselves for three years. For Selkirk the return stated that much of the housing in the landward part of the parish had been tied to jobs, and this had forced some of the old to migrate to the burgh. These statements do not give much quantitative support to the report. The report notes correctly that relief had risen in assessed parishes, but fails to point out that it had also risen in the unassessed.

Clearly the committee had not felt it necessary to stick closely to the evidence that had been collected: it had instead produced a report which expressed a particular line of thought. The general tone of the reply, though, is in tune with some aspects of the supplementary remarks of many of the returns. Pauperism, which was deplored, had increased, and had led to a weakening of the spirit of independence. Some laid the blame on unwise expenditure by the labouring classes. The minister of Galashiels (Roxburghshire) stated that economic developments had stimulated 'the industrious and the profligate to hard labour'; 'by overworking themselves they contract diseases and are exposed to accidents of different kinds, the effects of which reduce them for life to dependence upon the parochial funds'. 'Idleness and disease always spring from debauchery' said another, a harsh verdict for a world subject to the uncontrolled impact of tuberculosis, diphtheria and a host of other infections.

But the returns contain criticism of people other than the labourers, in particular of non-resident heritors, and their failure to contribute to relief unless assessed for it. The minister of Knapdale (Argyll) stated that nine out of the ten non-resident heritors, with a gross rental of £4,000 contributed nothing to relief. The minister of Athelstaneford (East Lothian) carried the attack to the tenantry: 'farmers who pay a thousand pounds, or £2000 of rent yearly reckon one penny to the poor funds on Sunday quite enough'. A note of future gloom was struck from Rannoch (Perthshire) that the Scottish system would be damaged 'if ever . . . the established Church is to any considerable extent broken with Divisions', if 'Proprietors . . . become lax and irregular in their attendance on Public Worship' and if there was to be an 'Excessive influx of Irish'. These, and many other criticisms and warnings found no place in the report.

In 1818 the committee produced a more planned report.[8] This document repeats the unwillingness of the earlier one to let the returns make their own points:

> The Committee take the liberty to add their own decided conviction, not only that the practice of legal and compulsory assessment for the support of the poor, is radically unwise and dangerous, but also that the crisis has already arrived when Scotland should in every quarter take the alert, and form precautions against the spread . . . of a baneful and national calamity.

We have a contemporary criticism of the report from the Reverend Robert Burns, a minister in Paisley.[9] He himself opposed assessment because it 'tended to cherish in the lower classes, a spirit of degraded and servile dependence'. He considered the report 'absolutely useless as a depository of facts'. The committee had used incorrect terms in its questionnaire, asking, for instance, for numbers of 'total' and 'partial' dependants on relief, in spite of the fact that few were totally supported: the terms should have been 'pensioned' and 'occasional'. The committee had also used the phrase 'industrious poor'; this phrase usually meant those in employment but not receiving a living wage, but it could also be used for the unemployed. In any case, as the returns to Kennedy had pointed out, almost all those on parish rolls as pensioners did something for their own support.

Burns himself is not a reliable witness on the state of the Poor Law. In spite of the fame of the case *Pollock* v. *Darling*, which was based on the practice, widespread in 1800–1, of making wages up to subsistence level from Poor Law funds, he could write 'In Scotland we know nothing of the very impolitick and pernicious practice of making up the deficiency of wages . . . by grants out of the parochial funds'. He also claims that 'the *doctrine of removals*' was 'happily unknown' in Scotland. It may be that he thought parishes did not remove potential paupers, rather than actual ones. Though as yet either form of removal was rare, instances can certainly be found. It is not clear whether Burns was consciously lying or merely adopting what was to become a common stance, claiming more virtue in Scotland than in England because of its closer adherence to Reformed doctrine.

Burns complained that the committee had misunderstood the information that he had sent in for Paisley, and probably for other places, so that its figures were faulty. So was the committee's arithmetic. Indeed the heading it gives to its most important table, the cost of paupers in the various synods, shows several weaknesses in numeracy. 'The average rate of relief (taking the mean betwixt the highest and the lowest in all the synods)' is one of its expressions. Since this table, with its dubious arithmetic, is the only general statement we have for regional Poor Law expenditure at this time, it is given in Table 7.1.

Table 7.1

Synod	Paid to each pauper per annum			% of poor
	£	s	d	
Lothian and Tweeddale	3	4	$8\frac{1}{4}$	$2\frac{1}{4}$
Merse and Teviotdale	5	15	$3\frac{1}{8}$	$3\frac{1}{4}$
Dumfries	4	2	$7\frac{1}{4}$	$2\frac{1}{4}$
Galloway	4	14	$5\frac{1}{2}$	$1\frac{1}{8}$
Glasgow and Ayr	5	2	10	$2\frac{1}{12}$
Perth and Stirling	3	3	$4\frac{1}{4}$	$2\frac{1}{8}$
Fife	5	11	$6\frac{1}{2}$	$1\frac{3}{4}$
Angus and Mearns	4	3	$3\frac{1}{4}$	$2\frac{1}{2}$
Aberdeen	2	2	$2\frac{1}{4}$	$3\frac{1}{4}$
Moray	1	3	$4\frac{3}{4}$	$3\frac{1}{4}$
Ross		16	11	$3\frac{1}{5}$
Sutherland and Caithness		16	9	$2\frac{1}{8}$
Argyll	1	10	$11\frac{1}{4}$	$2\frac{3}{4}$
Glenelg		16	3	$2\frac{1}{4}$
Orkney		19	$\frac{1}{2}$	$2\frac{1}{4}$

Even if these figures cannot be fully trusted, they show that the Border Synod of Merse and Teviotdale was not the only area where expenditure on the 'regular' poor was relatively generous. The large number of assessed parishes in the Lothians as well as in the Borders did not mean excessively high costs. In Glasgow and Ayr, and in Fife, expenditure was nearly as high as in the Borders. No area had an unusually high level of recognised poor. The figures for the Highland

Synods and the Northern Isles show that, with levels of poverty not strikingly different from those of the south, expenditure cannot have been meeting need.

The report claims that only three parishes were assessed before 1700, all of these in the Synod of Merse and Teviotdale. This is a very dubious statement. Town records show that some sort of assessment was established in Edinburgh well before 1700. It is not clear whether the report means permanent assessment, or the adoption of assessment only for a temporary crisis. If the latter it is a gross understatement, as can be seen from Chapter 2. Subsequently the General Assembly named two Border parishes as assessed before 1700, Fogo and Ettrick. Kirk Session Registers from neither survive. In fact the Border area did not furnish many of the forty-six parishes which can be seen to have raised assessment in the famine of the 1690s: the general growth of assessment in this area was a later event. But it is most unlikely that the parish ministers, when asked about the past in their parishes, consulted their KSRs: it is even unlikely that many of them were equipped to read seventeenth-century handwriting. It seems most likely that either ministers or the committee relied on guesswork.

The original returns to the committee are not known to exist, but a small handful were partly summarised in the report. The discrepancies between this sample and the generalisations of the report cannot have done much good to the reputation of the Church. The report states firmly that there had been 'no instance' of the removal of a pauper from one parish to another, 'involuntarily or by legal means'. Yet three of the Lowland parishes from which it quotes admit to the practice. It is also, of course, displayed in the legal processes of the eighteenth century.

A theme of longer-term significance is the hostility shown by the report to allowances ordered on appeal by the sheriff. There had been twenty-six cases of such intervention, all in the south, and it was alleged that more were threatened. A Scottish divine, interviewed by the Sturges Bourne Committee expanded on this.[10] Intervention by sheriffs, he stated, was becoming common and made it difficult for heritors to reduce the rates, because each successful intervention caused further claims. Furthermore, sheriffs paid no attention to the moral character of the applicant. (A sheriff's allowance was supposed to meet need, and it is difficult to see how a moral character should have a higher level of need than an immoral one.) The idea that poor relief should be only for the morally sound was becoming general in the first quarter of the nineteenth century.

The sudden interest of the two parliamentary committees in the Scottish Poor Law probably owes its arousal to two contributions, anonymous of course, to the *Edinburgh Review* in February 1817 and March 1818. These indicated a new contributor to debate, the Reverend Thomas Chalmers, minister then of the Tron parish in Glasgow, and still in his thirties. He had recently shown himself in General Assembly business as one of the most powerful orators of the time. Chalmers, who had converted to evangelicalism as a young minister in a small rural parish in Fife, took the evangelical dislike of poor relief to an exceptional level. The usual objection to relief was because of the demoralising effect on sturdy independence of any kind of outside help. Chalmer's view was that relief based on any kind of statutory provision was a moral evil. His March 1818 article was nominally a review of the Sturges Bourne report and the Scottish supplement to it based on the Kennedy material. Chalmers widened his theme to cover the whole topic of statutory relief. It would have been better for the English poor, he claimed, if there had never been legislation prescribing relief: a system such as the Poor Law destroys the natural notions which arise from human feelings and replaces them with artificial legal requirements. The English Poor Law should simply be abolished, and the country allowed to revert to the practice of the least corrupted part of Scotland where the support of the poor was based on the simple distribution of alms, voluntary giving between people who knew each other.

In his earlier article Chalmers did not discuss the basic problem of poverty, why there was so much of it, but offered a plan for the abolition of legally-based relief. Alms given freely from one person to another was part of the Christian way of life. But relief based on assessment and given by an organisation to people who claimed it as a right was a moral evil. For his immediate environment, Glasgow, where the support of the poor was in the hands of the General Session, not in the individual parishes of the city, his proposal was that this centralisation should be done away with and relief moved back to the individual parishes. Those paupers already accepted for relief should continue to get it from the general assessment but all new claims for help should go to the parishes and be met by money raised entirely voluntarily. Each application should be carefully scrutinised, a process which would discourage some claims, and the elders should do all they could to stimulate private giving. Eventually there would be a withering away of demands for aid. The assessment would no longer be needed for relief and could instead be used to support parish schools and to build thirty new churches.

It is difficult to see why it was acceptable to Chalmers to have assessment used to create new parishes and to provide schools but morally wrong to have it used to sustain the destitute. The fact that poor relief was an open ended commitment – need might increase suddenly – whereas payment for churches or schools could be calculated in advance and kept within a budget, might explain a preference for these alternative uses of money, but it does not seem to justify the moral denunciation.

The distinction between established claims and new demands gives away the source of Chalmers's plan. This was the programme of Malthus as set out in the second edition of his *Essay on Population* of 1803. Chalmers had been convinced by the argument and had added the moral coverage. Malthus stated that relief encouraged population growth and was defiance of the divinely arranged relationship between population and resources. His statement has already been quoted in Chapter 6: 'a man who is born into a world already possessed . . . has no claim of *right* to the smallest portion of food . . .'. Malthus proposed that this should be demonstrated by an Act of Parliament decreeing that 'no child born from any marriage taking place after the expiry of a year from the date of the law, and no illegitimate child born two years from the same date should ever be entitled to parish assistance'. There had been no political support for this drastic proposal and he now turned to Chalmers's more cautious idea of a cut-off of relief.[11] It is difficult to regard as entirely practical plans which assumed that the labour needs of society at a time of a man's maturity could be foreseen at the time of his conception, but dogma was more important than practicality.

Chalmers had come to the fore suddenly both as an orator and as the main advocate in Scotland of drastic deconstruction of the Poor Law. As a parish minister he was in touch with the leading figures on Glasgow town council and his new fame gave him the backing of the 'New Whigs', the young men in a hurry for office. After negotiations he was placed in a position to put into action his proposal of the 1817

Edinburgh Review article. In 1819 a new parish in central Glasgow, St John's, occupied by the better-off of the working class was carved out and withdrawn from the relief system of the city's General Session for all new cases. There were over 10,000 inhabitants in St John's, but more than a fifth of these did not adhere to the established Church. Chalmers's vision of a parish as a community giving Christian aid to one another was damaged by this and by two other features. One was the proliferation of voluntary charitable societies raising and distributing considerable sums on their own chosen definitions of worthy causes. The impact of some of these on the poor was general; for instance anti-mendicity societies discouraged begging; others were very selective. Some of the poor knew how to manipulate these societies and get from them what they needed.[12] The other difficult feature was the proliferation of pew renting. Rapid expansion of the city's population, particularly of the middle class, with no corresponding increase in church accommodation had put a premium on space. The city council, which raised and used the rents for pews, had drastically reduced or abolished the areas devoted to free or low-rent seating in the churches used by the middle class and greatly increased the rents of the rest, with the result that church attendance on Sunday had become prohibitively costly to much of the working class.[13] The poor, in any case, had usually pawned their Sunday clothes and could not attend. And of course the better-off congregations did not want the poor in church with them. They objected on grounds of hygiene to having dirty or disreputable figures using the same seats at different times. They were, unfortunately, right, with the prevalence of typhus in the city, in seeing this a risk to health. In St John's only some 7–8 per cent of the parishioners rented seats, but with Chalmers preaching there was a strong demand for places from people from other parishes.

Chalmers made some use of the pew-renting system. He charged high rents for the morning service, which was attended by a congregation drawn mainly from outwith the parish, and had low rents at an evening service held for the working class. This successfully combined financial and pastoral aims, but did not promote the parish as a social unit. To give close supervision to requests for relief he brought in men from outside to occupy the position of deacon. Most of these, but not all, were middle class. There were twenty-four, and the parish was divided between them. They were to receive requests for aid, and search out need and were expected to know their area well enough to discover what alternative sources to poor relief could be marshalled, whether family or neighbours could help. In many cases they found work for the claimants. It seems likely that they sometimes provided the aid themselves. Only if none of these resources could help was parish relief to be given, and then only if another deacon agreed.

We have no information on whether some claimants died before receiving relief, or removed to another parish. The parish gained population while the scheme was in operation, but that does not mean that people did not leave. There were no economic or social frontiers within the city. Indeed, it was a complaint by those who tried to help the poor that it was impossible often to prove in what parish they had acquired a settlement. During the four years Chalmers was minister the number of parish paupers dropped by a quarter. The old cases, left to be supported by the town's hospital, but later taken on by the parish, also decreased, but since most of these were already elderly that may have been by death. It is to be noted, too, that the numbers of poor in the rest of the city rose.

The deacons, on various occasions, claimed that the work was light. One put it at half an hour a month, another at two hours every three months. Our modern ideas of case work are based on a pattern of thorough investigation produced by the Charity Organisation Society much later in the century, but even after clearing the mind of such standards it is impossible to consider the time allotted by the deacons meant any real investigation. Search into possible means of support would have taken at least half a day. Some deacons admitted to giving their own money in particular cases, and several claimed to have found jobs for the claimants. But clearly in many cases the work of the deacon was to say no.[14]

Chalmers described the St John's development as an experiment but it would be more true to describe it as a demonstration of a fact of which he was already convinced, that even in a large industrialised parish poor relief could be cut down to small doles delivered personally, as it would be in a small rural parish. The idea of a genuine social experiment, that is the testing of a theory in practice under carefully controlled conditions, had not yet entered social study. Nor were the statistical techniques with which to evaluate it yet available. The development of the idea that statistics could be used to find truth rather than simply to support previously held positions is mirrored in the great investigations launched by Parliament into the relief systems and needs of the different parts of the United Kingdom in the 1830s and 1840s. Chalmers's faith in the power of the Scottish Church to solve social problems can be seen in the evidence he gave to the Royal Commission on the Irish Poor in 1830: he accepted Fletcher of Saltoun's estimate of 100,000 vagrants as normal in the 1690s, and explained their non-existence in the records of the early eighteenth century as due to the transforming power of the establishment of presbyterian church government.

The real aim of Chalmers's 'experiment', as is shown in his book, *The Christian and Civic Economy of Large Towns*, and in his articles in the *Edinburgh Review*, was the abolition of the English Poor Law. He was in alliance over this with Malthus, and brought his rhetoric as his main contribution to this cause. In his eyes the new system he had set up in St John's showed how England could proceed. It is probably because of the propaganda purpose of his writing that his description of the special virtues of the Scottish parish system is fairly low in factual reliability. Chalmers asserted that Scottish parishes did not 'hold themselves responsible to the entire subsistence of any of their paupers'. He also claimed that parishes not assessed spent less per pauper than those assessed.[15] The only general figures we have on this point are those in the report of 1818, in which the General Assembly displayed its innumeracy. Part of the table of 'average' costs per pauper by Synods is shown in Table 7.2.

Table 7.2

Synod	Assessed parishes			Non-assessed parishes		
Lothian and Tweeddale	£3.	4.	8¼	£4.	11.	7¼
Galloway	£4.	14.	5¼	£5.	1.	11¼
Perth and Stirling	£3.	3.	4¼	£4.	1.	5¼
Angus and Mearns	£4.	3.	3¼	£4.	17.	4¼

The figures given for the other Synods support or come near to supporting Chalmers's claim. In any case, without a knowledge of the size of the samples these comparisons are not meaningful. They are given here merely to show Chalmers's use of facts in argument.

Chalmers could be dogmatic even in areas of ignorance. For instance, he claimed that the other countries of Europe had no Poor Laws. He also suffered from a strong belief in Scottish moral superiority, writing 'in all parts of England the shameless and abandoned profligacy of the lower orders is most deplorable'. Perhaps it was from this belief that he wanted the English Poor Law to cease all support of illegitimate children. The levels of illegitimacy in the two countries are not known for this period: it was only in the 1850s that the Scottish belief in the superiority of the sexual morals of rural Scotland received the shock of actual figures of illegitimate births, but it is probable that already the levels of illegitimacy in some particular regions of Scotland were high.[16]

In 1823 Chalmers claimed that the St John's experiment was a success. The number of paupers supported by the session had fallen by over a quarter, and the older cases supported by the hospital had also fallen, probably by the natural process of death, so that the parish was prepared to take over the support of the residue directly. Relief based on assessment had disappeared from the parish. We do not know the social cost. If the deacons had been doing their work as Chalmers conceived it and if he had been able to find suitable men for the post from the parish, increased social coherence might have been put in the balance against the incidence of hardship. But Chalmers did not think in such terms and he had brought his elders and deacons in from his earlier Glasgow parish.

The system he had set up was sustained until 1832, but not by Chalmers himself for he left for a university chair and a more agreeable environment in 1823. Despite his propaganda only one other city parish followed the example, St George's, Glasgow, and not for long. Some large rural parishes, Dirleton (East Lothian), Ancrum (Roxburghshire), Langholm and Ruthwell (both in Dumfriesshire) are said to have tried the same system, but since their parish records do not survive it is not possible to evaluate the degree of success.[17] At this time Chalmers's was probably the most influential voice in Britain, and the poor response suggests that parishes found more obstacles to his plan than he realised existed.

One area where Chalmers's views received support in both the world of politics and elsewhere in the Church was his dislike of the idea that the poor could claim a right to relief. He claimed that this idea was new; any legal right was a work of the imagination. It was also undesirable, encouraging 'the rapacity of expectations'. It had apparently become more common, though still not frequent, for dissatisfied applicants for relief to appeal to the sheriff to overrule decisions by parishes. The 1818 report had complained of such overruling. The idea that the poor had a right to relief had frequently been asserted by the Court of Session in the eighteenth century. What was happening, encouraged by Chalmers, was the adding of a new qualification for support to the existing one of destitution, moral character.

Young T. F. Kennedy had entered the House of Commons in 1818. He was one of a distinguished group of 'New Whig' lawyers, mostly young, anxious to get on in politics and held back by the Tory dominance of Scotland. The most engaging and articulate of this group was Henry Cockburn, who has left us various memoirs and some correspondence. There were three others who, like him, became law lords, John Archibald Murray, James Moncrieff and George Cranston. Others included Francis Jeffery, who made his name through the *Edinburgh Review*; John McFarlan, whose father had written on Poor Laws, English and Scottish, and whose brother Patrick was to succeed Chalmers in St John's parish; George Joseph Bell who became responsible for the dominant legal textbooks of the century; and Alexander Dunlop, notable as a legal expert on parochial law. There were also Thomas Thomson, a minister who wrote for the *Christian Instructor*; James Abercromby, a useful source of political advice; and James Graham. Older men associated with this group included the second Lord Minto, the not very forceful politician who had helped Kennedy with his questionnaire; Sir Henry Moncreiff Wellwood, a power in the General Assembly; and the Judge David Monypenny, Lord Pitmilly. It was a strikingly talented clique. Several of these men are described by Cockburn in his posthumously published *Memorials of his Time* and others figure in his *Letters upon the Affairs of Scotland*.

In 1819 Kennedy introduced a Bill in Parliament to end the right of appeal to the sheriff on parish Poor Law decisions in Scotland. This was only one among many efforts in these years to whittle away legal rights to relief, but most of the efforts were for England. For instance, James Scarlett tried to place a legislative ceiling on the total of expenditure on Poor Law matters in England and to end relief to the able-bodied. These various attempts had failed for two reasons: the inability of their supporters to overcome the general acceptance by landed society that relief was desirable; and the determination by the government not to provoke popular disturbance. The year of Peterloo,

1819, was not the time to make life harder for the poor. The government systematically prevented any major change in the Poor Laws of England getting through the Commons.[18] Neither Kennedy nor the Scottish scene were important enough to get his Bill through.

The object of Kennedy's Bill was largely achieved by a different route. The economic problems of adjustment after the war had been particularly difficult in Paisley, a town of rapid growth where industry concentrated on the production of luxury textiles. Large-scale unemployment led a vast crowd of cotton operatives to put forward a claim for relief to the parish and, when it was refused, to the sheriff court, where it was granted. The parish, particularly handicapped in funds by a system of assessment that left out the property of absentee landowners, took the case to the Court of Session.[19]

It is surprising that after nearly 200 years of general operation there should still have been major uncertainties about the Scottish Poor Law, the most significant being the issue of whether people destitute but physically fit, the 'able-bodied' was the new phrase for them, were entitled to relief. Certainly people who appear to have been fit can be found getting relief in the eighteenth century. The resolution of Currie (Midlothian) Kirk Session to support all 'housekeepers' through the season of the 1740 harvest failure made no selection of the unfit. Help might be given to a man who had suffered an economic setback, such as the loss of a horse, or a domestic disaster, the burning down of his house or the birth of triplets. Most such instances seem to have been in unassessed parishes because most parishes were unassessed. In assessed parishes the Kirk Session was supposed to have free disposal of half of the collection money, and could use it for particular cases of need: there is very little sign of active supervision by heritors of the spending of this money, despite the Humbie decision.

Late in the century there are instances of claims that the Poor Law did not cover particular cases. For instance, there was a legal attempt to exclude foundlings from it, and in 1780 in a case at Dunnichen, where the heritors refused to pay a wet nurse for a family where the father was able-bodied, the Court of Session supported their interpretation of the law.[20] The help given by Edinburgh to the unemployed in the early nineteenth century was carefully based on voluntary subscription.[21] But it might be expected that the decision in *Pollock* v. *Darling*, though not unanimous, would have settled the matter. It did not do so because many people, notably lawyers, felt that destitution caused by harvest failure was in some way different from destitution caused by unemployment. Landed society, of which lawyers and Judges were a part, felt very strongly that harvest failure demanded drastic action. They did not think the same about a slump.

But there is a fair amount of legal opinion which supported the legality of relief for the unemployed. Two legal textbooks on the powers and duties of Justices of the Peace take this line, and so did the Professor of Law at Glasgow University, Robert Davidson.[22] Davidson clearly recognised *Pollock* v. *Darling* as authoritative, and stated that it gave 'the industrious poor' a right to relief, though he added a somewhat fatuous caution that the allowance should be 'moderate'. (No parish in Scotland would have given any allowance that it did not consider moderate.) Even Henry Cockburn, who wrote privately of aid to the unemployed as equivalent to having his pocket picked by them, admitted in the article he wrote for the *Edinburgh Review* that such aid was legal.[23] The voices of this period which state clearly that the unemployed were not entitled to relief were not those of accepted legal authorities.[24] Advocates, though, would state that the description in the 1579 Act of those eligible for relief, 'the poor, aged and impotent' should be interpreted as 'poor and aged' and 'poor and impotent'. This view is expressly stated in the 1859 edition of John Guthrie Smith's textbook on the Poor Law.

Richmond and others (conservatively estimated at 850) v. *The Heritors and Kirk Session of the Abbey Parish of Paisley* was settled by Lord Pitmilly in an Outer House decision against the operatives. The Judge did not enter into the issue of entitlement, a topic on which Cockburn and his friends were nervous, but stated instead that the decision of the sheriff was invalid since sheriffs had no appellant jurisdiction in matters of law and the parish was not a court of record.[25] This effectively left every parish in charge of its own relief decisions, except for the unlikely instance of some dissatisfied applicant managing to gather technical help and resources to enable him to appeal to the Court of Session. Such an appeal would not incur legal fees but it would require unpaid help, and the applicant would have to survive without resources until the court sat. (The eighteenth-century Court of Session processes on the Poor Law had been brought either by kirk sessions or by heritors, not by the poor.) The aim of Kennedy's Bill had largely been achieved. Kennedy had also wished to abolish appeal to the Court of Session, but this was seen as of minor importance.

The New Whigs were not fully satisfied. These men held very strongly, as did most property owners, to the sacredness of property, but they also saw themselves as working professional men. If they did not expect parochial aid in hard times, why should anyone else? There was, and it is no surprise, a failure to recognise that the law is of all employment, the least subject to the swings of the business cycle: people quarrel as much when trade is bad as when it is good. They feared that the Court of Session might override its own decision.

Kennedy had prepared another Bill with help from Chalmers. Its effect would be much what Chalmers had proposed for St John's parish. Assessment would be reserved for cases already receiving support, who would eventually die off. All others should rely on voluntary aid from the congregation under the management of the Kirk Session. There would be no appeal on any matter of relief from the decision of the session. Sessions would probably have to adopt something like the St John's system. Property would have no legal obligation to the poor, but presumably there would be enough rich and conscientious men, even if they had to be borrowed from other parishes, to control and help the deserving cases.[26]

Kennedy introduced the Bill into the Commons at midnight in April 1824, a time which meant that there would be little debate on the first reading and that the second reading would coincide with the General Assembly in May. The Bill produced indignant protests from several presbyteries and county meetings and the press carried considerable criticism. Even the *Scotsman*, a thoroughly Whig paper, did not offer support. Cockburn soothed Kennedy by labelling his opponents 'the whole fools in the kingdom', but in fact the opposition was from people who knew and worked the existing system, and could see the need for it.

The climax over the Bill came in the response of the General Assembly, still a body far more representative of educated Scottish opinion than the Members of Parliament. The Assembly was strongly opposed to the Bill. The best compromise vote that Chalmers, Moderator that year, could settle for was that it was inexpedient. Chalmers himself felt obliged to vote for this. Only one vote went the other way, that of John Archibald Murray. The Lord Advocate, who had been indignant at the surreptitious introduction of the Bill, was able to report that all public bodies in Scotland were against it, and Kennedy had to withdraw it.

The Whig clique had still one more weapon with which to reduce the effectiveness of the Scottish Poor law, the fact that it contained many of the brightest lawyers of the day. George Joseph Bell in 1829 brought out what was to become the standard textbook of Scottish law for the nineteenth century, in which he simply ignored *Pollock* v. *Darling* and asserted that only the disabled and impotent had a claim for relief.[27] Alexander Dunlop added an explanation that relied on Malthusian thought: in his *Parochial Law* he acknowledged the existence of *Pollock* v. *Darling* but explained that it had come in an era of inadequate economic understanding: 'the dread which was then entertained of persons . . . incurring the danger of starvation if not supported by compulsory provision, has been completely removed, by the greater knowledge which has been acquired, as to the true causes and remedies of pauperism'. He held that the Court of Session would no longer follow that precedent. Statutes of the seventeenth century that ordered the unemployed to be provided with work were merely 'regulations of police for the security of the public'.[28] He interpreted 'disabled' as a qualification for relief to adults to mean permanent disablement: a broken leg or an attack of typhoid would not count. It is unlikely that Malthus himself thought that knowledge of political economy would help an individual case of threatened starvation, but he could supply the intellectual justification for overruling the precedent. Lord Pitmilly went further and labelled the use of assessment to support the unemployed illegal, and stated that such claims were explicitly covered by the fact that the session controlled half the collection money.[29] The myth that the Poor Law did not support the unemployed and never had, became accepted historical belief.

NOTES

1. NLS MS 12177, letter dated 18 August 1815. For the whole attempt to reduce or destroy the Scottish Poor Law see my chapter, 'The creation of the disablement rule in the Scottish Poor Law', in T. C. Smout (ed.), *The Search for Wealth and Stability* (London, 1978), pp. 199–217.
2. The returns are in the possession of Lord Moncrieff of Tullybole, by whose kindness I have been able to consult them.
3. M. Blaug, 'The myth of the Old Poor Law and the making of the New',

Journal of Economic History, 23, 1963, pp. 51–84; also 'The Poor Law Report re-examined', ibid., 24, 1964, pp. 221–45.

4. June Irving, 'The Scottish Poor Law: response to the 1816 harvest failure', M.A. thesis, Department of Economic and Social History, Edinburgh University, 1982.

5. J. R. Poynter, *Society and Pauperism* (London, 1969).

6. SRO CH1/1/78–9. General Assembly papers.

7. This report can be found in various volumes of the Parliamentary Papers, most conveniently in *PP* 1817 VI, Report of the Select Committee appointed to consider of the Poor Laws.

8. *PP* 1818 V, Appendix to the Report of the Lords' Committee on the Poor Laws no. 30, Report of the Committee of the General Assembly on the letter to the Moderator by the Earl of Hardwicke.

9. The Revd Robert Burns, *Historical Dissertations with Regard to the Poor* (Edinburgh, 1819).

10. *PP* 1819 II, interview of Sturges Bourne's committee with the Revd Henry Duncan, 19 March 1819.

11. *An Essay on the Principles of Population* (London, 1803), pp. 531, 538.

12. Olive Checkland, *Philanthropy in Victorian Scotland* (Edinburgh, 1980) gives a picture of the scale and variety of charitable organisations at a somewhat later date.

13. Callum Brown, 'The costs of pew-renting; church management, church-going and social class in nineteenth-century Glasgow', *Journal of Ecclesiastical History*, 38, 1987, pp. 347–61.

14. The best account of Chalmers's views on poor relief is in his evidence to the Select Committee on the Irish Poor, *PP* 1830, VII pp. 279–339. For the St John's system see R. A. Cage and E. O. A. Checkland, 'Thomas Chalmers and urban poverty: the St John's Experiment in Glasgow, 1819–1837', *Philosophical Journal*, XIII, spring 1976, pp. 37–56. In his evidence to the committee for the Irish Poor Chalmers quotes a deacon as saying that 'the immediate readiness of the deacons at all times to procure employment . . . serves as a check against the lazy'.

15. The Revd Thomas Chalmers, *The Christian and Civic Economy of Large Towns* (1821–6), ch. 14, p. 234.

16. There is a detailed examination of the problems and scale of illegitimacy in Victorian north-east Scotland and of New Poor Law policy on the matter in Andrew Blaikie, *Illegitimacy, Sex and Society* (Oxford, 1993), ch. 4.

17. Stewart J. Brown, *Thomas Chalmers and the Godly Commonwealth in Scotland* (Oxford, 1988), ch. 3.

18. J. R. Poynter, *Society and Pauperism*. Kennedy's bill can be found in *PP* 1819 IB (180).

19. W. M. Morison, *Dictionary of Decisions* p. 10,577, vols xxv–xxvi, p. 10,577, *Richmond and others* v. *The heritors and Kirk Session of the Abbey parish of Paisley. Faculty Decisions*, 27 November 1821.

20. Court of Session papers in the Signet Library, 416; 56; June 1800, the case of John Brand.
21. ECA Papers on Relief of the Labouring Poor, 1809–10.
22. R. Davidson, *A Short Exhibition of the Poor Laws of Scotland, drawn from authentic documents* (Glasgow, 1816); G. Tait, *Summary of the Powers and Duties of a Justice of the Peace in Scotland* (Edinburgh, 1818), p. 368; G. Hutcheson, *A Treatise on the Office of Justice of the Peace, Constable, etc. in Scotland* (Edinburgh, 1815), vol. ii, p. 54.
23. *Edinburgh Review*, October 1824.
24. E.g. the Revd Robert Burns, *Historical Dissatations*. See also J. Anderson, *The Bee*, 1793–4.
25. *Faculty Decisions*, 29 December 1821.
26. Stewart J. Brown, *Godly Commonwealth*, ch. 4, part I. Kennedy's second Bill can be read in *PP* 1824 II (217). For discussion see *Caledonian Mercury*, May 1824, *Scotsman*, May and June 1824.
27. George Joseph Bell, *Principles of the Law of Scotland* (Edinburgh, 1829), p. 281.
28. A. M. Dunlop, *Parochial Law* (Edinburgh, 1835), pp. 325, 419.
29. David Monypenny, Lord Pitmilly, *Remarks on the Poor Laws* (Edinburgh, 1834), chs 7, 10, 11, 12.

CHAPTER 8

THE NEED FOR REFORM

The Scotland of the 1830s differed greatly from the country which in the mid-eighteenth century had, at least in the Lowlands, got the skimpy Poor Law to function effectively. The transformation of lowland agriculture after 1760 had led to a drastic tailoring of the rural population in the interests of productivity.[1] The large class of cottars, who had been attached to the old farms with small holdings of their own, had mostly been moved away, usually into villages where they provided labour for the farmers. Their semi-independent existence had been changed to landless and dependent positions, as hind, ploughman or day labourer. Since the labour needs of the new farming were sometimes less than those of the old, and often specialised, many men and women had had to cease being part of the agricultural system. They would be working on the roads, in industry or in domestic service, perhaps in some town. Agricultural productivity could now support a large industrial economy. Steam power meant that much of this was coming to concentrate in the larger towns, in particular those of the central valley. Population had expanded rapidly, encouraged by the opportunities of factory work for children and young people.

The productivity of the Lowlands had led to a deterioration in the Highland economy. Highland industry could not compete with that of the Lowlands and efforts to find new export commodities had failed. The Highlands were now exporting people, but not fast enough to restore the standard of living.

That the new economy did not produce an entirely beneficent world is clear to anyone who compares the tone of voice of the reports in the *OSA* written in the 1790s with that of the *NSA*, mostly made in the 1830s. The *OSA* has a buoyancy which the *NSA* lacks. By the 1830s many of the small industrial developments recorded in the *OSA* which had provided employment had succumbed to the competition of larger units. Service areas such as Dunkeld, which had developed in the Highlands had lost their function. Improved transport, mostly in the form of better roads, had largely removed the risk of starvation if a harvest failed, but there could still be great hardship. Capitalised farming made the farmers selective in their demand for labour: the weak, the old and the handicapped would be last in their choice. If there was no offer of work at a hiring fair, those not chosen knew they had to leave. The demand for female labour varied according to the type of farming chosen for productivity, but there were jobs in town. The hand spinning which had played an important part in household finances had given way to factory production.

The labour force faced a threat which though not new was on a new scale, the contraction of economic activity in a slump. In the past, war or famine had led to unemployment, particularly in the towns: this had, for instance, been conspicuous in the years 1740–2, when harsh weather and the opening of a European war had cut down many activities. But the slumps produced by the business cycle, in 1826–7 or 1837 for instance, were of a new intensity.

The risk of extreme poverty appears to have increased. Local specialisations of work could lead to unemployment for parts of the workforce, notably for older women and anyone with a physical handicap. Reorganised agriculture not only did not want the old, it wanted their cottages for men of greater work capacity, or it wanted these destroyed lest they be used by the unproductive. The old were encouraged to shift to the towns and try to pick up a living there. Safety was of low priority in the new factories and maimed workers had no legal claim on their employers, though some of the larger works, the colliery at Auchterderran (Fife), for instance, ran an insurance scheme for the employees.[2] The big open floors of the factories were places where infections spread easily: in particular tuberculosis was rife. Many factories were still powered by water, and had to shut down in drought, laying off all workers. Families might be deprived of male wage earners by old injuries from the Peninsular war, or by imprisonment or deportation for crime. 'Fever', probably typhus, raged through the poorer areas of the cities on an intensifying scale: cholera struck hard in 1832. It left Dumfries, for instance, with fifty-three extra orphans to care for.[3]

The economic and social world of industrialising society was very different from that in which the Poor Law had developed, and produced a different ideology. Property was still seen as absolute, but the attitude of those possessed of it to those not so endowed had become harsher. In particular the approach to destitution had become more hostile. Poverty was seen as predominantly the fault of those who experienced it. Failure to think ahead, failure to save every possible penny for hard times in the future, imprudent marriage, waste of resources on the occasional or regular alcoholic drink, the use of tea, sugar, snuff or tobacco, luxuries that the unskilled worker should do without, were seen as the main reasons for impoverishment. The fact that no amount of austerity and foresight could provide for loss of work by injury, disease, old age or the increasingly devastating slumps was ignored.

The climate of political and economic ideas is often described as *laissez-faire*. Business enterprise was to be completely free, and the right of employers to set wages, employ whom they found advantageous and sack those they did not were all part of the economic creed. Factory Acts were, in the 1830s, making a small dent in these assumptions, but the intellectual structure had not changed. At the same time the freedom of the workforce was limited, for the contract of employment was not an equal one. Only in limited terms was there acceptance of a right to strike and to form trade unions. Workers were evaluated not in terms of the expression of individuality but in terms of reliability in the labour force and of submission to conventions.

The gathering of large bodies of people of limited resources in the greater towns was seen as a threat to public order. The middle classes which dominated these towns held it as necessary to provide some sort of basic resource for the labour force when members were in difficulties. It tended to enshrine this support in substantial buildings. Sometimes there were special collections for unemployed workers, as in Edinburgh in 1809-10.[4] The towns had their hospitals for the reception of the poor, their charity workhouses, schools, infirmaries, bridewells, prisons, asylums and houses of refuge: each institution carried part of the poor, but still there were people who slid between the definitions of admission to them. And the numbers, within and outwith these institutions, grew.

Charity must necessarily depend on the climate of opinion, and a large part of the resources of the Scottish Poor Law was charitable – church collections, the extra generosity shown at the annual communion, legacies and endowments were what sustained poor relief almost completely in three-quarters of Scotland's parishes, and were a significant element even in those where relief was based on assessment. In the great towns, though relief had passed in the later eighteenth century into the hands of the town councils, church collections were still a noticeable element in the money available. It was not only in Scotland that articulate public opinion had come to claim that poverty was usually the result of moral flaws,[5] but in Scotland the low level of statute-based relief made these views particularly influential. They had been built into the teaching and preaching of the most influential figure of the 1820s and 1830s, Thomas Chalmers, whose restrictive idea of the proper role of poor relief had been systematically expounded to his theological students for many years. 'The appropriate remedy for the evils of want is to be found, not in the justice of man, but in the compassion of man' he had said.[6] When Chalmers left St John's, Glasgow, he went to an academic post from which, for the next twenty odd years, he impressed his views on those in training for the ministry. In particular Chalmers's rhetoric was aimed against raising statutory funds for poor relief, the method laid down in the statutes of the 1570s. The pauper supported by assessment had lost his independence, whereas the man or woman who relied on help from neighbours, kin, the charity of the parish or of past employers, or even on begging, deplorable though that was, was still 'independent'. The semantics behind this view are difficult to enter into today. A surprising gap in the line of argument is the failure to apply it to groups other than the poor, notably to the parish ministers themselves. Their incomes were derived from a tax on land in their parishes established in the seventeenth century. If such a source of revenue sapped independence, then perhaps it explains the failure of most of the ministry to put pressure on the landowners, who paid their stipends, to care adequately for the poor.

The new climate of opinion and the more rigid class system of the nineteenth century had brought into use a new vocabulary. The word 'poor' was taken to cover the whole working class: in the past the word for those of this class who had work had been the 'industrious poor'. 'Poor' also included the destitute. 'Able-bodied' was the term for those in work, but it also covered those incapacitated by sickness or injury not expected to be permanent, so a man in bed with pneumonia or a broken leg was referred to as 'able-bodied'. 'An independent man', a phrase which in the eighteenth century had meant someone who owned land or capital, and was therefore not dependent on decisions of others about a tenancy or employment, now meant a man who earned his and his family's living. The problem of defining settlement, statutorily an area of some confusion, had produced a new idea, 'industrial settlement' – a term not found in the statutes of the Poor Law. By this concept the Poor Law official of a town could refuse support to people who, though they had lived in an urban parish for more than three years, could not be shown to have earned their living throughout that period, or alternatively had not in person paid the rent. Another verbal newcomer in general parlance, though not a new word, was 'pauper', used not to denote an individual in poverty but one receiving aid from the Poor Law.

Scotland in the eighteenth century had experienced legislative inertia. Parliament had not been busy producing significant legal change, and had largely consisted of people unfamiliar with Scottish law. Henry Dundas had secured some minor desirable changes, but for the most part the country had escaped legislative notice. Well into the nineteenth century very little of parliamentary debate had concerned Scotland, but Scottish systems, issues and developments figure in Parliamentary Papers, often in a subsidiary role to changes planned for England or Ireland. But by the 1830s the legislative inertia of the eighteenth century had passed. Government now saw its role as interventionist; its duty to deal with evils and abuses. There were Passenger Acts, Police Acts, Factory Acts, Public Health Acts, and some of these extended, usually in a modified form, to Scotland. There had been in the years after 1815 an enormous public concern over the English Poor Law, and in the 1830s there had also been a demand for a Poor Law for Ireland, not so much for the benefit of the Irish poor but for the relief of English Poor Law authorities.[7]

The more extreme views on poverty in England had failed to get the English Poor Law abolished, but the expression of concern had been so great that an early action of the Whig government which came to power at the end of 1830 was to set up the famous Royal Commission on the working of the English Poor Law. This was appointed in February 1832. It was made clear that a rapid reply, and one which would lead to important legislative change, was expected. The commission circulated questionnaires to parishes, which for the most part were never returned. The main body of evidence came from twenty-six assistant commissioners who visited a collection of parishes selected on no statistical plan. Evidence flowed in, but the commissioners had written their report before all of it was available.

The report made a major inroad into the basic idea that the poor had a right to relief. The exercise of this right by the able-bodied was to be made only with the acceptance of the discipline of a workhouse, which meant confinement, sexual segregation and discipline. The 'workhouse test' thus meant that the offer of relief was conditional on the acceptance of discouraging conditions. Poor relief was removed from its parish base, which in many cases was too small for adequate classification of the poor, to the union of parishes, a unit capable of sustaining a large and regimented workhouse, and a central authority was created to make sure that the principles of the new ethos were adhered to.

The intellectual climate of the 1830s was dominated by political economy, and in the theories of this opinion the support of people not in gainful occupation or the possession of other resources was seen as a drag on the functioning of the economy. It was also an important time in the development of the statistical movement. Increasingly figures were seen as proving social opinions by providing a factual base. Figures were going to stay, to dominate investigations into social conditions and to provide a support for social theories. In the early days of this movement facts and figures were sought naively to support beliefs already held, as they are sometimes still today. The concepts of normal distribution and statistical significance were not at first appreciated. It was in this somewhat crude enthusiasm for numerical facts that the basis of the ten volumes of evidence, drawn from that collected by the assistant commissioners, was put together. Much was made of the fact that in one parish the bill for poor rates had surpassed the rental. No careful investigation was made into how widespread were the relief practices which were held to impede the free working of the economy, for instance, the grant of allowances to men at work who had large families. Instances rather than analysis were to be the base of rhetoric.

There had been strong pressure for major changes in the English Poor Law. The changes, when in 1834 they came, did not make as big an impression in Scotland in newspapers and comment as might have been expected. This was partly because the Scots had, since 1780, been commenting on the faults of the English system and congratulating themselves on their own model. Because their system did not share the conspicuous faults of the English one, they assumed that it was not in need of change. In any case the dramatic event of 1834 in Scotland was the passing of the Veto Act in the General Assembly in May. This marked the decision of the majority party in the Assembly, the Evangelicals, to defy the law on patronage.

The Veto Act forbade presbyteries to admit to parish benefices any proposed minister whose application was not supported by a majority vote of the male heads of communicating households in the parish. This was a repudiation of the system of patronage which had existed for most of the seventeenth century and also since 1712, by which specific patrons had the right to appoint. It was also, less obviously, a subversion of the system by which the main power of decision making in the Church lay with the presbyteries. The Veto Act did not at once produce trouble but sooner or later some candidate for the ministry, fully qualified in learning and dogma, would be rejected by the householders of a parish with no reason asked or given, and would go to law to claim what he saw as his rights and the rights of his patron. The civil courts would not regard as authoritative the vote of the General Assembly in matters involving property and stipends and would override the parish veto. The presbytery would then intervene on one side or the other, risking thereby either civil or ecclesiastical penalties which neither side would be slow to hand out. Each side would then encroach on the territory of the other, the state forbidding various ministers to carry out their ecclesiastical duties and the Church deposing ministers who obeyed the civil law. The battle between the Assembly and the civil courts was to reach a climax in May 1843 with the 'Disruption', when nearly 40 per cent of the parish ministers left the Church of Scotland to form the Free Church.

Although prepared to fight over the issue of patronage, the Church of the early nineteenth century had allowed its national position to be eroded in many ways. In earlier days it had provided almost all that there had been of local government except in the towns. Its sessions had disciplined the people, supervised the school system and been the source of what social welfare there was. No longer. Police Acts made a base for control of many activities and did much to suppress vagrancy and limit begging. The public health movement, initiated in the scare over the cholera epidemic of 1831-2, was also secular. In 1842 the investigation led by Edwin Chadwick into the spectacularly insanitary state of the larger Scottish towns saw no need to make links with the Church. The philanthropic approach to lunacy, which had produced asylums in the main towns, starting with Montrose in 1782, and pioneered a new standard of care, was also secular. The Church was being bypassed as new elements of provision and control were being set up.

The Church had also not prevented a purely secular manipulation of its parish rolls of the poor. Court fees in legal disputes were not charged on the poor. Most litigation was by people of property, untouched by this practice, but there was an area extending to those of limited means, divorce. Those who sought a divorce in the Commissary Court or those who resisted one might claim a place on the parish roll, even though such people would not be considered qualified for relief. Ministers and elders were prepared to issue certificates of poverty to those certainly not paupers.

There were some parishes where there was a real battle between ecclesiastical and lay. The *NSA* describes one such in Neilston (Renfrewshire) where the heritors attempted to prevent parishioners who could not pay seat rents from using the parish church. To fight this the kirk session had to go to the Court of Session for permission to have a second collecting plate for the expence of litigation.[8] It is claimed in the *NSA* that there were other similar local battles between parishes and landowners.

A different fight was being successfully carried on in Auldearn (Nairnshire). Here a landowner objected to what he called 'non-intrusionist' meetings being held in the parish church. (Non-intrusion was the somewhat misleading name adopted by the anti-patronage side of the Church in its struggle.) This landowner had obtained an injunction which prohibited committees being held in the parish church: the minister promptly declared that in that case the kirk session could not conduct Poor Law business. The support of the poor was thereby handed to the heritors: church collections for it ceased and the heritors had to take on assessment.[9] But on the whole there were few battles between parishes and their landowners except on the issue of patronage.

In several of the bigger towns the administration of relief had passed from the Church to the town council in the eighteenth century. In Edinburgh this had happened as early as 1740. Aberdeen in 1758 had set up a system by which the bulk of the funds for the poor, some 73 per cent, had come from church collections but was handled by a committee dominated by the council. In 1840 a quarrel between the session and the magistrates led the session to hold back funds, so the town was forced to adopt assessment. In Glasgow, except for the special arrangements made for Chalmers in St John's, relief was conducted by the lay organisation of the town's hospital.

We are not as well equipped with information about the situation in the 1830s as might be expected. The Church committee which organised the *NSA*, a work that might be expected to be a major source, chose, on the subject of the poor, not to ask for information in general but for reply to a leading question. This is evident from the content of the bulk of the replies, and indeed the question is quoted in the reply of the minister of Ayton (Lanarkshire): 'whether there is any disposition among the poor to refrain from seeking parish relief, and whether they consider it degrading'. This is very similar to questions in the 1818 General Assembly's report. There, question 8 asks 'is dependence on the assessment lessening in your opinion, the reluctance of the people to apply for aid?': and question 9, 'although there may not have been an actual assessment hitherto, is it your opinion that reluctance to apply for parochial charity is generally diminishing?' The working of the Poor Law is given scant attention by such loaded questions. Still, the *NSA* gives a picture of fairly routine working of the system. The percentage of the local population on some sort of relief varies between $2\frac{1}{2}$ and 5 per cent: little detail is given about the allowances paid.

There is a fuller report by the General Assembly of the Church, made in 1839 and based on returns from 879 of the existing 895 parishes. This contains a considerable amount of information.[10] The enquiry was particularly concerned with assessment. It pointed out that the returns it had received showed the average cost of a pauper to have been marginally higher in the non-assessed parishes than in the assessed, but the range in cost was so great as to make this a not particularly meaningful statistic. The report gives a historical survey which states that compulsory assessment 'was at a very early period permitted', and implies that the legislation of the 1570s put its main stress on voluntary sources. This shows a lack of elementary historical research. The Act of 1579 orders assessment generally: there is no question of mere 'permission'. The difference between the practice of the Scottish Poor Law and its statutory base had become wide, but that between statute law and the Church's view of it was even wider. Yet this report has a much stronger sense of history than had earlier Church statements. For instance, it recognised that assessment had been temporarily adopted by various parishes in the food crises of the seventeenth and eighteenth centuries. It was ignorant of evidence of early assessment not related to such crises.

What the report of 1839 shows is the growth of poverty in the 1830s. This had forced numerous parishes to take on assessment. By 1839,

226 parishes were assessed: of these 33 had become so in that decade, whereas in the 1820s only 11 had so changed. All types of parish give examples of an increasing inability to meet the needs of the poor. The manager of the poor in Edinburgh's West Kirk parish complained in 1843 that begging had gone up tenfold in the previous seven years, though there had been very little increase in population. The clerk to Stirling Hospital, an institution not for the sick but for the poor, also complained of a vast increase in need. There had been a striking rise in the number of cases of 'fever'. This now came in epidemic form, which suggests typhus. In Glasgow and Dundee the deaths from it had increased sharply. But it also struck smaller towns: Cupar (Fife), for instance, suffered frequently.[11] It was a major reason why the crude death rate had risen in the cities. It was not yet understood how the disease spread, but it was generally recognised as an indicator of extreme poverty and squalor. And fever deaths of wage-earners increased the number of families thrown on relief.

Other factors increased the burden on the Poor Law. An obvious one was the increase in membership of the various dissenting churches.[12] The Roman Catholic confession in Scotland was mostly of migrants from Ireland and their offspring, and such people earned low wages, which made it impossible for them to make much in the way of donations to other poor people. The various bodies of dissenting Protestantism in some cases directed part of their collections to their poor, but this meant the poor who were communicating members, not the congregation as a whole. In any case the first charges on funds were the salary of the minister and the costs of a chapel. Much of the charitable giving in church collections had not been entirely voluntary. The large amount of bad coinage received by Church in their collections is evidence of the felt need to be seen to give at least a halfpenny when leaving church. In 1772, for instance, Edrom (Berwickshire) had sold 6 pounds weight of bad halfpence. Farm wages had always supplied only a small income and in some areas these had fallen. It had become difficult for the wives of farm workers to contribute to household funds since the main activity that had sustained this, spinning, had now moved to factory production. The year 1836 had seen a bad shortfall in the harvest and the distress which this had caused merged with wider distress and unemployment in 1837. A particularly large group of workers, the handloom weavers, were now on bare survival incomes. Yet this craft continued to recruit, partly because a weaver needed the assistance of a child.[13] In Glasgow, the second most populous city in the British Isles, with a relatively large low-wage component, the level of real wages had sunk by between 15 and 24 per cent since the end of the Napoleonic wars.[14]

There were of course areas of improved provision and welfare. There had been expansion in the provision of infirmaries, dispensaries and lunatic asylums. There were specialised institutions for training the blind or the deaf and dumb. These helped the poor but it might be at high cost to the parish. An asylum might charge as much as £26 a year for a patient. Some big firms, collieries and other major works, supplied compulsory sick insurance for their workers. The Loch Catrine cotton company gave pensions to its workforce. In Blantyre the workers had since 1817 enforced their own assessment for the poor and in New Lanark the company supplemented a similar scheme. Edinburgh had a host of charities for particular groups, mostly sustained by a small stage army of the good, but these institutions supported only particular cases with special claims, not the mass of simple destitution. The most important institutions of the past that had given the working class some security, friendly societies, were in many areas in decline or broken up, because of the lack of sound actuarial information. The other institutions for the prudent approach to the future, savings banks, had always had a narrow appeal, and the deterioration of class relations meant that they were suspected of passing information on to employers which could make possible cuts in wages.

An important element in the structure of poverty was the immigration of the Irish. This had been in train for some decades, but was enhanced by the creation of steam navigation. Irish men and women could arrive in south-west Scotland in a few hours at the cost of 6 pence, and were regarded by employers as particularly valuable labour. Many had settled and married in Scotland. Even the second-generation Irish were treated as low-wage labour. Everywhere the Irish filled the bottom slots in a way that shows how little the Act of Union of 1800 had produced a sensation of a single nationhood. Their need to accept any wage, however low, pulled down the general level of wages for unskilled work. Glasgow and Dundee had become predominantly industrial cities and the Irish swarmed into them for work. By 1831 over a sixth of the inhabitants of Glasgow had been born in Ireland.[15]

There was confusion over the parish structure of the country. The church of Scotland had set up extra parishes with their role confined to religion and was raising funds for 200 new churches. These activities deflected part of charitable giving from the poor, and led to further arguments in the Court of Session over whether the collections in such churches should rightly go to the older established parishes. High pew rents in city churches, and even in some country ones, kept out much of the working class and also limited church funds.

There were increasing claims on parish funds in town parishes and in those rural parishes unlucky enough to be on a main road, through the system of passes. Passes were papers ordering the transfer of a pauper to his or her parish of settlement. Since paupers had to be infirm to claim relief they could not be expected to walk long distances, so carts and drivers had to be hired. There were, of course, abuses to the system, with parishes getting rid of claimants with very little evidence about their settlement. The system seems to have been a windfall for the carters.

The Irish could arrive cheaply, but they could also be cheaply dispatched once Ireland was presented with a Poor Law in 1838. A Poor Law, however inadequate, meant that there would be some system of support at the other end. Dundee sent so many Irish back home that it had found it profitable to negotiate special rates on the ferries to Dublin and Belfast. To the latter town a passage for the infirm could be got from 1 shilling and 5 pence, though the rest of the journey from Dundee by passes might send the total cost to 10 shillings. Passes cost half of the collection money in Channelkirk (Berwickshire).

Some part of the pass traffic was a racket. Currie parish, near to Edinburgh, reported cases being returned, ostensibly from Glasgow, on the same day that they had been sent. A similar story was retailed from Laurencekirk, on the road between Aberdeen and Perth. In an Annan case an old woman was carted off six or seven times, being simply taken out of one end of the town and sent in again at the other. There were tales of people sent around while dying. A man from Dalziel (Lanarkshire), dumped at the door of Rutherglen's treasurer, died two days later. In the south of England it was paupers who worked the racket. One woman, giving the name Jane Sinclair, but with no claim to Scottish nationality, commented to an observer that the name was never kept the same for different journeys.[16] She turned up afterwards as Ann Anderson.

There were also those categorised as vagrants. Surges of unemployment would send thousands onto the roads looking for work, and of these there were inevitably some who preferred begging to working. Those arrested by the police for vagrancy were not considered the responsibility of the Poor Law. The Police Act of 1840 allowed counties to raise funds for rural policing, and many lowland counties took advantage of this with a resulting sharp drop in complaints about vagrancy. Life in gaol was probably more comfortable, and the food there more adequate, than life on poor relief.

Begging done by outside vagrants might be regarded as criminal, but for many on relief it was necessary, since parish allowances were rarely adequate. Many towns specifically permitted their poor to beg, some at any time, others on a specified day, usually Saturday. Permits, as in Cumbertrees (Dumfriesshire), or badges, as in Irvine or Kirkcudbright, indicated who was a local pauper. Urban paupers might also make begging excursions into the country, from which many of them had migrated. There had been a move to the setting up of mendicity societies, which collected beggars, supported them or put them in gaol. These had mostly collapsed because the number of beggars outstripped resources. Kirkcaldy had suffered from a persistent old man who clearly enjoyed begging. When he refused to desist the police had gaoled him. He had then hanged himself, making the town less keen on the suppression of begging.

It was generally recognised that allowances were so small that the poor had to beg. What had to be agreed was the level of such activity that was to be tolerated. The attitude of the Church under the sway of Thomas Chalmers was that charitable relief was not corrupting. With this tenet dominant it was impossible to suppress begging. It is worth noting that Chalmers, ready to denounce the damage caused to a person's moral fibre by state support, does not seem to have considered the damage done to recipients of begged alms, or the damage done to the moral qualities of those who refused aid.

One of the difficulties of working the Poor Law in the countryside stemmed from the non-residence of many heritors. Estates had been built up by inheritance and marriage alliances, and often did not lie in a single parish. Often only one or two heritors were resident, the rest strangers to the parish. As such these did not provide much in employment, and might feel little obligation towards the local society from which they drew rents. They were not present at church, and so did not contribute to collections. Only if the minister wrote to them asking for money would they be aware of the needs of the parish, unless the parish had adopted assessment. And the period of strife over the Veto Act was not one when many landowners were likely to feel obliged to give when asked by the minister.

Non-resident heritors would be drawn into parish affairs if they and the resident heritors felt obliged to adopt voluntary assessment. Pressure for this system increased during the 1830s. A parish year by year would find its funds did not permit what was regarded as an adequate level of relief. For a few years it might tide over the gap by encroaching on its capital reserves, the legacies of the past. Sometimes these would be totally used up before any other course was considered, more often they were partially protected, and the heritors would be forced to recognise that assessment was inevitable. Voluntary assessment, though it cost as much as formal legal assessment, did not appear so permanent. Times might ease, and then it could easily be dropped. It had one basic weakness, though. The tenants could not be made to pay half the total sum, as they could with legal assessment. An effort to push the tenantry into such a scheme in North Berwick had failed and forced the parish to return to legal assessment. Voluntary assessment did not make a mark against the value of the estate, as legal assessment did, for any landowner could drop out of the system at will. That if he did so the parish would probably be on legal assessment in a couple of years could be ignored. If an estate was in the hands of trustees these might feel that they must resist any formal deterioration of its nominal income, and so prefer the voluntary to the legal assessment.

Adoption of legal assessment would usually mean at once, or very soon, a sharp rise in the money needed. There would be higher collecting costs. Tenants would have to be made to pay, either by real rent or by 'means and substance'. Decisions would have to be made where to cut off the obligation to pay, since nobody wished to drive the poorer end of the tenantry into needing relief themselves. Even if a limit was set at rent of £5 a year, there would be some just above unable or unwilling to pay, so summonses would have to be issued. The lesser tenantry had often helped the poor, giving them free potato ground, left-overs at the house and cast-off clothes. Now they would feel under less of an obligation to contribute to church collections since they were being taxed. They might encourage needy relatives to apply for relief instead of aiding them themselves. It was a normal experience for a parish adopting assessment to find its needs rise and its collections fall.

Parishes could mix the type of assessment according to tenure, and in burghal parishes distinguish between the 'landward' part and the town. This was given legal approval by a case for Dunbar in 1833, though it was contradicted by a subsequent case in 1838.[17] Neither decision appears to have had any effect in practice. Assessment was not levied on some persons, which meant that others had to pay more. In Edinburgh members of the College of Justice, that is all advocates and Judges, owners of some 13 per cent of the town's property, were exempt, despite their relative affluence. In Paisley non-resident heritors were not expected to pay, a ruling which had a disastrous effect on the amount that could be raised. The stipends of clergy of the established Church were free of assessment.

In asessed parishes the heritors often ousted the minister as convener of the joint committee of heritors and kirk session, but sometimes, as at Dunnichen (Angus) in 1838, there was a reverse movement re-establishing Church leadership. In Baldernock (Stirlingshire) the heritors had ousted the minister and session from poor relief, only to find themselves saddled by a charge of £20 a year for a lunatic in a Glasgow asylum. To reduce the imbalance between income and expenditure, they tried to cut the frequency of communion and to lay hands on a legacy left to the management of the minister.[18]

A significant part in the spread of assessment came from the story of the lunatic poor, as in Baldernock. Lunacy provided the area for the most generous and enlightened examples of care and also for the meanest and most inhumane. Lunacy is not a disease with an equal distribution: differences in diagnosis and definition as well as natural uneveness in incidence may lead to large numbers classified as lunatic in one area and very few in another. Since psychiatric illness appears to be partly familial and also the result of shock or strain, uneven distribution should not surprise.

The issue of care for the insane was a lively topic of debate in the early nineteenth century, stimulated by new methods practised at the Mount in York, and there was a current of optimism in the beneficial effect of early care. There was also a fear among the propertied that incorrect diagnosis, leading to the incarceration of someone of the gentry in an institution, might lead to loss of property. Most of this concern was confined to England, but the Royal Chartered Asylums being set up in Scotland showed the same philanthropic and optimistic beliefs. An unexplained document in the Parliamentary Papers of 1817 gives the numbers of alleged lunatics at large and confined in every

Scottish presbytery, and adds details on how many were partly or wholly maintained by poor relief. Edinburgh presbytery claimed 118 confined and 48 at large, while Glasgow had 27 confined and 150 at large, an unexpected difference in pattern given that the need for confinement was likely to be enhanced by the risks and crowding of industrial development.[19]

For one part of the Highlands, the presbyteries of Lorne, Mull and Abertarf, it was stated that there were no lunatics, whereas for the adjacent presbytery of Kintyre the statement was 104, a figure higher that that offered for any other highland area. Anyone who has had to deal with the varied responses to a questionnaire will understand that presbytery clerks in some places might choose to take the lazy way out by a nil return. Dalkeith presbytery stated 96 lunatics, two-thirds of them confined, figures which are explained by a near contemporary document, a supplement to a report on English madhouses in 1816, which shows a cluster of madhouses in Musselburgh (part of Dalkeith presbytery), some of which were used by other parishes for their pauper lunatics. The document comments on the standards of care in various types of accommodatiom, and has a general comment from the sheriff depute, Sir William Rae, that parishes all sought out the cheapest provision and none of their pauper lunatics was being treated with kindness.[20]

The problem was the sheer cost of good care. At the Montrose asylum the annual cost of a lunatic was £24. In some hospitals it might range even higher. In 1844 Carluke was paying £30 a year for a man in Greenock. Lunatics might repeatedly destroy their clothes, had to be watched so that no harm came to them, and to be kept clean. Some were treated by surgeons in ways that might not be recommended today but agreed with contemporary medical tenets. Indeed Glasgow asylum was criticised by the sheriff depute of Lanarkshire for having 'no general programme of bleeding, vomiting and purging'. In general much of the provision did not satisfy the humanitarian ethos of the day.

The presbyteries of the Synod of Aberdeenshire and Mearns had managed to reduce the high cost of asylum care from early in the century by raising money from the parishes to set up a capital fund, the interest of which could be used in grants towards the fees of asylums. Infirmaries and asylums also reduced charges to parishes which had donated to their building funds. But pauper lunatics remained, as the minister of Penninghame later complained, a 'grievous oppression'.[21]

Some of the big towns in the west had found a way of reducing costs by dumping their lunatics in Arran on backward farms. As a crofter today may find it more profitable to have his land under caravans rather than potatoes, so the tenantry of Arran preferred to accept the boarding of lunatics from Glasgow Barony, Glasgow city, Gorbals, Paisley, Greenock, Irvine, Ayr, Kilmarnock and Campbeltown to modernising their farming. By the 1840s there were at least 128 pauper lunatics from the urban parishes and towns stationed on primitive farms. The farmers did not make much profit from their presence unless they starved their guests. Paisley for instance paid 1 shilling a week for each of the nine lunatics that it supported in Arran, a sum which in the town would not have fed a pauper. The minister of Kilbarchan (Lanarkshire) later stated that his parish paid 4 shillings and 6 pence for a 'fatuous' couple on Arran, a more realistic but not generous level of support.

Arran is part of the presbytery of Kintyre, so the 1817 figures are explained by this story. The matter did not become generally known till 1844, when it was set out in the papers of the Royal Commission on the Poor Law, but as the 1817 figures show, was clearly of long standing. Dr Hutcheson of the Glasgow asylum had got wind of it and made an inspection. In spite of a large amount of pretence put up by the farmers he was able to see what was going on. Patients were said to have comfortable beds, and indeed these were present, but the patients had never seen them before. One man, alleged to sleep in style, actually slept in 'an old cart suspended over the cow house' with the fowls roosting around him. It was alleged that a lunatic had died of cold and starvation in an outhouse. Diet might be just potatoes and buttermilk, nutritionally adequate but at that time despised. The comment which reminds of the high standard being urged for the care of the insane was that the farmers said to be caring for them were 'ignorant and quite unfit for the task'. Many of the patients were considered dangerous.[22]

The scandal, once publicised, was briskly cleaned up by the sheriff. Its main interest today is the gulf it shows between humanitarian standards of enlightened care and the practices which unenlightened parishes might apply. It was not unusual for a parish to keep a lunatic chained or roped up – the Glasgow asylum said patients often came in with the marks of rope on their wrists and ankles. Dr Hutcheson was appalled that the patients on Arran were often put to menial tasks such as milking, and would receive clean linen only every two or three weeks. To the marginal poor of the cities this would not have been seen as hardship. But the legislature agreed with the higher concept of care. In 1840 an Act was passed ordering landowners to assess themselves for the care of their parishes' pauper lunatics and send them to asylums.[23]

In some areas nothing was done in response to the new law, but the directness of the way the Act was worded penetrated even some highland parishes where normal Poor Law activity was almost non-existent. In Tarbert (Harris) the existence of a lunatic forced the heritors into voluntary assessment. By contrast in Orkney lunatics were lodged by the sheriff in the gaol. In the Lowlands most parishes had to arrange for the care of those lunatics who were a danger to themselves or to others. Many parishes adopted voluntary assessment, but only for this category of poor. But this would eventually increase the number of legally assessed parishes, since voluntary assessment sooner or later would break down, as one or two heritors failed to keep up payments.

By 1840 the Poor Law was clearly in difficulties. Some big urban parishes were failing to raise enough in cash to keep even the existing allowances paid. Surges in unemployment had led to voluntary schemes for the unemployed: it was better to support them than to run the risk of riot. A typical sample of this was Rutherglen, which had raised money to provide both a soup kitchen and stone-breaking work. This work was not entirely satisfactory. To make use of the stone afterwards required the sort of development that towns were unlikely to undertake in depression. Many workers, particularly weavers, the most susceptible to unemployment, were not necessarily of the physique to break up rock. Such work might be suspended in winter, leaving the unemployed to wander in search of work, and, usually, to beg. Surges to unemployment followed on the completion of any major building or engineering project as the men were laid off: a typical example of this was the unemployment following on the completion of the Edinburgh and Glasgow railway.

Early in 1840 a new voice was heard on the subject of poverty; a substantial pamphlet of over 200 pages was published, *Observations on the Management of the Poor in Scotland*. It was by a distinguished medical man, Dr William Pulteney Alison, Professor of Medicine at Edinburgh university and recently President of the Edinburgh Royal College of Physicians. It was a hard-hitting attack on the level of provision for the poor. 'The upper ranks in Scotland do much less (and what they do they do less systematically and therefore less effectively) for the relief of poverty and of sufferings resulting from it than those of any other country in Europe which is really well regulated; and much less than experience shows to be necessary' was its stated theme. This was a particularly unpopular verdict, for only in 1838 had a very restricted Poor Law been set up in Ireland, which still allowed for a more generous interpretation of poverty than did the Scottish. Alison quoted from statements of the staff of the Edinburgh House of Refuge, set up in 1833 to help with the problem of vagrancy caused by the cholera epidemic: 'fully one third of the persons who apply for admission . . . belong to country parishes, and are *bona fide* objects requiring parochial aid . . . None of these ought to depend on voluntary charity.'

Alison's claims were disturbing to the self-image of the Scottish middle class. 'The grand object kept in view by almost every parish is the possibility of *evading* . . . the duty of relieving the poor.' 'A large proportion of the higher ranks resolutely abstain from every description of charity.' Alison wanted assessment in all parishes: only then would the poor of country parishes no longer be driven to migrate to the large towns. Scotland needed 'a legal system of relief which the poor are entitled to claim' and in the poor he included the unemployed. He pointed out that the money raised for relief had failed to keep pace with the level of destitution. In Edinburgh the requests for more money made by the city's Charity Workhouse, which ran the city's relief system, had been refused by the town council: in the suburban parish of the West Kirk the managers of the workhouse had refused to raise the rate from 11 pence in the pound to 1 shilling. Alison deployed the figures for the high and increasing level of fever cases and attributed this to unrelieved destitution.

Alison ascribed part of the meanness of Poor Law authorities to the distaste, cultivated by the Church, for the relief of what was called 'mere poverty'. Those who held this view often claimed that a better social investment than relief was moral education. This might, in the long run, be true, but was no help to the starving. It was also claimed that rate-based relief, by encouraging dependency, led to an increase in poverty. In some mysterious way, relying on voluntary charity did not encourage dependency.

The pamphlet also attacked the Malthusian argument that relief encouraged imprudent marriage and so overpopulation. Here Alison drew on the English evidence. In England relief had long been set at levels which enabled the poor to be 'comfortable', yet the country was not overpopulated. By contrast, inadequate or non-existent relief was likely to make people improvident.

The pamphlet ended with a survey of relief in other countries, in which Scotland compared badly with the rest of northern Europe. In particular it was pointed out that other countries supported the unemployed.

Alison had stated that the principles of the English Poor Law were 'infinitely preferable' to those of the Scottish. He had also recommended workhouses, not necessarily on the scale of those being developed under the New Poor Law in England, but able to act as some sort of moral control on those likely to spend relief money on drink, as well as a place to put those unable to care for themselves. He deplored the Scottish habit of denying relief to those regarded as immoral or of bad character, labels used for anyone driven to drink by despair.

The pamphlet was widely noticed, mostly in a hostile manner. The middle class of Scotland was not prepared to regard Scottish social institutions as inferior to those of any other country. Scots held that the truth of the dogma of the Calvinist religion together with the presbyterian church structure ensured the superiority of their institutions, particularly to those of England. There were very strong reasons for deploring the idea of any adjustment in the direction of the English example. It would mean higher standards of provision and therefore of expense, and it would mean, so it was suspected, the over-centralisation of the English Poor Law, with commissioners in Somerset House prepared to instruct every Poor Law Union how many ounces of oatmeal should go into every bowl of pauper breakfast. Scotland had for long been sheltered from legislative change. Its landed gentry had a much tighter control of local affairs than had the English, and were not ready to see this overridden.

In April 1840 there were several significant responses to Alison's broadside. One was entitled *Proposed alteration of the Scottish Poor Laws and of the Administration thereof as stated by Dr Alison in his Observations on the Management of the Poor in Scotland considered and Commented on by David Monypenny Esq.* – not a sprightly title. Monypenny was a strong Whig and a Judge under the title of Lord Pitmilly. The pamphlet is not a particularly well organised or effective one, and appears to have been written in a hurry. It picks up particular aspects of Alison's attack and distorts them: for instance, it claims that Alison wanted a uniform level of assessment for all parishes, everywhere higher than the current maximum. The most surprising statement is the assertion that, till recently, there had been doubt in Scotland (by which was presumably meant the legal fraternity) whether assessment could be compulsorily imposed, so far had legal casuistry departed from the statutes. The main emphasis, common to all the hostile writings that Alison provoked, was horror at the idea of any assimilation to England.

Pitmilly expanded on the evils of the system in England as if that country were still under its Old Poor Law. The Scots, he said, had an 'inveterate antipathy' to workhouses, yet these were the only way of dealing with the 'disease of pauperism' when it became really malignant. The English case showed the evils of granting relief to the 'industrious poor', that is the able-bodied unemployed. Somewhat illogically Pitmilly then stated that these people had always had help from the Scottish Poor Law out of the residual half of the collections left to the kirk sessions to administer. The smallness of Scottish Poor Law allowances was, he stated, because these were fixed in relation to other known resources.

One or two effective points were made. Pitmilly picked on an unwise statement that assessment did not lower the level of church collections. The evidence of many parishes shows that it did. Collections owed much to the class of tenant farmers and, as these had to pay half the assessment, naturally they reduced their contribution at the church door. Pitmilly said, probably with truth, that it was easy to tell whether a parish was assessed or not by looking at the scale of its collections.

Pitmilly drew heavily on the writings of Thomas Chalmers, in particular on his pamphlet *Reflections of 1839 on the now protracted experience of Pauperism in Glasgow, an experience of more than twenty years which began in 1815 and terminated in 1837*, and on the evidence he had given to the Royal Commission on the Irish Poor.[24] As might be expected, Chalmers laid emphasis on the system he had set up in St John's parish, which was now abandoned, and on the 'personal attention of the rich to the poor', the 'good feature' of the Scottish system. This 'friendly intercourse', which, according to some of his St John's deacons had taken up less than a half hour a month, was unlike the bickering of the English poor with their overseers. (It is difficult to see when in Chalmers's extremely busy life he had ever had time to spare on listening to the exchanges between English paupers and overseers.)

Alison's pamphlet also stimulated other men who shared his views. On 23 March 1840, at a meeting in the Edinburgh City Chambers with the Lord Provost in the chair, there was founded an 'Association for obtaining an official inquiry into pauperism in Scotland'. It produced at least two reports favouring a relief system near to that of England.[25] (The circumstances of its creation show the difference in attitude between the two cities of Glasgow, with its promotion of Chalmers, and Edinburgh.) Its mere existence stimulated a massive gathering of the Scottish upper classes. On 20 April in the Hopetoun Rooms in Edinburgh, there took place a vast assembly of landowners drawn from the whole country, chaired by the Earl of Lauderdale.

The meeting's main function, besides the expression of total satisfaction with the existing system of relief, was to set up a committee to monitor the activities of the association. The next day the association started to try to organise a meeting with this committee, but the committee refused to co-operate in any such thing, since its effect 'might be to alter the whole system of the Poor Laws in Scotland' without adequate opportunities for discussion. The committee had an exaggerated view of the speed and simplicity of legislation. Two days later the association was recommending an inquiry on the lines of the Royal Commissions that had investigated the Scottish universities and the legal system, but had decided not to apply to the government 'until it shall be ascertained whether the natural guardians of the poor in Scotland can fairly investigate the state of pauperism both in town and country'.[26]

It was the recommendation by Alison of features of the English Poor Law, and support for this by the association, that seem to have been the main offence in the eyes of those who had met in the Hopetoun Rooms. Indeed the association had gone so far as to ask the English Poor Law Commissioners whether they would undertake an investigation into Scottish pauperism. This was said to have led to some members resigning from the association, but this may not have happened. The source of the statement is the committee set up at the Hopetoun Rooms meeting, and it is unlikely to be a dispassionate report. There was a second meeting at the Rooms on 30 April, with Justices of the Peace and Commissioners of Supply from twenty counties present, which passed a firm motion stating that there was no need for an official inquiry: any changes needed in the Scottish system could be met by existing means and would be carried out by men acquainted with the system, 'being impressed with the conviction that much of what has been alleged concerning the condition of the Poor in Scotland, and the insufficiency of the Scottish system . . . proceeds on a misapprehension of the principles upon which all poor laws ought to be based'. But so as to have all possible information, the meeting encouraged counties and burghs to make detailed studies of their Poor Law needs and provision, and report back.

There were further pamphlet exchanges during the summer of 1840. Pitmilly produced *Additional remarks on the proposed alteration of the Scottish Poor Law*. In this he conceded that it ought to be legal under the Poor Law for paupers to be entitled to medical aid, and agreed that Poor Law money allowances might be smaller than was desirable, especially in the large towns – a minor fault that could be easily corrected. He attacked Alison's weak point, his inability to produce a causal link between destitution and fever cases. He also disapproved of plans to force assessment on rural parishes, which would thereby be forced to pay not only for their own resident poor but for those at a distance. Such a plan would reduce the right of these parishes to judge the needs of their own cases. Pitmilly agreed that there was some unrelieved distress, but that was inevitable if the Poor Law was to continue as it should, refusing relief to the undeserving. In England this was done expensively by the workhouse test; in Scotland without charge by investigating kirk sessions. (These remarks suggest some confusion between supporting undesirable characters and discouraging the able-bodied.) The urban problem in Scotland had been created by the incoming Irish, always useful scapegoats, or alternatively by crime, whisky and overcrowding. It would only slowly be cured. It did not help the process of cure that some 40,000 people did not attend church. The St John's system had shown that a voluntary system could work. When facing the problem of why this system had not been widely copied, Pitmilly claimed a general reluctance to change, a singularly weak explanation. In fact the system had for a while been tried in another Glasgow parish and in Canongate, and soon abandoned. One of the important features of the Pitmilly pamphlets is his firm statement that the poor had a right to relief.

Alison replied with further pamphlets.[27] A more important outlet for him though was the autumn meeting of the British Association in Glasgow, where he delivered a paper setting out the Scottish system of relief and giving instances of the actual level of allowances to paupers. He also gave figures of the level of seasonal unemployment. For women winter work was particularly scarce in many places. Some of his criticisms were based on local reports. There was one from St Andrews based on an investigation underway before the Hopetoun Rooms meetings, carried out by a distinguished committee. This had received considerable flak. Alison had remarked that it was 'almost treason' 'to suggest that the Scottish system was not perfect', but he stuck to his claim that the evidence from the 'great excess of poverty, destitution, suffering and dependence' above the number of accepted poor on parish rolls showed the failure of the system. He pointed out that heritors, who would be burdened with a large share of assessment, were the main judges of the level of relief and naturally tended to keep it down to prevent the need for assessment. There was a general assumption that allowances could always be supplemented by relatives or by occasional paid work, which was simply untrue. A more popular point made was that the inadequacy of relief in rural parishes, particularly in the Highlands and Islands meant that their impoverished people tended to migrate to the large towns in the hope of eventually getting on the poor roll.

Chalmers also spoke at the British Association meeting and with rhetoric much more effective than that of Alison. He had come to the conclusion that medical aid, especially for incurable cases, was an appropriate use of funds from assessment, but 'mere destitution' was not, since this usually arose from improvidence. In reply Alison pointed out that even this level of liberality would send up costs. He criticised Chalmers's selectivity in the approval of causation. 'Mere' destitution was often the result of causes outwith personal control, though some disablement resulted from imprudence. The debate seems strangely abstract: nobody who had ever faced destitution would apply to it the word 'mere'.

Material was also supplied to the meeting by Robert Cowan on death rates and in particular on fever deaths, comparing Glasgow's record with that of big English towns. Glasgow's death rate exceeded that of most places, but not Manchester, which at this time was regarded as the shock city of Britain. Cowan's evidence might well have created more alarm than it did: 52 per cent of the city's people had experienced 'fever', which was probably typhus. The depression of 1836–7 combined with a strike in the cotton industry had produced appalling conditions and led many to rely on a soup kitchen for their only support.[28]

In December the committee set up at the Hopetoun Rooms meeting drew up a report which was unanimously accepted by a further meeting, and was published in February 1841.[29] It was a document conspicuously satisfied with the existing state of affairs. The Scottish system of poor relief needed no change: in particular it was far superior to the English. That 'the mortality and wretchedness of the lower classes' was greater in England than in Scotland was one of its assertions, a somewhat surprising statement since there is no evidence that there had been any investigation south of the border. Only in Skye and some other places in the Highlands were Poor Law allowances too low, and for all such cases there were special reasons: it was, for instance, necessary to adjust local allowances by the level of the condition of local independent labour. Elsewhere the report denied that allowances were either inadequate, for they were fixed with a knowledge of other sources of income, or that they were much below those given out in England.

The report did not see the basis of the Scottish Poor Law as statutory but as religious. 'The Scriptures do not enjoin relief to all the destitute indiscriminately' it stated. What they required was that 'the deserving poor' should be supported, not by a compulsory assessment but by 'private charity'. This reference to the Bible as the Poor Law authority does not give chapter and verse: it seems to be based on recommendations of kindness to the poor. That it might be difficult to locate textual authority for the opinion does not mean that it was not sincerely held. Patriotism also entered into the landowners' view of Scottish institutions: 'the changes proposed by Dr Alison will be, not to assimilate merely the Scottish system to the English, but to subvert and abolish the former altogether'.

Twenty counties had been represented at the April meeting: there is no note of the membership of this one. None of the men present at the December meeting approved of the idea of an inquiry or supported the changes recommended by Alison and the association. Fourteen counties had appointed committees to investigate conditions and to report. Particularly approved were the reports that had already come in from Berwickshire, Fife and East Lothian. Hostility to the idea of a government inquiry had also been expressed by twenty-two presbyteries. The General Assembly had re-established the committee which had produced its 1839 report.

The Berwickshire county report still survives in several libraries. It is a well-organised and clear collection of the views and facts supplied by the thirty-two parishes of the county. Berwickshire, as a border county, was one giving relief at adequate levels to those qualified, but there was no wish to extend the right to relief to the unemployed, even though half the parishes recognised that there was a shortage of work in winter. The parishes unanimously stated that they had no wish to see an English-type system of workhouses installed.[30]

Most of the other reports produced by counties and burghs in response to the challenge of the association cannot be traced, but some indications of opinions expressed in them can be found in the press. That for St Andrews generated enough dispute in the press for some of its conclusions to be clear. It was obviously not a complacent report, even though the committee which drew it up contained an elder of the Church. Pitmilly was scornful of the fact that the committee had taken the unusual step of asking paupers for their views. The landowning committee gave a considerable amount of space to these local investigations, quoting generously from the reports of both East and West Lothian, Fordoun presbytery, Perthshire, Stirling and Dunfermline, and reprinting the questionnaire used by Edinburgh City parish. Alison had quoted from the report of another Dr Alison on conditions in Tranent, and Robert Chambers had made some critical remarks on cases in a scarcely concealed Peebles. There had earlier been a report of 1831 made by a Sheriff Barclay for Perthshire, which showed that the rise in fever mortality was not new.

The second report of the association criticised the statement of the Hopetoun Rooms Committee and also commented on the various county reports. It stated that the Edinburgh report on pauperism claimed that the absence, till recently, of an Irish Poor Law had kept population growth low, whereas the English Poor Law had encouraged population growth. This statement was made, of course, before the start of censuses in Ireland: even so it shows little acquaintance with that country.

Alison did not abandon the literary battle. In his paper to the Statistical Society of London, he pointed out that the apparently low level of pauperism in Scotland was the result of the failure of numerous parishes to enter many of their destitute on their rolls. He also made reference to published reports on particular towns and from the Association, which showed how low the level of Poor Law allowances was. For instance, he quoted from that by D. W. Stewart for Lockerbie which worked out at an average of £1.5 shillings a year, not a sum on which a person could survive.[31]

Much of the literature of the dispute gives the impression that neither side was truly listening to the other. Obvious facts were ignored, for instance the sheer impossibility of every case being known in all its sources of supplementary funding in a populous parish. But the Church of Scotland seems to have been losing some of its certainty. At its General Assembly in May 1841 the Committee on the Poor Law reported through the advocate Alexander Dunlop. The general line was that relief should be only a supplement to other charity, and that it should not be extended to the unemployed: 'the only effectual means for permanently improving the physical condition of the working classes . . . consists in religious, moral and intellectual cultivation' it stated. But the report recognised that there was destitution even among those entitled to relief. Landowners could not be expected to be adequate judges of the amount they themselves had to provide. Some sort of inquiry was needed and this should not be conducted exclusively by either landowners or by the Church.[32]

By 1841 the relations between landowners and the Church had deteriorated drastically in the course of the conflict precipitated by the Church's Veto Act. There was little likelihood of the General Assembly setting up a major inquiry within the terms of this recommendation. Indeed the report was heard only through indignant interruptions. The Church was heading for the great split of the Disruption, while the political climate was becoming more tranquil. The weakened Whig ministry of Lord Melbourne, which had been the cause of much of the alarm fuelled by fear of a public inquiry similar to that rigged in 1834 over the English Poor Law, fell at last and in September 1841 a Conservative government under Sir Robert Peel was formed. Early in its life Peel and his Home Secretary, Sir James Graham, were exchanging notes about the need for minor legislative changes in both the English and the Irish Poor Laws. But they took it for granted that nothing need be done for the Scottish.[33] In December 1842 they had to change their minds.

NOTES

1. T. M. Devine, *The Transformation of Rural Scotland* (Edinburgh, 1994), pp. 141–6.
2. *PP* 1844 XXII, *Poor Law Inquiry, Scotland*, pp. 322, 378, 403.
3. *PP* 1844 XXII, pp. 553–8.
4. ECA, Papers on the Relief of the Labouring Poor, 1809–10.

5. See, for example, Mary Lindemann, 'Urban growth and medical charity: Hamburg 1788–1815', in Jonathan Barry and Colin Jones (eds), *Medicine and Charity before the Welfare State* (London, 1991), pp. 113–32.

6. Thomas Chalmers, *On the Sufficiency of the Parochial System, without a Poor rate, for the Right Management of the Poor* (Glasgow, 1841), p. 152.

7. J. Poynter, *Society and Pauperism* (London, 1969); *PP* 1830 VII. *Report from the Select Commission on the Poor in Ireland*. In general for Chalmers's views on the Poor Law, see Steward J. Brown, *Thomas Chalmers and the Godly Commonwealth* (Oxford, 1982), ch. 3, ch. 6 part 1.

8. P. Shaw, *Digest of cases decided in the Supreme Court of Scotland 1800–1869*, *vol. II* (Edinburgh, 1843–52), 1 June 1831; *NSA* VII (Edinburgh, 1837), pp. 342–5, for differences between minister and heritors in Neilston.

9. *PP* 1844 XXI *Poor Law Inquiry Scotland*, pp. 537–8.

10. *PP* 1839 XX *Report by a Committee of the General Assembly on the Management of the Poor in Scotland*.

11. *PP* 1844 XX *Poor Law Inquiry, Scotland*, p. 430, Evidence of Dr Perry.

12. A. Drummond and J. Bullough, *The Church in Scotland, 1688–1843* (Edinburgh, 1977), pp. 220–2; Callum Brown, *A Social History of Religion in Scotland* (London, 1987), ch. 2.

13. Norman Murray, *The Scottish Handloom Weavers, 1790–1850* (Edinburgh, 1978), chs 2 and 3.

14. R. Cage, 'The standard of living debate: Glasgow wages 1800–50', *Journal of Economic History 1983* 43, pp. 175–82.

15. T. M. Devine, 'The Urban Crisis', in T. M. Devine and Gordon Jackson, *Glasgow*, vol. 1 (Manchester, 1995), p. 407.

16. *PP* 1833 VI, p. 19. The Annan case was reported by the Royal Commission in 1844. See Chapter 9.

17. P. Shaw, *Digest*, vol. II, *Heritors of Dunbar* v. *Magistrates of Dunbar*, 4 July 1833.

18. Anne Gordon, *Candie for the Foundling* (Edinburgh, 1992), pp. 162–3.

19. *PP* 1817 XV *Summary shewing . . . the number of Lunatics in each Presbytery*.

20. *PP* 1816 VI *Third Report on Madhouses:* Appendix.

21. *PP* 1844 XXII *Poor Law Inquiry*, Scotland, p. 527.

22. *PP* 1844 XXII, p. 949.

23. 4 and 5 Vic. cap. 60.

24. Printed in his *Collected Works*, vol. xvi Appendix. Chalmers's evidence to the Select Committee on the Irish Poor, *PP* 1830 VII pp. 280–331 is the best exposition of his views, and not distorted by rhetoric.

25. Association for Obtaining an Official Inquiry into the Pauperisation of Scotland. *An Account of the founding of the Association and abstract of W. P. Alison's pamphlet* (Edinburgh, 1840); *Report of the Committee of the Association*, 11 January 1841; *Second Report of the Association* (Edinburgh, 1841). There is also *Report of the Edinburgh Lord Provost's Committee on the best mode of an inquiry into the condition of the poor in Scotland* (October 1840).

These pamphlets are in EUL.

26. *Report of a Committee appointed on the 20th April 1840, at a general meeting in Edinburgh of landed proprietors connected with the different parts of Scotland called in consequence of the establishment of an association for obtaining an official inquiry into pauperism in Scotland* (n.d).

27. D. Monypenny, *Proposed alteration of the Scottish Poor Laws . . . as stated by Dr Alison in his 'Observations on the management of the poor in Scotland' considered and commented on*; W. P. Alison *Illustrations of the Practical Operation of the Scottish System of Management of the Poor* (London, 1840); *Observations on the Management of the Poor in Scotland and its effects on the health of the great towns* (Edinburgh, 1840); *Observations on the Management of the Poor in Scotland . . . Reply to the pamphlet entitled 'Proposed alteration of the Scottish Poor Laws . . . considered and commented on by David Monypenny . . . by W. P. Alison*, (Edinburgh, 1840); *Reply to Remarks by a Member of the Committee opposed to an official inquiry* (an appendix to the second report of the Association).

28. Papers given at the Glasgow meeting of the British Association, September 1840 are summarised in *Chambers's Edinburgh Journal*, vol. 9, pp. 323–4. Alison's is printed in full as 'Illustrations of the Practical Operation of the Scottish System of management of the Poor' (London, 1840) and Robert Cowan's as 'Vital Statistics of Glasgow' (Glasgow, 1838); see also Stewart J. Brown, *Godly Commonwealth*, pp. 292–3.

29. *Remarks addressed to the Edinburgh Committee on Pauperism* (Edinburgh, 1841).

30. *Report on the State of the Poor in Berwickshire* (Edinburgh, 1841).

31. 'Further Illustrations of the practical Operation of the Scotch System of Management of the Poor', *Journal of the Statistical Society of London*, 4, pp. 288–319.

32. J. Baillie, *Report on the Proceedings of the General Assembly of the Church of Scotland for MDCCCXLI* (Edinburgh, 1841), Monday, 24 May, p. 34, 'Report of the Committee on Pauperism', pp. 34–46.

33. British Library, Add MS 40446, ff. 251–6 Correspondence of Sir Robert Peel, especially 26 December 1841, Sir James Graham to Peel.

CHAPTER 9

THE END OF
THE OLD POOR LAW

The depression which brought the old Poor Law to its end can be seen starting in April 1841 in the textile industries. Handloom weavers in particular were already out of work in hundreds. Depression spread to other industries as the spending power of people dried up, and this faced shopkeepers with a lack of customers. By early in 1842 there was mass unemployment and many businesses faced bankruptcy.

As always the industrial towns and villages were dilatory at dealing with the social issues of depression. When a slump became unmistakable a collection would be raised and funds would come in, but by then the unemployed were pawning their furniture and bedding or taking to the road. The frequency of depressions in the early nineteenth century bred a certain callousness: there had been 1819, 1826–7, 1829, 1831 and 1837. The minister writing the description of Paisley in the *NSA* in 1837 referred to 'the Dark Cloud' hanging over this textile town. A still darker one appeared in 1841. Workers in low-wage industries, particularly in handloom weaving, had had little chance to redeem their possessions since the last depression.

By May 1841 the depression was deep enough for the General Assembly to accept the idea of some sort of inquiry into the working of the Poor Law.[1] Towns were setting up soup kitchens: in some places these had become almost permanent, in Torryburn (Fife) one had been operating since 1832. After special collections had been raised many towns set up work schemes for relief of the unemployed. These might involve road making, repair of river banks or other local projects, but the fallback activity was usually stone-breaking. In Glasgow in 1842 there was the unusual choice of stone-breaking or muslin weaving. Here at least there was recognition that some of the unemployed might not have the muscle power to be effective at stone-

185

breaking.[2] Wages for such work would not usually rise above 1 shilling a day, and often were adjusted to the size of the worker's family. Sometimes such work was available only to married men. It was rare for any of these schemes to make provision for single women before the Act of Parliament of 1842, which forbade the employment of women underground, forced recognition that women as well as men could have dependants and be unemployed.

The depression of 1841–2 had an early devastating effect on one particular town, Paisley. Paisley's population had grown very rapidly, as incomers arrived drawn by its highly developed textile industry. It specialised in fine stuffs, especially in the elaborate and beautiful Paisley shawls, at risk of changing fashion, but also in other fine dress fabrics. Some of the work was sent out to the industrialised villages of Renfrewshire. The increased sophistication of machinery had eaten away at the value of the workers' skills in the previous twenty years, and by the 1840s many of these men could earn only 7 shillings sterling a week. The decline of the weavers from the position of aristocrats of the working class is one of the saddest tales of industrialisation. In Paisley they still retained some of the attributes of leadership: a value on skill, and a commitment to radical but peaceful politics – in the 1840s this meant Chartism – and organised prudence and self-support by friendly societies, of which there were thirty-six in the town.

The drying up of trade meant that by July 1841 there were already 2,000 workers on some sort of relief: by February 1842 the figure had risen to over 14,000. The Paisley shawl was a luxury that middle-class women were showing they could wait for. A relief fund had been opened with a committee to handle it, but not much in the way of subscriptions had come in because most of the town's businesses and those people who lived on investment income had been hard hit by the collapse of the Cart Navigation Trust. This had been the town's 'safe' investment. Almost all friendly society funds had been placed in it, so the societies had also collapsed. At every level of industrial society people faced a total lack of cash, so that there was no hope of raising further relief sums. The payments by the general relief committee had been made without a requirement of work, and it is probable that some unsuitable cases had received money.

Paisley, despite its obvious vulnerability to changes in fashion, had an inadequate system of Poor Law funding. The town was assessed but did not raise money from non-resident landowners, so approximately a quarter of the property escaped contributing. This meant that not only did an affluent section not share the cost of relief, but also that consciousness of this basic injustice discouraged resident landowners from setting a high rate or making extra voluntary contributions. The number of recognised poor increased as unemployed men deserted their families and took to the road. Still, special funds for the unemployed had come in from the county and from organisations all over Scotland. Sir Robert Peel, the Prime Minister, had been closely watching the situation in the town. He had received letters from a Dr Handyside, secretary of the association formed in Edinburgh to sustain Dr Alison's efforts for a government inquiry into the Poor Law. He had commissioned a special report from the Sheriff Depute, and Sir James Graham, the Home Secretary, was receiving regular returns of the numbers on relief from the town's provost. Donations had come in from abroad, even from the United States. Yet destitution in Paisley seemed a black hole able to swallow everything. The town itself had raised only £3,000 for the unemployed. By May 1842, even though the relief scale had been reduced from its initial generous level of 5 shillings a week for a family of five, the money was simply running out.

Laissez-faire was official government policy, but the General Relief Committee of Paisley hoped that the information sent would push the government into intervention. Indeed the dangerous nature of the situation might have justified drastic action. The General Relief Committee was made up of highly politicised individuals, most of whom were convinced that the government's policy of retaining the Corn Laws had been a major cause of the depression. There was the Anti-Corn Law League, an unscrupulous body, ready to pounce on any slip, and keen to make political use of any disaster in its campaign against the government. Paisley had a long tradition of radical politics. One of the leading Chartists in Scotland, and certainly the most vocal, was a Church of Scotland minister there, the Reverend Patrick Brewster. The new founded county police was undermanned and the town police was suspected of radical sympathies. There was no adequate force that could be trusted to deal with riot and looting, if order should fail. And the total end of relief supplies was near.

Peel's response to the crisis was calculated to disguise the government's involvement. He raised a small sum by private subscriptions from very public figures, £500 from the Queen, the same from the

Marquis of Abercorn, the principal landowner of the town, and lesser amounts from himself, Sir James Graham and the Minister of Defence, Lord Stanley. The money was entrusted to an English Assistant Poor Law Commissioner, Edward Twistleton, who went north in March 1842. After a short period of living incognito in Paisley while he gathered the details of the situation, Twistleton made his position and his fund clear. He was prepared to help but he would do things his own way. To make the money go as far as possible he would offer relief only in basic food and in return for a working day of ten hours. The food offered was bread, oatmeal and potatoes supplied wholesale. This was minimal aid to the workers, and no help to the shopkeepers who faced bankruptcy.[3]

Twistleton soon departed but not before he had set up a committee to handle his fund, and to receive at last aid from the government. Because of the commitment of most of the local clergy to the earlier more generous relief, his committee consisted entirely of laymen. The insistence on work may have been psychologically valuable, but it involved an increase in expense. In May Graham had persuaded the moribund Manufacturers' Relief Committee, a London-based organisation which had been active in 1826, to revive itself and raise funds for the unemployed. The committee sent over £12,500 to Paisley, more than a third of the total funds it raised, and it was the prospect of money from this source which enabled Twistleton to carry through his unpopular policy.

In July the Queen was persuaded to send out a general letter calling for more subscriptions and the money collected went to aid over sixty towns, the share out made by a committee in Edinburgh. In Paisley Twistleton's relief committee was forced into a final restriction in aid and knocked off the lists of those eligible all Irishmen who had not resided there for twelve years, single men under forty and those who had been on relief for a year. The Queen was persuaded to promote the shawl industry by buying specially designed types and several 'shawl dresses', fashion garments which did not catch on. Gradually work returned.

The whole disastrous period had destroyed much of the validity of the views expressed by the Hopetoun Rooms meetings. It was also no longer possible for the cabinet to maintain the policy of inertia in Scottish affairs on the grounds that the Scots could best manage their own affairs. A town of 57,000 people had been in danger of starvation:

widespread poverty had been shown as barely relieved in many other manufacturing towns. Rural police had been forced to patrol the roads to prevent armies of unemployed workers begging with menace in small towns and rural areas.

In January 1843 Peel set up a Royal Commission to look into the working of the Scottish Poor Law, in spite of the hostility of land-owning society. As convener he chose the second Viscount Melville, an experienced Tory minister now on the shelf, and, to balance him politically, another peer, Lord Belhaven, who had acted as High Commissioner to the General Assembly for the recent Whig govern-ment. There was a landowner and inactive advocate, James Campbell of Craigie and an ex-member of Parliament for Perthshire, Henry Hume Drummond. There were also two ministers of the Church of Scotland, Patrick MacFarlan, whose father had written on the Poor Law, who had succeeded Chalmers in St John's parish and was to be a Moderator of the Free Church's General Assembly, and James Robertson, whose cure of souls lay on the fringes of the Highlands and who had vainly tried to soften the Church's attitude over patron-age. There was also Edward Twistleton.[4]

The membership of the commission was discussed in both Houses of Parliament in March, in the Lords with muted approval. It was pointed out that there was no 'gentleman' on it who was familiar with the conditions in large towns. This remark ignored Twistleton, who could not be accused of ignorance and counted as a gentleman – he rated an esquire after his name. In the Commons, Edward Ellice criticised the commission as composed entirely of landowners and ministers, both classes deeply involved in the current system. Nobody pointed out that much of the ineffectiveness of the Poor Law had been the result of the work of advocates.

At the time of these debates the commission had already started work. Its remit does not make clear the aim of the government. What had shown up as the shocking inadequacy of the Scottish Poor Law was its failure to support the unemployed. That there were other failures had not yet been revealed, and the rhetoric of the committee of the Hopetoun Rooms meetings strongly denied this. There is no special emphasis on the unemployment issue in the instruction of the commission: this merely said that the commission was 'to inquire into the practical operation of the Laws which provide for the Relief of the Poor, and what Alterations, Amendments and Improvements may beneficially be made'.[5] It could be argued that the Paisley crisis had been outwith the operation of the Poor Law, but it is difficult to escape the conclusion that the government expected the commission to recommend some sort of provision for the unemployed in the Poor Law.

The activity of the commission gives a remarkable view of the conscientious behaviour of the governing élite of Scotland. First of all the commission dispatched a long questionnaire, seventy items in all, to every parish. The parishes took their time over answering, but eventually almost all responded, unlike the English parishes, of which in 1833–4 only 10 per cent had replied. The Scottish replies fill three folio volumes of the Parliamentary Papers.[6] The questions cover economic features as well as Poor Law policy. There were nine questions specifically concerned with events in 1842, and other questions asked about policy for the unemployed. Some questions required quantitative answers they were unlikely to get, such as the average age of marriage for the two sexes, the trend over early marriage, the number of children whose families could not afford schooling for them, the trend in bastardy. The economic side has furnished a book on the standard of living of the working class.[7] The commissioners, all together in the main towns, elsewhere in groups or singly, met either the minister or the session clerk of every Church of Scotland parish and these meetings and others, and discussions, fill another three folio volumes each of over 800 pages in the *Parliamentary Papers*.[8]

The commissioners also interviewed ministers of other denominations, over 140 medical men, some factors and landowners, eight men who had been skilled workers and one woman. They were to claim that they had met men of every class, but they had not yet absorbed enough of the statistical movement to have aimed at a balanced sample: 872 ministers interviewed contrast with nine people with working-class experience. The only destitute people they talked to were some in Edinburgh refused relief because of uncertainties over settlement, who were produced by Dr Alison, and a woman in Shetland. They had also visited over 4,000 paupers in their own homes, noting what they received in support, their family structure, the state of the house, furniture, bedding and general cleanliness. They had given relatively little time to hearing the views of the landowing class.

The commission paid particular attention to hearing the two leading spokesmen on Poor Law issues, the Reverend Thomas Chalmers and Dr W. P. Alison. Alison's specimens of people denied relief gave them some insight into the problems of the lower layers of society, but they did not meet the rock bottom layer. Alison's sample had addresses where they could be found, which means that they had some way of paying rent. The commission, in this like all members of the middle and upper classes, did not meet the people for whom a later social investigator, Charles Booth, set up the standard of the 'cab horse charter', the need to have assurance that they would share the security of the cab horse, shelter for the night, food and work for the day.[9] Alison obviously knew that such people existed in the big towns; Chalmers obviously did not, for if he did he could not have stated, as he had to the British Association, that people could always manage to be decently clothed and to send their children to school.

The commission spent sixteen months on its investigation, travelling all over the country. It asked for further details about the replies to the questionnaire, and delivered some thirty further questions to every rural minister. In the larger towns members let their respondents also raise whatever points they thought important.[10] In the first three months it concentrated on the big towns and cities of the central valley, and also spent some time in May catching ministers who had attended the General Assembly from the Northern Isles and the Highlands. After that it divided. Belhaven and Twistleton did most of the far north; Craigie, sometimes accompanied by McFarlan, did the Western Highlands and Islands. The commission got together for Aberdeen. In the late winter most of the commission were looking at the Lothians. They had secretarial support which recorded everything said to them. They rarely revealed their own opinions, and listened patiently to a great deal of cant from the clergy. Twistleton appears to have lost his temper once. A doctor was denying that the law meant an obligation to support the poor, and made unjustified criticisms of the English amended Poor Law. Twistleton replied, 'You would condemn the English system as a mechanical system of offering relief to able-bodied persons in a workhouse to prevent them from starving, while you would approve the Scottish system as a moral system in giving them no relief at all in cases of extreme destitution?'

Despite the heavy burden of interviewing the commissioners took time to pursue allegations of particular cruelties, indecencies or other abuses. They succeeded in showing cases of gross overcrowding, but in other instances they came up against alternative stories or successful covering. Still, the general impression of distress, inhumanity and squalor comes clearly from the evidence.

Initially the commission appears to have held that Alison's attack had been unjustified. But it received numerous statements from men who clearly knew what they were talking about and which were incompatible with this view. For instance, the manager of the Edinburgh Charity Workhouse had calculated that out-relief payments came to £1. 6/ a year per pauper, and only 12 shillings and 8 pence if that pauper were a Roman Catholic. Asked about the opportunities left for charitable giving he replied that he had 'never heard it argued seriously that limiting the allowances to a pauper had a tendency to increase the charity of friends and neighbours'. A Kirkcaldy manufacturer described the system as not feeding but starving the poor. James Heriot, convener of the Commissioners of Supply for Fife, gave 'the principle of the Scotch poor law' as 'to under-supply the paupers and to let them get the rest of what they want from their neighbours'. Remarks such as these were difficult to reconcile with the bland satisfaction of the reports of the General Assembly or the rhetoric of the Hopetoun Rooms meetings.

Twistleton was more ready than the other members to ask uncomfortable questions. When the Reverend Mackenzie of Rogart described the effect of assessment and the recognition that the poor had a right to relief as producing a 'dogged and sullen disposition . . . disrespectful of superiors' he elicited the fact that the minister knew no assessed parish. When the minister of Dysart, admitting that the poor were very poorly provided for, said that the heritors always gave whatever was asked for, he asked why then did the minister not ask for more: the minister was unable to answer. But it is clear that many ministers preferred to keep the poor in semi-starvation rather than annoy their heritors: there were many ways, as eighteenth-century disputes had shown, in which a heritor could make the life of his minister difficult. It was only when backed by the voice of the General Assembly, as over patronage, that most ministers were prepared to stand up to their heritors.

On 18 May, before the commissioners set off northwards the Church of Scotland broke in two: the threatened 'Disruption' had arrived, and there were now the Church of Scotland and the Free Church. This event alone would have meant that the existing Poor

Law, run largely by the Church, could not go on. The Church of Scotland now held only a third of the population of the country in its membership, active or inactive.

The views of the ministers in the different branches of presbyterianism on the causes of poverty and of how it should be relieved varied very little. There was general agreement on the desirability of keeping allowances low, expecting paupers to be aided by kin or neighbours, discouraging intemperance or vice by cutting off allowances and disapproving of raising funds by assessment. An extreme example of the negative approach to relieving poverty is shown by the minister of Nielston, who claimed that the existing Poor Law was 'perfect if rightly acted upon' because 'there is every check that wisdom, candour and prudence can devise, to prevent the community being imposed upon by idle and slothful individuals'. The positive obligation of giving relief seems to have escaped him. It is exceptional to find a minister such as the Reverend Nevison in Middleby (Dumfriesshire), who had come to the conclusion that Chalmers's views on poverty were wrong.

Scotland had no uniform system of assessment. It could be based on 'valued rent', which meant using the 1667 land valuation, or on 'real rent', what was actually being paid, or on 'means and substance', which was an attempt at an income tax. These methods could be mixed: the heritors of a parish might pay by valued rent which gave advantage to those whose estates had been modernised to raise productivity, while their tenantry paid by real rent. Since in many areas farms had been reconstructed tenants could hardly pay by the old valuation. Towns might use means and substance – usually calculated by guesswork. Peel's ministry had only recently re-established the Income Tax of the war period and many people disliked answering questions about money. As the Member of Parliament for Dundee, where this system was in use, said to the commission 'It is extremely disagreeable for gentlemen to sit in judgment on their neighbours'. Rental, real or valued, was something generally known and did not involve 'inquisitorial' questioning. The Dean of Guild of Dundee was uneasy about means and substance because he had noticed that the separate assessment for the police, based on rental, caused much less trouble than that for poor relief on means and substance. In Selkirk, where assessment was on rental, a large number of summonses had to be issued to get the money in. To avoid bringing legal cases against the low paid, who could not afford to contribute, most towns did not try to raise money from those of low rent. A Court of Session decision over a case in Cargill (Perthshire) in 1814 had declared illegal the practice of having separate systems of assessment and Poor Law funds for the landward and the burghal parts of a mixed parish, but the decision had been reversed in 1833.[11] Neither decision appears to have made any difference to practice. A typical sample of mixed practice was Hawick, which in 1843 was using valued rent for the landward part and real rent in the town.

By 1843 assessment covered all parishes or towns with inhabitants numbering 11,000 or more. It usually meant that the Church ceased to administer relief, though parishes can be found that carried on with the kirk session making the decisions. In Kilmaurs (Ayrshire), for instance, the session had run assessment for eight years. But usually the heritors appointed and salaried a collector. This was one of the reasons the cost of the poor went up on the adoption of assessment, and parishes which had fixed a rate often had soon to raise it. In any case since half the assessment was laid on the tenantry these were likely to reduce their casual charity or their contribution to church collections, and this also sent up the poor rate.

Parishes that needed assessment had often delayed adopting it, as the commission found. While delaying they might, as had Glenisla (Perthshire) and Kilwinning (Ayrshire), first use up money that had been left in legacies, and so no longer receive interest on it.

In some places the heritors had asserted that this process was legally necessary – one of the many legal myths that cluttered Poor Law administration. In Cults (Fife) the heritors had refused assessment until the legacies had been consumed. In Tongland (Stewartry), Biggar (Lanarkshire), Freockheim, Kirkden, Glenisla, Guthrie, Lunan (all Angus), Kilmany (Fife) and Dunlop (Ayrshire), considerable capital sums had disappeared in the avoidance of assessment. In Glenelg (Inverness-shire) £700 had simply gone and could not be accounted for. Dunfermline also had lost a considerable sum by muddle.

Despite the fact that half the assessment was paid by the tenantry or householders, these had no representation or share in decision-making. For a ratepayer there was no representation unless he happened to be an elder. A solitary exception to this was Rutherglen (Lanarkshire), where the ratepayers voted for a governing committee which worked with the magistrates. Normally all decisions were made by the kirk session and the heritors together. In a few places the session had withdrawn from action. In Neilston (Renfrewshire) and Denny (Stirlingshire) disputes of several years' standing between session and heritors had led to the session leaving the heritors to carry on alone, and again this had forced on assessment.[12]

It was sometimes claimed that the Church could undermine the position of the heritors by creating extra elders to dominate voting. But evidence for this was rare, and a more common form of controlling the vote was to allow in those holding small feus as heritors. In Campbeltown, where poor relief had aroused much hostility, one heritor was alleged to dominate meetings by the use of proxies from seventeen such feuars. But the commission did not find much demand for regulation of voting practices or for committees of ratepayers, though various people pointed out that dissenting bodies should in some way be drawn into the system.

Assessment sharpened the local desire not to support those without settlement. Legally someone who had supported themselves for three years in a parish, or who at least had not received relief nor been noticed begging, was 'settled' there. But the large industrial towns added to these requirements evidence of rent paying or 'industrial settlement', and not all workers in a parish paid rent directly or had held jobs which could be traced. These extra requirements knocked out the claims of many applicants whose native parishes correctly thought that the relief of such people was the concern of somewhere else.

Theoretically, parishes where a person had settlement could be called upon to recompense another parish which had had to support him. Indeed in southern Scotland this system worked reasonably well, but elsewhere it did not. Creich (Sutherland) had simply ignored a demand for 30 shillings from a southern parish. Petty (Inverness) had ignored many demands. Poolewe (Ross) had received various bills, but had never paid. 'Our answer was that we had no funds' said the minister. Northern and Highland parishes refused to pay demands which, whether correct or not, were based on a much more generous relief scale than that which they operated. South Uist's reply to a demand for £2.2/6 from Govan for support of a man and his child, was that there were 'no funds whatever in the parish for such a purpose'. A similar answer, though accompanied by a denial of settlement, had been made by Stornoway to Greenock over the support of an insane sailor. He had been sent to Stornoway when that parish refused to pay, and the parish was threatening to send him back. The legal myth that supported this intransigence was that Stornoway was not obliged to support the man since it was not assessed. Iona was said to be a particularly resistant parish, but there were numerous legal myths that supported other places. South Uist decided it had no obligation towards a woman who had been away for a year. Quarff (Shetland) refused demands from Peterhead and Aberdeen because the individuals had been in good health when they left, implying that the sickness was the responsibility of the receiving parish, as indeed it might have been. Dunrossness (Orkney) took the same line. Not all Highland parishes had had reliable baptism registration some forty years earlier, so it was possible to deny that an individual belonged there. Halkirk (Caithness-shire) had not refused to pay demands for its emigrants but had paid at the rate they would have received at home, and in that county the normal yearly allowance was between 12 and 13 shillings, which did not go far in matching the relief given. And not all the refusals to pay were from the Highlands. Greenock had had trouble with Largs, Dumfries and Glasgow.

The response of the big towns to cases where payment was not forthcoming or settlement was denied was simply not to enter the claimant on the roll. In Edinburgh cases of unclear settlement were considered only at monthly intervals: the gap in support had recently led to the creation of a House of Refuge for temporary support. It was supposed to be able to carry 1,500 cases, but had to manage with more when there was severe unemployment. It was an important buffer for the inadequacies of the system and made the brutality of the insistence on industrial settlement bearable. Glasgow also had such an institution, particularly used for the housing of boy delinquents and there had been a night asylum there for the emergency homeless since 1838. This city also gave some support while settlement was being investigated. Greenock supported some native poor without clear settlement but refused to take on the Irish. It had built a House of Refuge but had not the funds to run it. In Glasgow the gaol had, in the recent slump, housed forty voluntary prisoners.

The pass system enabled lowland parishes to get rid of paupers who had no settlement there. But in some places it was abused, and paupers were shuffled to and fro. Transfer of paupers to English parishes had some awkward features. English people could gain a Scottish settlement, but Scots could not gain English. Scottish border parishes complained of English authorities dumping people on the street. In returning the compliment the Scottish grievance was that paupers had to be carted well beyond the nearest local authority to places less well clued up: otherwise the cart would be confiscated.

Already in the eighteenth century some parishes in the Northern Isles had been using a system of caring for the poor which had been adopted in Orkney in the famine of the 1690s, the compulsory quartering of paupers on households in turn.[13] This meant that sums of money did not have to be extracted, and probably secured a better diet for the poor than was likely elsewhere. In North Ronaldsway paupers went round the various farms two or three times a year, eating fish and potatoes with the families. In Sandsting (Orkney) the length of stay in each household was determined by the size of the land-holding or by the rent paid. Mid Yell (Shetland) households had to offer a night for every pound of rent: elsewhere it might be a night for every mark of land and a mark was somewhere between $1\frac{1}{2}$ and 2 acres. Alternatively tenants might give 20 ounces of meal for every mark to paupers in their own houses. In Walls (Orkney) besides the quartering, each pauper received an allowance for clothes, a generous arrangement for often the need for replacement clothing was ignored.

Quartering brought out differences in standards of cleanliness. A merchant in Delting, not an enthusiast for it, gave his view on housing a blind woman, probably verminous, who turned up every six weeks with a blanket. In one of the few statements recorded from the poor themselves she said 'I like the course of life well'. Some households disliked it enough to refuse to take part. Orkney parishes complained that the recent severe depression had seen vagrant beggars coming to them from southern Scotland and Ireland and parishes did not wish to house these people.

Most of Scotland served its poor with money allowances, not always carefully calculated in relation to need. David Stuart, the distributor of stamps for Dumfries, gave the commission the results of an estimate he had worked out of what was the minimum that would keep paupers in food and clothing. A single woman would need 8 ounces of oatmeal a day and 3 pounds of potatoes a week. Provided the cost of potatoes did not go above 1 shilling and 2 pence a hundredweight, this, with some clothing, would mean a total cost of a little under 7 pounds a year. It can simply be said that almost nowhere except in the Borders did paupers receive anything near this sum. The commission did not try to encourage other areas to spend this much. It took the line that relief should be related to local levels of pay, and that paupers should not receive as much as independent labourers. Indeed in Skye, where the population hit an extreme level of poverty, the estimate of the distributor of stamps would have been grossly unfair to the rest of the people.

Paupers admitted to the hospital, as it was called, or workhouse of the big towns were adequately if austerely maintained. The dietary of Paisley's hospital cost $19\frac{1}{2}$ pence a week per head, a sum very similar to that of a contemporary prison diet. That of Edinburgh's House of Refuge, which was designed for short-stay people, came to 14 pence a week and would probably have been inadequate for prolonged stay. It was the paupers on out-relief there who were half starved, and since the residential housing was limited it was these who were increasing in number. Edinburgh's allowances were said to be 'not enough for food alone'. One minister described families receiving only 6 pence a week, which might cover rent but nothing else. Things were better in Leith, where 2 shillings and 6 pence a week was a normal allowance. Glasgow sent orphan children out to board, and this cost 22 shillings and 6 pence a quarter, and even more if they were under three. In these cases the town was having to pay the true cost. But its poor on sessional relief received only between 4 and 6 shillings a month. If some of that sum had to go on rent a married couple would have had less than 1 shilling a week for food and fuel for two. In Greenock the depression had forced parishes to recognise that those whom they nominally supported had been, to a large degree, dependent on further help from working-class neighbours. Unemployment had destroyed that system, so allowances should have been increased, but had not been. An instance of inadequacy was the case of a widow who received 2 shillings a month from her kirk session and a further shilling from the local benevolent society. Her rent was 2 shillings a month, so she had too little for food. Edinburgh Council had been asked by the Workhouse Committee to raise the level of the assessment: it stood at 6 per cent of rents and requests for a further $\frac{1}{2}$ per cent in 1837, and 1 per cent in 1838 had both been refused. The inevitable result of this refusal was starvation allowances to those on out-relief.

The large towns all contained populations with no legal claim to relief there. Dr Alison had stated that he knew of forty-eight destitute families who had not been settled long enough in Edinburgh to claim relief, but who would not return to their native parishes because these had too little to offer in funds and opportunities. He also gave detailed information of forty-three claimants who had lived at least seven years in Edinburgh and had had relief denied or delayed.

Not all the level of hardship was evident to the local authorities. Edinburgh had only one inspector to investigate claims. The minister of one of its central parishes had been horrified to discover 'a great many females' with 'no visible means of subsistence' in a state of positive starvation'. He had visited ten rooms with 'not a particle of furniture' because the charity workhouse would refuse to admit claimants so long as they had not converted all their furniture into cash. It was this minister who graphically described the difference between the social problems in Edinburgh and those he had met in his earlier rural parish, Methven (Perthshire): in the latter he said 'I never saw a case of destitution that I could not relieve before the sun went down' but in Edinburgh there could be a thousand that he could not help.

The treasurer of Edinburgh's Charity Workhouse gave an explanation of the policy of refusing support to sixty-nine cases denied aid because of doubtful settlement. He was brought to the commission's notice by Alison.

> It is a most delicate thing to relieve these people, because the moment you do they think their claim is admitted. And supposing the woman belonged to any other parish in Scotland, the fact of our giving so much money to her would have been made use of by that other parish, in order to show that we had indirectly admitted her claim.

A similar fear persuaded parishes to grant allowances which could not really support life: if adequate allowances were known to be available there would be an influx of claimants from elsewhere.

An Aberdeen magistrate was critical of the town's policy: allowances were 'not half of what would support the poor in the humblest manner'. A seceding minister stated that the poor were almost starved. For those on the roll the allowance averaged 5 shillings a month, which was more than many claimants received in Edinburgh. Aberdeen kept a special, private list of 'shamefaced poor', people who dreaded their status being known: these received money from the communion collections. The city claimed to be much affected by the agricultural reforms carried out by northern landowners, which 'effectively exiled' unwanted peasantry from the new big farms.[14] The city also was undersupplied with poorhouse accommodation. A doctor at the infirmary said that disease was enhanced by malnutrition, and also by intemperance.

In small towns and in rural areas, except in the Borders, allowances were in no way near to the cost of living. Brodick, paid £2 a year, and Kingarth (both Bute) did not usually get so high. Alness (Ross) had as its highest allowance £1 a year but the average there was below 10 shillings. Gorbals would give a woman with children between 4 and 5 shillings a month. Kirkmichael (Ayrshire) had as its highest 10 shillings a year, Kirkwall would give up to 18 pence a quarter. For Auchtermuchty (Fife) the allowances to the poor were described as 'more fitted to insult their poverty than to relieve it'. The minister of Kilchrenan (Argyll) described the allowances as at starvation level, the highest being less than £2 a year: a similar comment came from Kirkcaldy, but in Fearn (Aberdeenshire) the highest was 6 shillings. In Kirkintilloch the allowance would pay the rent, in Dingwall and Kiltearn it was not enough for this. In Oban it would keep a pauper in coals, in Iona it would mean a pair of shoes. In Ardrossan where an octogenarian received 1 shilling a month and his rent, the minister described him as very comfortable on it.[15]

Places of moderate size were not so extravagantly mean as some rural parishes. In Stirling a widow with two children would get a peck of meal weekly and 7 shillings and 6 pence a month: this would have fed the family, just. The highest allowance in Inverness was 1 shilling a week, and paupers there were known to have gone without food for twenty-four hours. Particular hardship in many places, including Inverness, was experienced by widows with large families.

The surprising meanness of many small towns was not so damaging to the poor as the excessive frugality of the big cities, for in small places people did not flit from one squalid room to another, neighbours were known, kin often within reach. Ministers spoke the truth when they said that other sources were available, though these might fail in severe depression and even in good times be not enough to close the gap. In the larger towns there were charitable societies, who gave relief, but often their standards of aid were known to those administering the Poor Law, and allowed for. Sir David Brewster, Principal of St Andrews University, opposed the work of the Ladies' Society there on the grounds that it merely let the heritors off their legal obligations.

The town with the honour of being the meanest in Scotland was Campbeltown. Here the usual allowance was 1 shilling a week but at a suddenly held meeting in 1842 forty-eight on the roll, mostly widows with children, had been struck off and told they could have badges allowing them to beg. Some of those so denied aid could not face the life of beggary. A considerable number of ministers held that virtues, forced on to the poor by the low level of support they received gave the Poor Law a moral quality which a more generous system would have denied. A total absence of indulgence in drink was in itself a virtue. Independence on the part of the working class justified the suffering caused, though whether the various means by which the poor gained enough to eat made them more independent than did the receipt of relief was not considered.

Meanness to widows was common, and many parishes refused to support a woman with an illegitimate child; this was the subject of a particular item in the questionaire. In the Synod of Lothian and Tweeddale 28 per cent of the parishes, twenty-three out of eighty-two, claimed to deny such women aid. The minister of Dolphington (Lanarkshire) regarded support of these women as 'one of the most painful points . . . We are obliged to do it . . . but we do it with a grudge . . . giving a premium to vice.' His views were an echo of those of Chalmers, who had said to the commission 'I don't like to legalise bastards in any way': in his view moral offenders should 'be left to feel their own weight' and not be merged with other paupers. The minister of Muiravonside held that support to such women would lead to a drop in the collections. The moral point of refusing aid to the mothers of illegitimate children was, however, somewhat blunted by the fact that in this Synod 17 per cent of parishes denied relief to respectably married widows with one child. In Aberlady (East Lothian) a widow with five children had been struck off the roll because the youngest child had reached the age of two and she was now expected to earn.

Tough though parishes might be on mothers of illegitimate children, they had ceased to take much action about the fathers. The heritors' clerk in Yetholm (Roxburghshire) said that the heritors had abandoned efforts to get hold of such fathers. Stitchel (also Roxburgh-shire), which did not support the mothers made no effort to enlist the fathers' aid, but the minister of Methven (Perthshire) claimed that because the parish did not support the mother, the fathers could be expected to provide. The minister of Walston (Lanarkshire) had had to leave uncharged the father of a bastard because the man had a large legitimate family: if he were to take off it would leave a heavy burden on the parish.

Various rural parishes had noticed, with some concern, the recent legal process concerning the parish of Ceres (Fife). Here a widow with six children had been enabled to outwit the barriers to an appeal system created in the 1820s and had brought a case for a higher allowance in the Court of Session and won. Even so the increased allowance laid down by the court had been delayed: it had taken a year and a further application to the court before it was raised from 2 shillings and 6 pence a week to 4 shillings, a sum still not enough to feed the family.[16] Stranraer had raised its allowances in response to the decision. Other parishes had not taken action in response, but several were worried by the case. The convener of Mearns noted a new tendency of the poor there to claim for full maintenance, not for just what the voluntary system would allow.

It might have been expected that in the industrial towns friendly societies would have been a valuable protection against destitution, and also that in the better-paid occupations use would have been made of savings banks: 6 per cent of working men and women belonged to friendly societies and 3 per cent had savings bank accounts.[17] In periods of economic tranquillity these institutions could be a valuable resource, but the story of Paisley had shown that they could fail in a crisis. Besides, many of the societies were only temporary or too local to be a safe investment, and even the great affiliated orders, which covered large areas, based their payments on inadequate actuarial information. There were, also, proletarian suspicions about savings banks. Various informants told the commission that workers had suspicions that information about holdings in savings banks would be passed on by bankers to employers, with effect in lowered wages. A gentleman in Eyemouth wrote 'If once the labouring classes had the impression that Savings Banks were encouraged as a means of keeping them off the parish poor-roll, then they would become prejudiced against them.'

The issue of morality could be a convenient excuse for keeping expenditure down. The statute of 1649 had ordered that there should be discrimination in relief on this ground. The certainty of ministers and sessions on the moral quality of those on relief is, still, somewhat surprising, for Calvin had strongly stated that it was not possible for anyone to know whether another person was or was not 'justified' and so to be redeemed. The visitor of the Perth Destitute Sick Society was strongly against giving the same allowance to good and bad characters. A deacon of St John's parish (Glasgow) stated that attention was always paid to the moral character of a claimant before relief was given, though some relief had to be given to the immoral 'if the party had a claim'. Morality might mean simply abstinence from alcohol. In Dalkeith it meant regular church attendance. It was pointed out by a Glasgow minister that parish churches there no longer had a parochial congregation, so that it was difficult for a minister to know his flock, but clearly the deacon felt he knew where people stood. Certainly it was easy to identify the mothers of bastards. Oban went further and had struck from the roll a woman whose daughter had had an illegitimate child. Given the low level of allowances there, this attack of virtue may not have made much financial difference. Alyth (Perthshire) claimed to 'distinguish between characters' as much as possible'. Crall (Fife) had kept a woman off the roll because she was 'cohabiting'. Westerkirk (Dumfriesshire), a parish with a startlingly high level of illegitimacy in the eighteenth century,[18] had decided economically that some distinction should be made about whether marriage had or had not taken place, even though the needs of the women and their children were the same. Similarly the minister of Auchtertool (Fife) had kept the allowance of a woman of bad character below that of others. In Stirling, where the commissioner Drummond was taken to view some of the poor in their homes, he noted that different levels of support were being given, and that 'some of those who were in the best circumstances, had, at the same time the highest allowances': presumably the parish was favouring those not driven by poverty to drunkenness or prostitution. The Reverend Patrick Brewster of Paisley quoted to the commission a remark by the Lord President of the Court of Session, that allowance to the poor 'is not a pillow, to keep them from starvation but such . . . as may prevent them being injured by its scantiness'. Clearly many parishes felt that this was not the case, for no parish set a level for those it regarded as virtuous as more than just sufficient for survival: all those discriminated against were being supported at a level below survival.

Many paupers were obliged to live in very primitive conditions which could deteriorate into squalor when they fell into sickness. The commissioners heard of a particularly gruesome case from a doctor in Scone. There a lodging house for adult paupers was kept by one known locally as 'Dirty Meg'. A dying man, described as 'fatuous' was found in bed with 'the excrements and other evacuations of his body'. Another lodger at Dirty Meg's, put there by the parish, had declaimed in public against the 'filth and nastiness', attempted suicide and died. By the time of the commission's visit the parish, under pressure from the local great house, had changed its policy and acquired a better lodging house.

The commission also came across another local scandal in Oban. This parish had given up assessment in 1842, and as a result reduced the level of support that it gave. There followed the death of three-quarters of its bedridden poor. One of these was said to have lain on the floor on some straw for thirteen weeks. Allowances were said to have been between between 14 pence and 4 shillings a month, which would not have been enough for any nursing care. Doctors had given their services free. There may have been some unusual epidemic to explain the deaths, but it seems more than merely possible that the outbreak of meanness among the heritors was responsible.

In no parish did the medical and nursing aid extend to midwifery. The issue of whether the woman in childbirth was or was not married did not therefore arise. Since most of the women receiving relief were too old for childbirth the gap in provision was not particularly serious. By contrast a great many parishes were relatively generous in their support of funerals. In Kilmuir (Inverness) this was the only relief that the parish had given in three years. Many parishes supplied coffins for paupers and in some there were grants for a pint or two of whisky and some oatcake for funerals, as in Killearn (Stirlingshire).

Parishes which gave relief in money as most did might have views on how it should be spent. Allowances might be reduced if they led to intemperance. There was debate over whether they should be spent on the 'luxuries' appreciated by the working class, tea and tobacco. The natural desire for these may have been accentuated by the fact that both contain addictive drugs. The minister of Penninghame considered spending on tea, tobacco or snuff 'unreasonable', but the minister of Kells (Stewartry) took it as a sign of 'comfortable' support that his poor drank tea and ate wheat bread. In Duns the heritors' clerk said that if money was spent on tea there would not be enough for support. The minister of Eddleston claimed that tea drinking was 'the chief cause of increased expense', but since it had not led to an increase in allowances the burden fell not on the assessment but on the paupers. Dumfries poorhouse granted tea to all old women, an ounce a week with a quarter of a pound of sugar: men got the same only if they were 'ailing'. Nobody was allowed to spend allowance money on spirits, but it is difficult to believe that this prohibition was fully observed. The agent of the Earl of Stair took tea drinking by labourers as a sign of improvidence. In Dornoch the greatest want of the poor was said to be snuff, but in Snizort there were tobacco addicts. The expenditure which had caused the greatest wrath among heritors was in Nigg (Mearns) where the widow Ferries had given 1 penny a week of her 4 shillings a month allowance to the Church's Sustentation Fund for supporting 'non-intrusionist' clergy in the struggle over patronage.

Some special forms of aid were revealed in the interviewing. Both Edinburgh and Glasgow had institutions for the care and training of the deaf and dumb, and occasionally a generous heritor or kirk session might send a child for such help.[19] Malcolm of Poltalloch had paid half the care of such a child sent from Knapdale (Argyll). The commission met with several instances of generosity by individual landowners, but the landowning class as a whole did not come well out of their investigation.

The commission made particular enquiries into the special arrangements set up to cope with the mass unemployment of 1842 in the large towns. Paisley had clearly been out of line in not insisting on work in return for relief. But providing work was not easy. Edinburgh had had the advantage of the construction of the railway tunnel in Scotland Street, which had used considerable manpower; there had also been quarrying and stone-breaking. The city had demanded nine hours work a day, not a particularly tough requirement by contemporary standards, and payment had related to the number of dependants. The city had been helped by gifts amounting to £3,661 from other Scottish parishes and a further £2,100 from the manufacturers' committee in London, a reminder of the considerable sums which voluntary charity could produce from the middle classes. Glasgow had raised £8,000 for the 1837 slump and £12,000 in 1842. Greenock had supported 11,000 families but had been less effective than the two leading cities in extracting work in return for aid, and had eventually abandoned the requirement. This town had delivered food to families according to their size. Aberdeen had raised £2,500 for the unemployed. The relatively small town of Dunfermline had received £200 from the London committee but had raised over £1,000 on its own. Altogether the aid from the London committee, distributed by a committee in Edinburgh, had gone to sixty-one towns, the bigger towns receiving several separate grants. Of applicants only Langholm and Selkirk had been refused on the grounds that they were not manufacturing centres. Most of the towns had run soup kitchens to aid the families of the unemployed. In Largs the heritors had kept weavers employed, though the resulting cloth had had to be sold at a loss.

It had been a crisis reduced but not totally resolved. From almost all parts of Scotland, even as far as Orkney, came complaints of a surge in vagrancy. Men had taken to the road in numbers that the new rural police could not control, looking in vain for work and begging. Nowhere, other than Paisley, had poor relief broken down, but it was clear that there had been great hardship, and in many places family life had been disrupted. The men supported by the schemes for special work had been only a part of the unemployed, and there had been unwillingness to support working women. These facts were the unstated reason for appointing the commission, and, though not mentioned in its remit, the issue of relief to the unemployed was a major part of its investigation.

In the commission's questionnaire item 49 was 'Is relief given to able-bodied men on account of unemployment, or of temporary sickness?' The coupling together of two separate issues made room for confused double answers and sometimes received them. In the Border Synod of Merse and Teviotdale 40 per cent of the sixty-three parishes admitted to supporting the unemployed, though many qualified this by stating that it was only occasional. More helped with temporary sickness. In the Synod of Glasgow and Ayr 44 per cent supported the unemployed, often occasionally: in Angus and Mearns the same percentage gave support. In the largely rural Synod of Moray 30 per cent supported the unemployed. It is clear that many parishes recognised that there was a chronic lack of work for women, particularly in winter, and supported them in unemployment. Able-bodied female inmates were essential to the running of the Edinburgh Charity Workhouse, and it was cheaper to have them there as inmates than as employees. But it also seems that many Border parishes, though recognising a shortage of winter work, did not see this as grounds for a change in the law for unemployed men.[20] In practice the ban on relief to the unemployed was by no means as total as stated in legal textbooks or asserted by clergy and lawyers. But the ban received support from the handful of skilled workers interviewed by the commission.

The commission often asked those it interviewed for their views on important issues, and the most important of these was whether the unemployed should be supported by the Poor Law. Many respondents indicated a strong dislike of the system of relief for both applicant and dependants only within the workhouse which, although it was the aim of the English commissioners, was nowhere near being achieved. Alison and the association he had encouraged were a minority here in wanting an approach to the English system. Those who felt that support of the unemployed was inevitable and did not want the English system had no easy mechanism to promote for distinguishing the genuineness of need. Many of those interviewed fell back on the idea of there being discretion in the law: local authorities could decide that unemployment was severe and allow aid to those experiencing it. The city treasurer of Edinburgh thought that sheriffs might be empowered to lift the ban on relief to the able-bodied in times of severe depression. One of the Glasgow inspectors for the relief fund said that there was always some unemployment, but he had before seen nothing like 'what had occurred these two or three years', and recommended discretionary power. A secession congregation's minister in Paisley felt that the unemployed had 'as strong a claim in nature, humanity and religion as any other class of poor'.

Many of those interviewed had no practical suggestions to offer on the problem of the unemployed except to urge that large bodies of such men should be dispersed, and that in the long run a better-educated working class would not suffer on the same scale. It was sometimes suggested that some small contribution would be sufficient to protect the labouring population from starvation. Any relief for the able-bodied which did not consider character was 'fundamentally erroneous'. These were views with which most of the commissioners had much sympathy.

The failure of the commission to deal with the problem of the unemployed, except in bland statements, was inevitable, for it is clear from the evidence it took that the great bulk of educated men in Scotland were proud of the fact that the Poor Law excluded them from relief, even though a substantial minority held that some form of discretion for occasions such as the last few years would be desirable. The commissioners were more decisive on matters with which they had some direct acquaintance and could reinforce their views with the dogmas of political economy. They did not accept the view of some witnesses who thought that the only way to prevent rural paupers being landed on the towns was to compel the imposition of assessment in every parish, so that highland parishes could not claim that they had no funds with which to reimburse the parishes actively supporting their paupers. The loud complaints of towns that agricultural labour surplus to the needs of modernised agriculture was dumped on them were dismissed. In several places the commissioners investigated the length of residence of paupers when they applied for relief and found it simply untrue that many claimed relief as soon as they could show a three-year residence. They also repudiated the belief that rural workers came to town expressly to get relief. In those places where they inquired into the past of every pauper, it was clear that the movement to town had been based on legitimate motives, expectation of work or the maintainence of family links. The commission did not investigate the claim made in Dundee that rural parishes secretly supported indigent migrants until they had acquired a legal settlement, nor the claim made by some rural parishes that Dundee and Perth encouraged migrants to ask for relief before they had acquired settlement, thereby making themselves liable to deportation if they became destitute later.

A common statement from ministers was that it was bad for the poor to know that there was a legal right to relief. In practice, in the remote parts of the Highlands or in the appalling poverty of Skye, such knowledge did not have any value. But elsewhere cultivated ignorance was tantamount to the removal of any right. Lord Pitmilly and other lawyers had, however, made it plain that the right to relief certainly existed. Still a minister could do much to make it ineffective. In a number of parishes the commission found that ministers were unwilling to call on the heritors to fulfil their legal obligations. The episode in Oban where a curtailment of funds had been followed by a sudden rise of deaths among the bedridden poor showed that paupers could not effectively assert their rights. A missionary minister in Kilmalie (Inverness-shire) said that, even before the

Disruption, the Poor Law had not been in operation. 'It is not the custom here', said the minister of Fodderty (Cromarty) 'to ask the heritors for help'.

We have no details of the discussions that took place as the commission prepared its report: the only indication of individual opinion is the fact that Twistleton disagreed enough to submit a separate minority report. There is considerable blandness in the main report, and an unwillingness to undertake change. The commission justified its refusal to lay down a standard level of adequate relief on the grounds that local wage levels varied considerably and it was important that those classed as poor should not receive a higher income than that available to active labourers. The commission's summary statement was 'we believe it will on all hands be admitted, that in many parishes the poor are adequately cared for'. 'Many' is not a precise word. Cumulatively it could be said that in most Border parishes allowances were adequate, and that the same was true in a handful of other places. In the big towns those admitted to the charity workhouse or hospital were adequately fed and clothed, but those on out-relief were not given nearly enough to live on. In a more truthful statement the commission admitted this by saying that in many parishes the funds were insufficient – and explicitly including Edinburgh in the statement. It admitted that much of the Poor Law was a dead letter. It also demolished Chalmers's vision of happy class relationships based on charity by stating that inadequate funding did not make for friendliness. The line of argument taken at the Hopetoun Rooms meetings, that the Poor Law worked adequately and economically, was shown by the evidence to be untrue, though the commission was unwilling to admit this.

Twistleton in his minority report is clear that, in general, allowances were inadequate. He states this with vigour: 'the inadequacy of allowances does not come from lack of knowledge but lack of funds and this owing in no small degree to theories respecting the effect of any provision for the poor, even when it is restricted to the relief of the aged and infirm'. This is as near as any member of the commission came to denouncing the effect of the social dogmas that Chalmers had injected into the clergy which elevated the natural ungenerousness of humankind into a virtue.

The report was set up under four subheadings: the persons entitled to relief, the body administering it, the funds available and the nature and extent of the relief. This structure brought the issue of the unemployed to the front. The commission accepted the Whig story that these had never been entitled to aid, and added a mythical historical dimension of its own: 'the important distinction made by the poor laws of Scotland between the respective titles to relief of able-bodied and impotent paupers was held for centuries to be the distinguishing excellence of these laws'. The sentence brings an image of public opinion polls in the seventeenth century, but is, of course, simply an example of the use of fictitious history to cover up gaps in knowledge. What the Poor Law had been over 270 years lay in several hundred parish records and no one was going to look into these. The only authorities available to the commission were either lawyers or clergy, and both professions had been busy misrepresenting the past.

More important than opinion in the past was opinion in the present. Various of the people interviewed, usually laity, had spoken strongly to the commission that the reasons for destitution should not matter: what mattered was relief. But the commission, by its determined effort to interview the minister of every parish of the Church of Scotland, weighted its evidence with a preponderance of opinion strongly opposed to the idea of the unemployed receiving poor relief. Almost every minister had accepted Chalmers's doctrine that to support an unemployed man was to destroy his personal independence. Various people interviewed had suggested some system by which the ban on the unemployed could be lifted in periods of severe economic depression, but these the commission rejected, although it admitted that the scale of destitution possible in an industrialised society was much greater than it had been in the past. It also rejected the idea of adopting the English scheme of workhouses and the workhouse test, pointing out the severity of the discipline needed to make such a system work.

Though the Church of Scotland's kirk sessions had ceased with the Disruption to be in any way representative of the majority of the population, the commission had no alternative to offer as administrative unit for the Poor Law in unassessed parishes. In the assessed it recognised the need for some representation of ratepayers who were neither heritors nor elders, but elsewhere heritors and elders were to carry on. Not the feuars, though. In towns, parishes should be combined for funding and for the definition of settlement. The commission took the trouble to point out that the urban complaint of old people coming to towns to get settlement and relief was largely unjustified: most incomers had valid reasons and worked for several years in their new location. All the same, it recommended extending the period by which settlement could be gained to seven years, and excluded all but native-born Scots. The commission did not see any need to compel parishes to pay for medical aid.

Since the commission had admitted, and its evidence conspicuously showed, there to be an inadequacy of money allowance, how was improvement to be achieved? It took the line that it could all be done by publicity and education. Each parish was to appoint an officer who would handle every case. The parish where a claim was first lodged was to support a pauper until the issue of settlement was decided, when it could reclaim its outlay from the parish responsible. There was to be a central Board of Supervision, entirely of unsalaried gentlemen, to which all parishes should report and which, once a year, would report to the Secretary of State. There need be no appeals from parish decisions about relief to the civil courts; the influence of reason and good feeling aided by public opinion would provide a moral force which it would be impossible to resist. Presumably the various scandals which had come to light all lay in places not yet reached by moral force. This was a possible tenet for Campbeltown and Oban, but Edinburgh and Glasgow, both cities well supplied with newspapers and other manifestations of information and education, had been shown to be resolute in their refusal to make their scales of out-relief realistic in the face of obvious need. On this aspect, the commission had simply shirked its duty and placed a bland confidence in a public opinion which in the past had conspicuously failed to compel observance of the law.

Twistleton's minority report recognised this failure. He wanted legislation to secure adequate allowances. Assessment seemed to him the fairest method, and there should here be more uniformity. He wanted all towns of over 5,000 in population to have a poor house, and he wanted medical aid a normal feature of relief. Houses of refuge should have wards for the able-bodied and there should be discretion to raise money by assessment in slumps to put up work schemes for the unemployed. He did not go so far as to recommend the English New Poor Law's system of the workhouse test.

The report, the minority report, the evidence of the interviews and the replies to the questionnaire were all published in the summer of

1844 in six folio volumes, all of more than 750 pages.[21] The report did
not gain as much publicity as did its evidence. There was little news
value in a general recommendation that almost nothing should be
done, whereas the seamy aspects of social life contained many disreputable stories. Indeed, a fair selection of the more shocking
instances had been quoted in the report. Not all, though. The
commission had not pointed out that in Aberdeen where all the
ministers had left the established Church, collection money had
beforehand been syphoned off for the new Free Church.[22] The
scandal of lunatic farming in Arran was a story that spread widely.

The publication was ignored by the *Edinburgh Review, Blackwood's
Magazine* and the *Westminster Review*. It received a scathing article in
the *Quarterly Review* by a writer convinced that a commission over-
whelmingly made up of landowners and clergy was not to be trusted.[23]
The writer wanted a much nearer approach to the New English Poor
Law, and took the trouble to point out the failure of Chalmers's
system: it had not been copied, except in one urban parish and had
been abandoned even in St John's. *Chambers's Edinburgh Journal*
quoted some grisly examples of squalor and attacked the belief,
sounded by so many churchmen, that 'the systematic relief of poverty'
was 'a pure evil'. It pointed out the collaboration of many landowners
with the clergy in saving expenses. The *Journal* also suggested a
connection between the quality of poor relief in the cities and the high
levels of 'fever' deaths, comparing the levels in Glasgow and Edinburgh with those in the English industrial cities.[24]

As might be expected Dr Alison made a rapid contribution. In a
substantial pamphlet of 302 pages, he gave a summary of the report's
recommendations, liberally illustrated with quotations giving the opinions of various of those interrogated by the commission and vivid
illustrations of the actual condition of the poor. He also pointed out the
self-contradictory nature of the report: not only on the major issue of
whether support for the poor was adequate, or on the attempt to
suppress begging while denying the poor living allowances, but on
ancillary matters such as statements that the relief schemes for the
unemployed in the recent slump had been satisfactory (p. 58) or
unsatisfactory (p. 60). He followed up the association between destitution and fever deaths and implied that the figures used by the
commission were not those generally acknowledged. He was scathing
of the concept that pressure from public opinion led to reform,

considering how little effect it had as yet exerted, and spent considerable space attacking the thesis of Chalmers on the need to sustain the
independence of the working man by denying him material aid. The
pamphlet usefully gave the basic information of evidence and report in
approximately a twentieth of the print of the official publication.[25]

The General Assembly of the new Free Church set up a committee
to consider the report. The Church of Scotland followed suit only at
the end of its General Assembly, with a committee 'to consider the
poor'.[26] Considering the quantity of literature on the Poor Law
produced in 1840–2, the relative neglect of the report is surprising.
Some part of it may have come from a distaste for the revelation of
ignorance. Many middle-class lay people had not realised how little
the poor were expected to live on and the squalor that resulted. That
ministers in the big towns had assured the commission that if poor
relief were to be left entirely to the Church it could raise the funds to
run it suggests a lack of practical knowledge even among people in
close touch with the system. The Lord Advocate was later to point out
that only a quarter of the funds used in relief came from charitable
giving, and the reason that the system in the big towns had been run
by the councils since the mid-eighteenth century had been because the
Church could not provide enough for it.

There is room for research in private papers to discover the impact of
the report and evidence on the clergy. Many divines had affirmed to the
commission their belief that destitution was confined to the immoral,
yet the evidence was clear that it was impossible for women, on the
wages they could expect, to save for old age, and that, for most men, the
cost of supporting a family ruled out any saving. The minister of
Coldingham, who was aware of this, had stated that 'hinds' tended to
'break up' in their forties, a time when they still had dependent
children. Yet a hind still had to provide for himself, for his children
in some cases, as well as saving for his own old age. The minister of
Alloa took a more common view: 'the great destitution of the poor
results from their low moral state'. Besides caring for cases produced by
the normal hazards of life in the mining areas, parishes had had to
support women whose work as coal bearers had been stopped by the
Mines Act of 1842: and many of these women had dependants. It was
generally accepted that the unemployment of 1841–2 had been un-
precedented, but there was no good reason to believe it could not
happen again. It would be interesting to know if the level of allowances

surprised members of the middle class, since it was, as Alison pointed out, the natural result of the legal changes of the 1820s which handed over the Poor Law to the unsupervised decisions of heritors.

Late in the parliamentary session in July 1844, Sir James Graham was asked in the Commons if he would produce legislation in the next sessison. He fended off the question, saying that he had not yet read the report and evidence, a fair enough reply. He did assure the House that the sheriff had cleared up the Arran scandal.[27] After questioning in the next session he promised a Bill 'after Easter'. The Bill he produced went much further than the report. The central Board of Supervision was to contain two salaried members and to have much greater power over parish officials. Appeals against parish decisions were to be allowed by the board, so that heritors ceased to decide what financial burden they would have to bear. Neglect of cases could lead to criminal prosecution of the parish official involved. Settlement was to be gained by five years' residence without begging and could be acquired by English or Irish migrants. Given the large proportion of Irish in Galloway and in some industrial towns, to have restricted relief to the natives would have caused great hardship. There was still no reciprocal way for Scots to gain settlement in England, and, for Ireland, the matter was obscure because the Irish Poor Law Act of 1838, made in a hurry, had not mentioned settlement. While settlement was in debate relief was to be allowed in the parish or town where the claim was made. Shuttling of sick claimants by passes was to end, and removal of the English was to require a medical certificate. Parish funds could be used for medical or educational aid, but this was optional. Assessment by valued rent was to end, and small rent payers were to be exempt.

Graham stated that he would have liked a general assessment for the poor but felt that it would come in time. The whole emphasis of the Act was gradualism. By steady pressure the Board of Supervision would even out differences and raise the level of provision to that of a restricted but acceptable life. Since this would involve a reduction in the powers of two major social groups, the clergy and the landowners, in a country unaccustomed to legislation, his cautious approach was probably justified. The English Poor Law Amendment Act of 1834, intended as a drastic change, was still not working as intended in many parts of the country, and England was more accustomed to the idea of centralised authority than was Scotland. 'The poor of Scotland,' Graham said in the Commons, 'labour under hardships which . . .

the legislature may to some extent remove'. He was, he added, replacing an illusory right of appeal to the Court of Session with a real right which would carry no legal charge.[28]

The evidence of the commission had caught the attention of various Members of Parliament, who were deeply shocked by it. This injected a note of urgency into the debate on second reading and in committee. Several members would have liked a more drastic reform; Edward Ellice for instance wanted medical aid to be statutory. It was made plain that, at such a late stage of the session, amendments would mean postponement for another year. The critics gave way and on 4 August the Bill passed into law[29] and the Old Poor Law of Scotland came to an end.

The significance of the change from the Old Poor law was that it was followed by other legislative changes which together gave Scotland a modern system of government with some degree of representation. The Board of Supervision was the most powerful of a system of boards set up, and it used opportunities for intervention which steadily increased its powers. At the same time it was obliged to enlarge the element of democracy. Modern government thus arrived.

NOTES

1. J. Baillie (ed.), *Report on the Proceedings of the General Assembly of the Church of Scotland for 1841* (Edinburgh, 1841).
2. *PP* 1844 XX *Poor Law Inquiry, Scotland*, p. 410.
3. T. C. Smout, 'The strange intervention of Edward Twistleton: Paisley in Depression, 1843' in T. C. Smout (ed.), *The Search for Wealth and Stability* (London, 1979), pp. 218–42. See also I. Levitt and T. C. Smout, *The State of the Scottish Working Class in 1843* (Edinburgh, 1979). For Twistleton's period in Paisley see *PP* 1843 VII.
4. It is sometimes claimed that the commission was set up in response to the Disruption of the Church of Scotland (see, for instance, R. Cage, *The Old Scottish Poor Law* (Edinburgh, 1981), p. 140. But the timing of the Disruption, May 1843, makes this impossible. It is clear from the Peel papers in the British Museum, in particular Add. MS 446/251–6, Graham to Peel, 6 December 1841, that there was a sudden change in Graham's view of the adequacy of the Scottish Poor Law.
5. The remit of the Royal Commission on the English Poor Law had been to 'make a diligent and full inquiry into the practical operation of the laws for the relief of the poor . . . To report whether any, and what, alterations, amendments or improvements may be beneficially made . . . and how . . . best carried out'.
6. *PP* 1844 XXIII–V *Poor Law Inquiry, Scotland*.

7. Levitt and Smout, *The Scottish Working Class*.

8. *PP* 1844 XX–XXII. In vol. XX are the interviews held in the large towns of southern Scotland, and also those conducted with ministers from the Highlands and Islands who were in Edinburgh for the General Assembly. Vol. XXI covers the meetings held in the northern Synods, Ross, Argyll, Orkney, Shetland, Caithness, Glenelg and Aberdeen. Vol. XXII covers the Synods of Angus and Mearns, Perth and Stirling, Fife, Glasgow and Ayr, Galloway, Dumfries, Merse and Teviotdale, and Lothian and Tweeddale. Each volume has a full table of the interviews, which can be used to locate particular parishes.

9. Donald Macleod, 'Thomas Chalmers and Pauperism', in Stewart J. Brown and Michael Fry (eds), *Scotland in the Age of the Disruption* (Edinburgh, 1993), pp. 163–76.

10. Levitt and Smout, *The Scottish Working Class*.

11. P. Shaw, *Digest of cases decided in the Supreme Courts of Scotland 1800–52*, 3 vols, Vol. II (Edinburgh, 1843–52), p. 1,255, *Heritors of Cargill* v. *Tasker*, 29 February 1816: p. 1,256, *Curry* v. *Sir N. M. Lockart*, 5 March 1814; p. 1,256, *Heritors of Dunbar* v. *Magistrates of Dunbar*, 4 July 1838.

12. *NSA* vol. VIII part 2, pp. 136–8, vol. VII part 1 pp. 342–4.

13. Frances J. Shaw, *The Northern and Western Islands of Scotland* (Edinburgh, 1980), p. 201.

14. T. M. Devine, *The Transformation of Rural Scotland* (Edinburgh, 1994), Ch. 8.

15. Out-relief allowances in England were said to lie between 2 and 3 shillings a week.

16. P. Shaw, *Digest*, p. 1,245, *Duncan* v. *Kirk Session of Ceres*, 4 February 1843; W. P. Alison, *Remarks on the Report of her Majesty's Commissioners on the Poor-Laws of Scotland, presented to Parliament in 1844 and on the dissent of Mr Twistleton from that Report* (Edinburgh and London, 1844), p. 169.

17. Levitt and Smout, *The Scottish Working Class*, pp. 131–7.

18. Rosalind Mitchison and Leah Leneman, *Sexuality and Social Control* (Oxford, 1989), p. 148 for earlier comments on such occasions.

19. Gordon Phillips, 'Scottish and English Institutions for the Blind, 1792–1860', *SHR*, vol. LXXIV 1995, pp. 178–209.

20. *Report on the State of the Poor in Berwickshire* (Edinburgh, 1841), pp. 31–2.

21. *PP* 1844 XX–XXV. *Poor Law Inquiry, Scotland*.

22. A. MacLaren, *Religion and Social Class: The Disruption Years in Aberdeen* (London, 1974), pp. 55–6.

23. *Quarterly Review* vol. 75, December 1844, pp. 125–48.

24. *Chambers' Edinburgh Journal* vol. 2, July–December 1844, pp. 110, 200, 365.

25. W. P. Alison, *Remarks on the Report of Her Majesty's Commissioners*.

26. *Scotsman* 25 May 1844; SRO CH1/2/142–4, Principal Acts of the General Assembly.

27. *Hansard* vol. 76, Commons, 31 July 1844.

28. *Scotsman*, 16 and 19 July 1845.

29. 8 and 9 Vict. cap 83.

CHAPTER 10

HOW THE POOR LIVED

The commissioners took trouble to see the poor in their own homes, and the scale of these visits, over 4,000, makes it unlikely that they saw only picked and presentable cases. In particular they came unexpectedly upon lunatics who, though wild in conduct, had not been sent to asylums. In Glasgow Barony, Twistleton and Craigie met 'a maniac sitting naked by the fire' and in Beith (Ayrshire), Twistleton arrived to meet the excitement caused by the escape of another. In Skirling (Peeblesshire) a female lunatic had just been attacking her people. More often the commissioners saw the poor creatures tied up or confined. By this time probably not even half the lunatics regarded as potentially violent had been sent to asylums as required by the recent Act. There were other features which the local Poor Law authorities might have preferred unseen – the family of four in a pig sty in Annan, the half naked children in Glenelg, the thirteen children and four women farmed out to a lodging-house keeper and kept in one room 12 feet square, with another twenty-six, one with 'typhus' in one 14 feet square in Glasgow Barony, the house in Hamilton totally without food, the unemployed man in Glasgow who had no shoes and therefore could not dig, and so had been denied emergency relief, the six people in a bed in Kirkintilloch with two blankets between them. Readers might also have been shocked that in Annan funds for the poor were raised by having a public drinking orgy. Craigie noted a horse and pig sharing the room of a family: the unusual creature was the horse, obviously a valuable resource. It was not unusual for paupers to keep pigs – in Dairsie this was how paupers paid their rent – but it was rare that they could afford to eat them. In Stranraer Twistleton met an Irish widow in a house with three lodgers, three pigs, a large basket of bones and a quantity of potato peelings: she probably had a link with some inn for odd jobs. It was said in Nairn that many of the poor kept a pig within doors: this usually meant in the only room.

The commission was anxious to relate the condition of the poor to the standard of living of the common labourers locally. This was not easy. In some areas, notably the Highlands, such labourers hardly existed. There were other difficulties. Were handloom weavers, trapped in an occupation that rarely brought in more than 5 shillings a week and that included the wage of a juvenile, labourers? In Kilsyth the poor, almost destitute of bedclothes, were considered only marginally worse off than weavers. In Kirkmichael (Ayrshire), too, there was not much difference in condition between poor and labourers. For Dumfries a doctor declared the condition of the poor to be 'much inferior to that of labourers' while a Justice of the Peace said it was similar. At Rhu (Dunbartonshire) the minister declared 'a considerable gap' between the poor and the lowest of labourers, at Crossmichael (Dumfriesshire) the poor's condition was similar to that of the lowest labourers, in Scone (Perthshire) the standards were 'nowhere near'. In Stenton (East Lothian) the poor were stated to be better off than the class above them because of medical aid and dietary supplements given during periods of convalescence. Clearly there was no general answer, nor even regional coherence. There were too many local variations. Medical relief was not available in most parishes. In Merse and Teviotdale Synod only a third of the parishes could send a patient to a dispensary, and this figure depended largely on widespread use of that in Kelso. In the Synod of Glasgow and Ayr in thirty out of one hundred and three parishes there was some organised medical aid, but in most cases this was merely the right of a parish to send two patients a year to the Glasgow Royal Infirmary: for lesser illnesses or more sufferers there was nothing.

Comments from the commissioners on the state of housing are brief but telling. There are references to broken windows, sometimes to a lack of windows, to holes in the roof, damp floors: often the houses were very dark. In Bowmore a chained lunatic was held in a dark closet in a loft. In Stranraer an eighty-year-old Irishman lay in an unheated outhouse which had no window or fireplace, complaining of the cold. In Stornoway a house was so dirty and so much in danger of collapse that Craigie refused to enter it. Others were so full of smoke that he kept outside. In Fort William a family who did not own a bed slept on the ground in a hut with gaps between its boards.

Clearly housing for paupers was a low priority and their comfort not an important issue. From the poor's own view it was of less importance than food. Only in the Borders was it taken for granted that the poor should be kept in some sort of comfort. Some landowners let paupers occupy rent-free houses but such landowners were unlikely to take much trouble over repairs. In any case the landowners' policy of getting rid of cottars and pulling down the houses that they had occupied meant that in many rural areas there was a lack of housing for those not employed locally.[1] This shortage was a major cause of the migration of older people to towns. But some of those no longer wanted as labour were too old to have a realistic hope of town employment and had to stay in the country.

Food, on inadequate allowances, was a more urgent need. A doctor in Huntly (Aberdeenshire) remarked to the commission 'the poor do not suffer much from want of medical assistance; they suffer most from want of clothing, insufficient food and bad housing'. Another in Craignish (Argyll) said that the poor might do well enough if they were satisfied, like many others, with one meal a day.

In most assessed parishes and in some not assessed, it usually took time for someone slipping into infirmity and consequent poverty to get put on the parish poor roll. Edinburgh, for instance, considered applications for relief only monthly. Further delay would occur if there was any uncertainty about settlement. Cumulative delay would force the applicant to pawn furniture – Edinburgh did not consider people as destitute if they still had furniture. There would not be any retrospective payments: once at the pawnbrokers the furniture would stay there. So, although some households had enough furniture, we get sudden glimpses of deprivation in the commissioners' notes: a widow with four children in Kirkintilloch all sharing the one bed; in Tiree a brother and sister owning only 'a wretched bed, very little bedclothes and a little straw'. Twistleton and Macfarlan in Greenock noted that one of the paupers had 'parted with most of his things', another had 'parted with almost everything' and a third had a 'house completely stripped'. In Paisley a pauper's furnishings were two stools and a heap of straw. In Edderton (Ross), though several pauper households were well equipped, a widow lived alone in a house the roof of which was 'no protection from rain or snow' and had as possessions 'a broken chair, a stool and a table': another had 'two old chairs, a table and some straw on the floor'. In Ullapool a family of five, one of them an idiot, lived rent free in a garret with no possessions but 'a miserable bed'. A family in Glenelg was said to have no bed. Some of the notes of furniture made by the Commission remind the reader of the possessions of Edward Lear's Yonghy-Bonghy-Bo:

> Two old chairs and half a candle, –
> One old jug without a handle –
> These were all his worldly goods:
> In the middle of the woods
> These were all the worldly goods
> Of the Yonghy-Bonghy-Bo.[2]

But the Yonghy-Bonghy-Bo was written some twenty years later as nonsense humour. The commission's lists were compiled from observed fact. The cases quoted here are of the more extreme type, but there were many such and their existence shows little organised attempt to improve things. Parishes simply accepted deficiences in housing and furniture.

Most parishes had for some time insisted that before being placed on the roll paupers should agree to the surrender of their possessions to the parish after death. This requirement still existed but many parishes told the commissioners that they did not actually carry it out. It was mainly a technique for discouraging applications by those not truly destitute. Old people might have an attachment to individual objects of furniture beyond their saleable value. The quantity and condition of much pauper furniture suggests that it was not usually worthwhile to try to pawn it.

By contrast in some parishes the poor were well equipped. In Ceres (Fife) several had two furnished rooms: in the case which had won its appeal to the Court of Session for a more ample allowance a widow and seven children had a fully furnished room and a second room containing looms: four of the family had some earning power. In Selkirk there were several well-furnished pauper houses, some even containing a clock. Mclean of Ardgour's tenantry were described as living in cottages with proper ceilings and wooden floors, with an eight-day clock in every house. These were not paupers. The local banker who described these to the commission was aware that many other people were less well off. He had no doubt that 'a great many of the petty larcenies here proceed from absolute want', and spoke feelingly of privation from want of fuel.

A particular item often pawned was blankets. There was perhaps some hope of recovering such relatively inexpensive possessions, but usually the hope was vain. In Dunbar the commission noted shortages of food and bedding. There was a relationship between the two features, for those who could not subsist on their allowances might be driven to pawning. Some parishes recognised the particular need for blankets. Huntly had a special store of blankets to lend. Kirkmichael and Eaglesham (Renfrewshire) gave out blankets. In various parishes such as Killarlity (Inverness-shire), there was a Ladies' Charitable Society which provided blankets to those lacking them. But the heritors knew in detail what these societies did and adjusted the allowances to paupers accordingly: the end result of the charity of the ladies was a subsidy to the heritors.

The people treated most generously by the various parishes were those obviously incapable of supporting themselves, once such cases became known. In this category came a considerable number of lunatics, who, if placed in an asylum, could place a heavy burden on parish resources. Some parishes had sent deaf and dumb children to special endowed institutions. There were very few blind people supported by the Poor Law, perhaps because both Edinburgh and Glasgow had made a success of protected workshops in which they could earn their own living.[3] We also hear of a blind boy in Laurencekirk who had been trained to sing and earned his living as a precentor and singing teacher. Orphans with no near surviving kin were much better provided for than those with a widowed parent, for they were farmed out and those receiving them insisted on allowances that covered the whole cost. As a sample, in Ardrossan a widow with six children washed clothes for three days of the week, receiving 3 shillings, while the parish gave her the same amount: the family thus received less than shilling a head a week. In Dundee five orphan children were boarded at 8 shillings a month each. In Scone three orphan sisters were boarded at 15 shillings a week: their rent was paid by the nephew of the householder: the children all attended school and the householder got occasional work.

Many of the poor were able to do some work to augment meagre allowances. There were periods when farmers needed extra labour, so we hear of an eighty-year-old woman shearing corn in the snow in Newtyle (Angus). The limits on people's earning power came often from the usual problems of age: failing sight, arthritic fingers or unsteady balance. Men's work was less often available than women's, because most work usually given to men involved an amount of muscle power the older ones no longer possessed, but there were anyhow many fewer men than women on relief. The evidence collected by the commission shows a wide range of types of work which could be done by some.

In rural areas the poor might feel that they had a claim on past employers for aid or work, and this claim was often accepted. Tenants might supply some food, or the opportunity to get it by a small loan of land or of light work. In Brechin (Angus) the poor would cadge wool from local farmers and make it into clothes or blankets. In many areas tenants would allot half-acre potato plots in return for the collection of manure for them. Sometimes this meant composting vegetable matter such as bracken in a corner of the house, more often searching out, scraping up and bringing within doors dung to store through the winter. This was not a particularly salubrious practice: as Dr Alan of Forres said, 'The filthiest places where these deposits are made, are always found to be the chief seats of disease'. The reward was a stock of food for two-thirds of the year. Despite the contemporary view of potatoes as an inadequate diet, this was better than that obtained in most towns.

In Scoonie (Fife) a widow had been provided with a mangle by the parish, and thus equipped she could earn her living. Some women supplemented allowances by knitting; whereas a young woman could produce three pairs of stockings in a week, each earning 3 pence, an old woman might knit one pair if her eyesight was sound. Some could still earn by spinning, perhaps 2 pence a day, but most of the pensioners had been born too late for this to be a common skill. The market for hand spinning of linen existed in only a few places. A woman in St Monance (Fife) was strong enough to hawk fish in the country. In Ferryport (also Fife) there was the opportunity of gathering bait for the fishermen. Making nets in many places, at a halfpenny a yard was said, not very credibly, to bring in 6 pence a day. In Thrumster (near Wick) twisting heather ropes brought in a few pence. Cutting muslin, and making fringes paid well. In Auchterless (Aberdeenshire) some women earned well at tailoring, stay making, ironing and waiting at parties, but these activities required unusual skills and a level of cleanliness not often possible in the houses of the poor. Along much of east coast Scotland women could wind bobbins for the factories. Sixteen hours' work a day might bring in 2 shillings a week, but few had the stamina and physique to earn that much.

Some of the work was exceptionally unattractive and low paid. Oakum picking had not yet acquired its association with prison life, but was finicky and unrewarding. So was picking over cotton in Lochrannoch, at 4 pence a week. Straw plaiting reported in Stromness was in decline, and there were not many other jobs for women there. In Canisbay (Caithness) women could spin hemp. Unexpected work mentioned to the commissioners included selling treacle candy, ironing, and waiting at parties. But several places already experienced a lack of work for able-bodied women which would mean that it was very difficult for the infirm to earn. One way of getting a few pence for those who had some furniture was to take in lodgers: there were always some single labourers needing a bed who did not expect much in the way of cleanliness. The parish of Lochwinnoch (Renfrewshire) was trying to persuade a woman to accept an allowance rather than house vagrants at 2 pence a night, but like Dr Chalmers she valued independence.

There is one striking omission in the information given about pauper employments: there is barely a mention of prostitution. This is surprising. The topic had recently been the content of two detailed studies, one based on Edinburgh, the other on Glasgow.[4] The study of Edinburgh had shown that a considerable number of women went into this profession because of the low level of wages in domestic service, dressmaking and other specifically women's work in a city lacking a major industrial base. We know of brothels at various social levels. Many female paupers may have been too old to be sexually alluring, but this is not a necessary qualification for the profession, and in any case there were numerous young widows with children needing more than they could get in relief. It is possible but unlikely that the commissioners did not know of these activities, and it is possible that they avoided mentioning them in material which was to be printed, though the readership of their evidence can never have been expected to be wide. It is also possible that generalised statements about immorality were code references to this topic, which readers were expected to interpret. The word 'dissipation', used for instance by an Edinburgh police surgeon, may have been in such a code. But the main use of 'immorality' appears to indicate drunkenness. Some at least of the women taking lodgers for 2 or 3 pence a night may have been offering other services.

Only one respondent, a police superintendent in Perthshire, raised the subject of tinkers, who might, because of a lack of fixed habitation, have been classified as without settlement, or considered immoral from failure to go through marriage services.

It is somewhat surprising that, in a relief system regarded as only for the disabled, there was, in most parishes, no regular provision for medical or surgical aid. Medical or surgical intervention did not at that date do much directly to improve the health of those treated, except when it was a case of mending broken bones, but it alerted a parish to the likely need of nursing, promoted cleanliness and gave psychological support to many who suffered from loneliness or neglect. The bigger towns had infirmaries or dispensaries which were free to the poor, and since some parishes subscribed to these they can be seen as indirectly paying for medical relief. Aid to the poor from infirmaries was limited, for these institutions were likely to discharge those they regarded as incurable, and in any case they would not receive anyone suffering from infectious disease. It was further alleged that the Glasgow infirmary discharged Highlanders and the Irish into steamboats for homeward journeys before they were fully recovered.

A question in the questionnaire circulated to all parishes asked how much had been spent on medical aid in 1842. Though some parishes ignored this question, most made a reply. In the Borders Synod of Merse and Teviotdale, 42 per cent of the sixty-two parishes had had no medical expenditure and a further eight had used the dispensaries in the towns to which they might or might not have made a subscription. In the Synod of Glasgow and Ayr, 44 per cent had had no such expenditure, in that of Aberdeen 69 and in Argyll 60 per cent.

The lack of expenditure did not mean that there had been no medical aid, merely that it was not paid for. Doctors and surgeons pointed out that their services were often taken for granted as a free gift, that the system was in fact a tax on the profession. A Berwickshire surgeon complained not only that he was not paid for work with paupers but that in one case he had had to support a patient for three months. A surgeon in Fraserburgh said that most parishes in that area made no provision for the sick poor and did not even subscribe to the Peterhead infirmary. Another in Kirkcaldy said that he had never been paid for work with the poor but that there was a generous lady in Aberdour who helped them. Various medical men stated that a lack of extra food and a diet of only potatoes delayed recovery. They also, not unreasonably, thought that parishes should pay for medicines to the poor. 'Attendance on the poor,' said a surgeon in Wick 'was a heavy assessment on the medical profession', and one in Alford (Aberdeenshire) stated 'medical men are more taxed for the poor than any other class in the country'. They were not alone in being burdened: in Inverurie two druggists supplied free medicines, and apothecaries in Portmoak and Comrie charged only half price. But a parish was usually more ready to pay for drugs than for a doctor's time and travel. Birse (Aberdeenshire) had paid a medical fee, once; Kirkhill (Inverness-shire) would pay for nursing but not for medicines; Barry (Angus) would sometimes pay for medicines; Cupar (Fife) used an elder who was a doctor without paying him, but would pay for medicine. Some parishes, for instance Bothwell (Lanarkshire) would pay a medical fee only if the visit had been specially commissioned. Even in the relatively generous border area there were parishes that did not help with medical costs, for instance Melrose, Ladykirk, Annan.

The medical profession was not the only source of medical aid. Several ministers had medicine chests and medical books; some even had had medical training. The minister of Contin (Ross) used his medical chest and explained that Highlanders were prejudiced against doctors. In Applecross the minister met needs which, given the remoteness of the peninsula, had no likelihood of other help. He also supplied extra food to the sick. Several ministers vaccinated children, as the Church had encouraged them to do when the technique first became available.

Some beneficent landowners subsidised surgeons to attend on the poor. The Duke of Sutherland did this in parishes where he was the sole heritor, and in Inveraray the Duke of Argyll sent his own doctor out, as did the heritors of Kinfauns (Perthshire). Malcolm of Poltalloch paid a regular salary and an allowance for drugs to a surgeon, and several landowners in Harris together made up a salary of £70 for a medical man. Some of the larger collieries, such as that at Dalgety, ran compulsory insurance schemes which included medical aid.

It was generally thought that convalescence would be helped by improved diet, but only a few parishes made provision for this. Craill and Kilwinning (Ayrshire) made extra payments, and Neilston reported having very recently accepted the need. The elements of this special diet would not gain approval from a modern nutritionist but doubtless were cheering items for the patients: tea, sugar, wine and even beef in Kinghorn (Fife), cordials and cash in Kilmalcolm (Lanarkshire), whisky toddy, wine or beef tea in Lasswade (Midlothian), tea, sugar, wine, porter and butcher's meat in Innerwick (East Lothian) and cordials, coffee, tea, sugar and wine in Whitsome (Berwickshire). Kilmarnock believed in the therapeutic qualities of wine for fever cases; the allowance was four glasses of port for men, three for women and two for older and one for younger children.

Some of the poor lived in isolation, and were consequently at risk, in failing health, of not receiving parish help. The days of reliable registration of deaths had not yet arrived and we cannot tell if death rates were unexpectedly high. But there is a coincidence in time between economic depressions in the early nineteenth century and serious epidemics of 'fever', probably typhus, in the larger towns, 1827–8 and 1837–9.[5]

The general evidence of the commission was that it was rare, outwith the Border region, for paupers to receive enough to live on with any element of comfort or of dignity. The 2 shillings and 8 pence that Mr Stuart of Dumfries had carefully calculated as necessary for long-term care was simply not what people received, in kind or in cash. The commission did not gain any clear impression of how much beyond the meagre allowances paupers received from begging. It was simply not practical for rural parishes to repress begging, and for the most part they did not try. In towns policy varied. Several, for instance Haddington, Bo'ness and Peebles, allowed the poor to beg on Saturdays; Falkirk preferred Fridays. Nairn allowed anyone, local or incomer, to beg, but many places tried to prevent incomers doing so. Rathven (Banffshire), for instance, allowed begging only by local people, Banff forbade it altogether but did not try to enforce the prohibition on the landward part of the parish.

The households in which the poor lived varied in structure. Widow Robertson in Dundee, aged forty-five, received 5 shillings a month, all of which went in rent. She had three children with her, girls of twenty and sixteen and a boy of eight. The older girl had two illegitimate children and worked in a spinning mill for 4 shillings and 9 pence a week. The other daughter was 'silly in mind' and unable to work. The widow 'teased' rope; when she could get work she earned 1 shilling and 6 pence a week. The money thus coming in weekly to support six people was less than 10 shillings and irregular. There was no arrangement to increase the allowance when work was not available. Not surprisingly the boy was not at school. The single room in which the six, and a lodger, lived was dirty and poorly furnished.

In Dumfries Thomas McQueen, aged twenty-five, who made baskets, had had a fever for seven weeks and had received 2 shillings and 6 pence. He was lucky in this since he would not have counted as disabled. He had two young children. His wife kept the household by selling baskets and begging.

In Yetholm Mary Holiday, aged seventy-four, received 2 shillings and 3 pence a week. She 'kept house' for William Faa, aged ninety-four and known as the King of the Gypsies. He owned his house and supported himself by alms from those who came to fish, and also by fishing himself.

In Falkirk four orphans, one of unsound mind, were boarded with a bedridden man of seventy-eight and his wife of forty-seven. This couple also had five of their own children, aged from nine to twenty-one, living there in two rooms. The orphans received 26 shillings a month and the man 1 shilling a day. Rent was 3 pounds 15 shillings. The money came to more than 1 shilling a week per head, the relatively generous level being based on the fact that there were orphans involved.

In Coldstream a man of seventy-two who had once been a prosperous farmer and his wife of seventy received 2 shillings and 6 pence a week. Their insane daughter got 3 pounds a quarter. They had a granddaughter living with them and an unmarried son. He earned 9 shillings a week and paid half of this as board. The parish also supplied coals.

One house in Kilmuir (Inverness-shire) which Craigie visited was that of Mary Macfarlan, aged ninety-three. 'Says God takes care of her. She can earn nothing for herself. McLeod of Kingsburgh gives her some money and she lives upon the public. Very poor bedstead, with straw, chest, stool, small pot. No window. She was spinning with a distaff. Very fine old woman – quite alone.'

In Duirnish (also Inverness), 'Ann Campbell, widow, aged 74. Has one son who is ill with the falling sickness; he fell into the fire and got himself burned about five years ago . . . Lives on the charity of neighbours. Very small house. Two bedsteads, very bad, little bed clothes. Some stones to sit on . . . She is the widow of the last of the McCrimmons, the pipers'.

In Dundee Craigie and McFarlan met the seventy-five-year-old Donald McIntyre, who was 'getting on very soberly'. He

was a fisherman but since he became unfit for that tried weaving. He gets very little work, and could not do much. His wife has been stone blind these eighteen years, and now getting into bad health otherwise. There is a brother . . . aged 60 who is bedridden. They have one and sixpence a week for the whole, plus money to pay their rent. They live chiefly on potatoes . . . and sometimes the bedridden man can't eat potatoes . . . No doctor has seen him. No doctor could be of any use to him.

The Scottish Poor Law had been created in a conspicuously rural and unindustrialised society. In the early modern period probably less than a tenth of the population had lived in anything that could be called a town, and even in the burghs many people had to do farm work for part of the year, for the town's stock of cattle had to be cared for and its grain crop harvested. In rural Scotland almost every household had a close link with a holding of land, even though, as in the case of the main classification of people, cottars, this was not enough to support a family. Farming skills and farming experience could be taken for granted. The scale of the agricultural sector of society was such that the issue of unemployment, except for short periods of harvest failure or wartime dislocation, hardly arose. It was entirely reasonable that the Acts of 1574 and 1579 did not follow their English model in ordering the creation of work for the unemployed and that later Acts should not distinguish between people who could not work and those who could not obtain it.

By the 1840s the social and economic structure of Scotland had been transformed. The eighteenth century had seen a sharp increase in the size of the main towns and cities: new trades and new trade routes had led in particular to a rapid growth of the Clyde towns and the ports of Leith and Dundee. New infrastructure of government and economy had led to the rapid growth of Edinburgh. Scotland was now the second most urbanised country in Europe. Town growth had obtained its manpower from the land. People had always walked to work in towns, but many more now did so. In the last quarter of the eighteenth century began the great reorganisation of Scottish agriculture. Landowners, seeking greater productivity, redrew the maps of their estates with new shapes and sizes of farms, and the labour force of the new farming no longer had its own holdings but relied on skill and muscle to bring in an income. The class of cottars disappeared. Instead there were hinds, ploughmen, orramen and other definitions of agricultural workers. Many of these had been the children of cottars, but there was no place now in the countryside for cottars or anyone else who did not hold a job.

In the same quarter century began the restructuring of industry. The great water-powered mills, the successors of which can be seen in the massive buildings of New Lanark, concentrated work on textiles in the valleys of rivers, to be followed in the early nineteenth century by steam-powered industrial concentrations in the larger towns. The towns swelled as people moved into tenements hastily run up and without sanitation. In this newly urbanised population there was a significant proportion of people who had cut all contact with rural society. In particular there were cohorts from both the Highlands and Ireland. In western Scotland approximately a quarter of the workforce was either Irish born or of Irish extraction.[6] Whereas the labour needs of the new improved farming were fairly constant, the demand for manpower in industry was liable to sharp fluctuations. Unemployment had become a major risk.

The picture that the evidence of the Royal Commission gives us of the life of the poor is therefore incomplete, for it is a picture of those of the poor recognised as coming under the remit of the sixteenth-century's definition. Yet the word poor must naturally cover those destitute from unemployment. Though the unemployed are often mentioned as a problematic issue, there is very little about their way of life in the evidence of the commission. Two years before they had been a vast population, partly contained within the towns by emergency relief measures but in many cases wandering the roads of Scotland. Some were still on the move through Scotland as 'vagrants'. These were not visited or interviewed by the commission. Others hung out in the slums of the cities unemployed, and in some cases unemployable. And the slums had given rise to shocked comments by Edwin Chadwick in his sanitary report of 1842.[7]

So the commission's evidence leaves us with an important section of the poor not investigated. A sample of the urban unemployed are among the people Dr Alison brought to the commission's notice. But for the most part they are known only indirectly – in the unwilling recognition by many of their social superiors interviewed that some sort of discretion over the entitlement to relief was desirable, in the mortality from fever which Chadwick had pointed out was greater in

Dundee, Glasgow and Edinburgh 'than in the most crowded towns in England', in the structure of the tenements in the cities, in the statistics for tuberculosis which had become a special Scottish plague and in the statistics of emigration.

The picture of the life of the poor, incomplete as it is, bears little relationship to many of the descriptions given, particularly by the clergy of the established Church, but also by others, in surveys and pamphlets, in the vast bulk of Thomas Chalmers's writings and in the reports of the General Assembly. Class divisions were already deep and were manifested in the geography of towns, where select suburbs for the middle and upper classes reduced for them the likelihood of contact with squalor and begging. Social inequality was seen as divinely programmed: the president of the Society for the Destitute Sick pointed out to the commission that 'the differences in external condition among men are calculated to ensure a great purpose, in a state of moral discipline, in the culture of the moral affections'. It requires a fairly ruthless theology to hold that the destitution of the unemployed was divinely organised, but the physical segregation of town areas made it possible for many to be ignorant of conditions until the commission unveiled them. Many landowners, including most of those with very big estates, set a policy of generosity for their factors to carry out. It was possible for them to hold to such a policy of personal generosity but to be vigorously opposed to the prospect of basing the Poor Law on assessment. A strong reason for this stand could be that assessment would affect the nominal value of their estates. They might also hold, as most of the clergy did, that relations between social classes should not involve compulsion. The statement in the Hope-toun Rooms meetings that assessment was incompatible with the precepts of the Bible was not advanced to the commission. Ministers were, for the most part, not capable of breaking away from the notion of the 'independence' of the worker that had played a major part in Chalmers's social thought.

The commission, for all its extreme caution over change, was successful in leading to a more adequate concept of the level at which the poor should be supported, which inevitably meant the extension of assessment. Its failure to take on the issue of the unemployed is understandable, given the weight of opinion that it heard expressed. Seeing the views of the clergy, who were the main component of opinion that it met, it could hardly have aligned the Scottish system with the English, but it might have taken up the suggestion, made in many areas, of some sort of discretionary system available in severe economic depressions. As it was, it sent Scotland into the era of industrialisation with a fundamentally inadequate system of relief.

NOTES

1. T. M. Devine, *The Transformation of Rural Scotland* (Edinburgh, 1994), ch. 8.
2. Brian Alderson (ed.), *A Book of Bosh. Lyrics and Prose of Edward Lear* (Harmondsworth, 1975), pp. 180–4.
3. Gordon Phillips, 'Scottish and English Institutions for the Blind, 1792–1860', *SHR*, 75 (1995), pp. 178–209.
4. W. Tait, *Magdelanism* (Edinburgh, 1842); Ralph Wardlaw, *Lectures on Female Prostitution* (Glasgow, 1842).
5. T. M. Devine, *Exploring the Scottish Past* (East Linton, 1995), pp. 130–1.
6. J. Handley, *The Irish in Scotland, 1788–1845* (Cork, 1843), chs 4, 5 and 8; R. H. Campbell, 'Irish paupers in Wigtownshire after 1845', *Scottish Archives*, 2 (1996), pp. 47–62.
7. M. W. Flinn (ed.), *E. Chadwick's Report on the Sanitary Condition of the Labouring Population of Great Britain 1842* (Edinburgh, 1965).

BIBLIOGRAPHY

There is a great deal of information about the working of the Poor Law scattered through the accounts of individual parishes in the *OSA*. There is also information in the papers of incorporations held by the NLS. Parish material is available in the KSRs, available through the SRO.

Alison, W. P., *Observations on the Management of the Poor in Scotland and its effects on the health of the great towns*, Edinburgh, 1840.

Alison, W. P., *Illustrations of the Practical Operation of the Scottish system of Management of the Poor*, London, 1840.

Alison, W. P., *Observations on the Management of the Poor in Scotland. Reply to the Pamphlet entitled 'Proposed alteration of the Scottish Poor Laws . . . considered and commented on by David Monypenny'*.

Alison, W. P., *Remarks on the Report of Her Majesty's Commissioners on the Poor Law of Scotland, presented to Parliament in 1844 and on the dissent of Mr Twistleton from that Report*, Edinburgh and London, 1844.

Alison, W. P., *Reply to Dr Chalmers's Objections to an improvement of the legal provision for the poor in Scotland*, Edinburgh, 1841.

Association for obtaining an Official Inquiry into the Pauperisation of Scotland, *An Account of the founding of the Association and abstract of W. P. Alison's pamphlet 'On the management of the poor in Scotland'*, Edinburgh, 1840.

Association for obtaining an Official Inquiry into the Pauperisation of Scotland, *Report of the Committee of the Association*, 11 January 1841.

Association for obtaining an Official Inquiry into the Pauperisation of Scotland, *Second Report of the Association*, Edinburgh, 1941.

Baillie, J., *Report on the Proceedings of the General Assembly of the Church of Scotland . . . for MDCCCXLI*, Edinburgh, 1841.

Barron, D. G. (ed.), *The Baron Court Book of Urie 1604–1708*, SHS, Edinburgh, 1892.

Bell, George Joseph, *Principles of the Law of Scotland*, Edinburgh, 1835.

Birnie, Graham M., 'Tradition and Transition; the Scottish Poor Law, Harvest failure and the Industrious Poor, 1799–1801', M. A. Thesis, Department of Economic and Social History, Edinburgh University, 1976.

Blaikie, Andrew, *Illegitimacy, Sex and Society*, Oxford, 1993.

Blaug, M., 'The myth of the Old Poor Law and the making of the New', *Journal of Economic History*, 23, 1963, pp. 51–84.

Blaug, M., 'The Poor Law report re-examined', *Journal of Economic History*, 24, 1964, pp. 221–45.

Brown, Callum, *A Social History of Religion in Scotland*, London, 1978.

Brown, Callum, 'The cost of pew-renting; church management, church going and social class in nineteenth century Glasgow', *Journal of Ecclesiastical History*, 1987, pp. 347–61.

Brown, Stewart J., *Thomas Chalmers and the Godly Commonwealth in Scotland*, Oxford, 1982.

Burns, Reverend Robert, *Historical Dissertations on the Law and Practice of Great Britain and particularly Scotland with regard to the poor*, Edinburgh, 1819.

Burton, J. H. B., 'Poor laws and pauperism in Scotland', *Westminster Review*, xxxvi, 1841.

Cage, R. A., *The Scottish Poor Law, 1745–1845*, Edinburgh, 1981.

Cage, R. A. and Checkland, E. O. A., 'Thomas Chalmers and urban poverty: the St John's experiment in Glasgow, 1819–1837', *Philosophical Journal*, XIII spring 1976, pp. 37–56.

Calderwood, Anna B., *Buik of the Kirk of the Canagait*, SRS, Edinburgh, 1961.

Cameron, J. C. (ed.), *The First Book of Discipline*, Edinburgh, 1972.

Cavallo, Sandra, *Charity and Power in Early Modern Italy*, Cambridge, 1995.

Chalmers, Reverend Thomas, *On the sufficiency of the Parochial System, without a Poor rate, for the Right Management of the Poor*, Glasgow, 1841.

Chambers's Edinburgh Journal, vol. 9, 1840.

Checkland, Olive, *Philanthropy in Victorian Scotland*, Edinburgh, 1980.

Cowan, Robert, *Vital Statistics of Glasgow*, Glasgow, 1838.

Cramond, W., *Records of Elgin*, vol. 2, New Spalding Club, Aberdeen, 1908.

Davidson, Robert, *Short Exhibition of the Poor Laws of Scotland*, Glasgow, 1816.

Devine, T. M., *The Transformation of Rural Scotland*, Edinburgh 1994.

Dingwall, H., *Late Seventeenth-Century Edinburgh*, Aldershot, 1994.

Drummond, A. L. and Bullough, J. B. D., *The Church in Scotland 1684–1843: the Age of the Moderates*, Edinburgh, 1973.

Dunlop, Alexander Murray, *The Law of Scotland regarding the Poor*, Edinburgh, 1854.

Englander, David, *Poverty and Poor Law Reform in Nineteenth-Century Britain, 1834–1914*, Harlow, 1997.

Ewing, Reverend James, *Report on the Management of the Poor in Glasgow*, Glasgow, 1812.

Fawcett, Arthur, *The Cambuslang Revival: the Scottish evangelical revival of the eighteenth century*, London, 1971.

Fergusson, James, Lord Kilkerran, *Decisions of the Court of Session from the year 1738 to the year 1752*, Edinburgh, 1775.

Fleming, D. Hay (ed.), *Register of the Minister, Elders and Deacons of the Christian congregation of St Andrews*, 2 vols, SHS, Edinburgh, 1889.

Fletcher, Andrew, of Saltoun, *The Second Discourse, concerning the Affairs of Scotland written in the year 1698*, Edinburgh, 1698.

Forbes, William, *The Duty and Powers of Justices of the Peace . . .*, Edinburgh, 1707–8.

Goodare, J., 'Parliament and Society in Scotland 1560–1603', Edinburgh University Ph.D. thesis, 1989.

Gordon, Sir Alexander, *Address to the Inhabitants of the Stewartry of Kircud-bright . . . respecting the Laws relating to the Poor*, Edinburgh, 1820.

Grant, Patrick, Lord Elchies, *Decisions of the Court of Session from the year 1733 to the year 1754 collected and digested in the form of a dictionary*, 2 vols, Edinburgh, 1813.

Grell, Ole Peter, 'The Protestant imperative of Christian care and neighbourly love' in Ole Peter Grell and Andrew Cunningham (eds), *Health Care and Poor Relief in Protestant Europe 1500–1700*, London, 1997.

Gunn, C. B. (ed.), *Records of the Baron Court of Stitchill 1655–1707*, SHS Edinburgh, 1905.

Edinburgh Review: the vols for 1820 and 1821 contain several articles on Poor Law matters.

Hamilton, T., *Poor Relief in South Ayrshire*, Edinburgh, 1945.

Hardy, J. (ed.), *The Session Book of Bonkle and Preston*, Alnwick, 1900.

Hindle, Steve, 'The problem of pauper marriage in seventeenth-century England', *Transactions of the Royal Historical Society*, 6th series, 1998, vol. viii, pp. 71–89.

Home, Henry, Lord Kames, *Remarkable Decisions of the Court of Session from the year 1736 to the year 1752*, Edinburgh, 1776.

Home, Henry, Lord Kames, *Select Decisions of the Court of Session from the year 1752 to the year 1768*, Edinburgh, 1780.

Hufton, O., *The Poor of Eighteenth-Century France*, Oxford, 1974.

Hutcheson, G., *Treatise on the Office of Justice of the Peace, Constable and Commissioner of Supply etc.*, Edinburgh, 1806.

Irving, June, 'The Scottish Poor Law's Response to the 1816 Harvest Failure', M. A. thesis, Department of Economic and Social History, Edinburgh University, 1982.

Jütte, Robert, *Poverty and Deviance in Early Modern Europe*, Cambridge, 1994.

Kerr, R. and Lockie, J. R., 'Scottish beggars' badges', *Proceedings of the Society of Antiquaries of Scotland*, v.xcv, 1961–2.

Kirk, James (ed.), *The Records of the Synod of Lothian and Tweeddale*, Stair Society, Edinburgh, 1977.

Kirk, James (ed.), *Visitations of the Diocese of Dunblane 1586–1589*, SRS, Edinburgh, 1984.

Leonard, E. M., *The Early History of English Poor Relief*, Cambridge, 1906.

Lindemann, Mary, 'Urban growth and medical charity: Hamburg 1788–1815' in Jonathan Barry and Colin Jones (eds), *Medicine and Charity before the Welfare State*, London, 1991.

Macfarlan, Reverend John, *Enquiries concerning the Poor*, Edinburgh, 1782.

McIntosh, Marjorie K., 'The poor in late medieval and Tudor England', *Continuity and Change*, vol. III, 1988.

MacLaren, A., *Religion and Social Class: the Disruption Years in Aberdeen*, London, 1974.

MacLeod, Donald, 'Thomas Chalmers and pauperism' in Stewart J. Brown and Michael Fry (eds), *Scotland in the Age of the Disruption*, Edinburgh, 1993, pp. 163–76.

McPherson, J. M., *The Kirk's Care of the Poor*, Aberdeen, 1940s.

Malcolm, C. A. (ed.), *The Minutes of the Justices of the Peace for Lanarkshire, 1707–1723*, SHS, Edinburgh, 1931.

Mechie, Stewart, *The Church and Scottish Social Development, 1780–1830*, Oxford, 1960.

Mitchison, Rosalind, 'A parish and its poor. Yester in the second half of the seventeenth century', *Transactions of the East Lothian Antiquarian and Field Naturalists' Society*, 14, 1974, pp. 15–28.

Mitchison, Rosalind, 'The making of the Old Scottish Poor Law', *Past and Present*, 63, 1974, pp. 58–93.

Mitchison, Rosalind, 'The creation of the disablement rule in the Scottish Poor Law' in T. C. Smout (ed.), *The Search for Wealth and Stability*, London, 1979, pp. 199–217.

Mitchison, Rosalind, 'North and South: the development of the gulf in poor law practice' in R. A. Houston and I. D. Whyte, *Scottish Society 1500–1800*, Cambridge, 1989, pp. 199–217.

Mitchison, Rosalind, 'The Athelstaneford case', *Transactions of the East Lothian Antiquarian and Field Naturalists' Society*, 23, 1996 pp. 45–7.

Mitchison, Rosalind, *Coping with Destitution: Poverty and Relief in Western Europe*, Toronto, 1991.

Monypenny, David, Lord Pitmilly, *Remarks on the Poor Laws*, Edinburgh, 1834.

Monypenny, David, Lord Pitmilly, *Proposed alteration of the Scottish Poor Laws . . . considered and commented on*, Edinburgh, 1840.

Monypenny, David, Lord Pitmilly, *Additional Remarks on the proposed Alteration of the Scottish Poor Laws and of the Administration Thereof*, Edinburgh, 1841.

Morison, W. M., *The Decisions of the Court of Session . . . digested under proper heads in the form of a dictionary*, 42 vols, Edinburgh, 1811.

Morren, N., *Annals of the General Assembly of the Church of Scotland*, 2 vols, Edinburgh, 1838.

Muirhead, A. T. N., 'A secession congregation in the community: the Stirling congregation of the Reverend Ebenezer Erskine 1731–1754', *Records of the Scottish Church History Society*, v. 22, 1986.

Murray, Norman, *The Scottish Handloom Weavers, 1790–1850*, Edinburgh, 1978.

Parliamentary Papers, 1816 VI 'First report of the Select Committee on the Better Regulation of Madhouses in England'.

Parliamentary Papers, 1817 VI Reports from the Select Committee on the Poor

Laws with an Appendix, the Report of the Committee of the General Assembly.

Parliamentary Papers, 1817 XV Summary of returns from the parochial clergy in Scotland. Number of lunatics in each presbytery.

Parliamentary Papers, 1819 II Reports (1817) from the Committee on the Poor Laws.

Parliamentary Papers, 1830 VII Report from the Select Committee on the State of the Poor in Ireland.

Parliamentary Papers, 1833 XVI Select Committee on Irish Vagrants.

Parliamentary Papers, 1834 XXIV–XXXIX Material from the Royal Commission on the English Poor Law.

Parliamentary Papers, 1839 XV Report by a Committee of the General Assembly on the Management of the Poor in Scotland.

Parliamentary Papers, 1843 VII Report from the Select Committee on Distress (Paisley).

Parliamentary Papers, 1844 XX–XXV Report and evidence from the Poor Laws Inquiry (Scotland).

Paton, H. (ed.), *The Session Book of Dundonald 1602–1731*, Edinburgh, 1936.

Phillips, Gordon, 'Scottish and English institutions for the blind, 1792–1860', *SHR*, 74, 1995, pp. 178–209.

Post, J. D., 'Famine mortality and epidemic disease in the process of modernisation, *Economic History Review*, 29, 1976, pp. 14–37.

Post, J. D., *Food Shortage, Climatic Variability and Epidemic Disease in Pre-Industrial Europe*, Ithaca, 1985.

Poynter, J., *Society and Pauperism*, London, 1969.

Quarterly Review, 75, December 1844, pp. 125–48 contains articles on the Scottish Poor Law.

Remarks addressed to the Edinburgh Committee on Pauperism, Edinburgh, n.d.

Report of a Committee appointed on the 20th April 1840 at a general meeting in Edinburgh of landed proprietors connected with the different parts of Scotland called in consequence of the establishment of an association for obtaining an official inquiry into pauperism in Scotland, n.d.

Report of the Edinburgh Lord Provost's Committee on the best mode of an inquiry into the condition of the poor in Scotland, Edinburgh, 1840.

Report on the State of the Poor in Berwickshire, Edinburgh, 1841.

Report on Committee on pauperism, see Baillie, J.

Riis, Thomas, *Aspects of Poverty in Early Modern Europe*, 3 vols, Stuttgart, 1981–90.

Slack, Paul, *Poverty and Policy in Tudor and Stuart England*, London, 1988.

Smith, J. Guthrie, *A Digest of the Law of Scotland relating to the Poor*, London, 1860.

Smout, T. C., 'Famine and famine relief in Scotland' in L. M. Cullen and T. C. Smout (eds), *Comparative Aspects of Scottish and Irish Economic and Social History*, Edinburgh, 1976, pp. 21–8.

Smout, T. C., 'The strange intervention of Edward Twistleton' in T. C. Smout (ed.), *The Search for Wealth and Stability*, London, 1979.

Steven, Maisie, *Parish Life in Eighteenth Century Scotland*, Aberdeen, 1995, ch. 10.

Stewart, John (ed.), *Selections from the kirk session, presbytery and synod of Aberdeen*, Spalding Club, Aberdeen, 1846.

Tait, G., *Summary of the Powers and Duties of a Justice of the Peace in Scotland* 2 vols, Edinburgh, 1815.

Torrie, Elizabeth P. D. (ed.), *Gild Court Book of Dunfermline 1433–1597*, SRS, Edinburgh, 1986.

Townshend, Joseph, *A Dissertation on the Poor Laws*, London, 1782.

Turnbull, George, *Report on the present state of Pauperism in Berwickshire*, Edinburgh, 1838.

Tyson, R. E., 'Famine in Aberdeenshire, 1695–1699: anatomy of a crisis' in D. Stevenson (ed.), *From Lairds to Louns: County and Burgh Life in Aberdeenshire 1600–1800*, Edinburgh, 1986.

Woolf, Stuart, *The Poor in Western Europe in the Eighteenth and Nineteenth Centuries*, London, 1986.

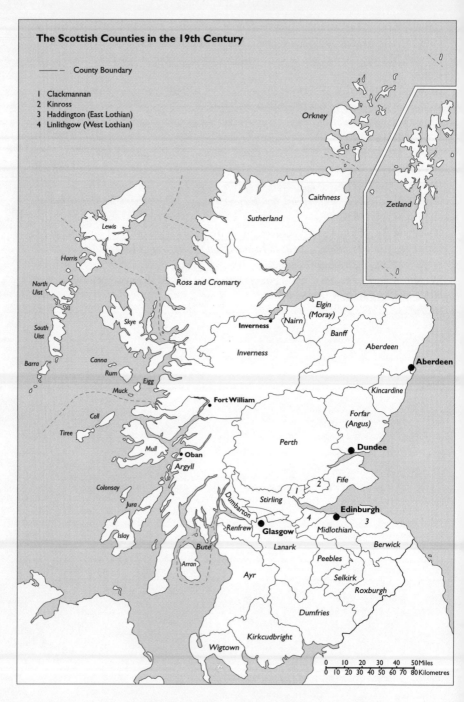

The Scottish Counties in the 19th Century

— — — County Boundary

1 Clackmannan
2 Kinross
3 Haddington (East Lothian)
4 Linlithgow (West Lothian)

Orkney

Zetland

Lewis

Harris

North
Uist

South
Uist

Barra

Canna

Rum

Muck

Eigg

Coll

Tiree

Mull

Colonsay

Jura

Islay

Bute

Arran

Sutherland

Caithness

Ross and Cromarty

Skye

Inverness

Inverness

Elgin
(Moray)

Nairn

Banff

Aberdeen

Kincardine

Forfar
(Angus)

Fort William

Oban

Argyll

Perth

Dundee

Fife

Stirling

Dumbarton

Renfrew

Glasgow

Lanark

Midlothian

Edinburgh

Berwick

Peebles

Selkirk

Roxburgh

Ayr

Dumfries

Kirkcudbright

Wigtown

Aberdeen

0   10   20   30   40   50 Miles
0 10 20 30 40 50 60 70 80 Kilometres

*I am grateful for this to the work of other members of the department
of Economic and Social History, Edinburgh University.*

GLOSSARY

almons	alms
babbie	baby
bairn	child
bede house	almshouse
boll	bulk measure for grain
call	Invitation to a parish charge
cess	tax or assessment
compear	appear in court
coffers	subtenants
delate	accuse
desuetude	disuse
discharge	forbid
ell	measure, approximately 37 inches
fasheit	bothered
feuar	holder of land in feu
fiar	accepted price for exchange between grain and money
firlot	measure of capacity, a quarter of a boll
forestall	anticipate market sale
forpet	a fourth part
harn	coarse linen cloth
heritor	landowner with obligations of church support
hind	married farm servant
impeishit	impeded
incorporation	guild
landward	rural
lauchfull	lawful
lint wheel	spinning wheel for flax
mart	a beast killed for winter food
merk	two-thirds of a pound Scots
misterfull	destitute
mortification	legacy
orraman	odd job man

outhald	force out
outwith	without
peck	capacity measure for grain
remit	terms of reference
reset	house or shelter
roup	auction
skybes	low rogues
sorner	one who begs or quarters himself
stent	tax or rate
teind	tithe
thirlage	compulsion on tenants to use a particular mill
tyke or tick	bag
verra	truly
victual	grain or meal

INDEX